HISTORICAL DICTIONARIES OF ANCIENT CIVILIZATIONS AND HISTORICAL ERAS
Series editor: Jon Woronoff

1. *Ancient Egypt,* Morris L. Bierbrier, 1999.
2. *Ancient Mesoamerica,* Joel W. Palka, 2000.

Historical Dictionary of Ancient Mesoamerica

Joel W. Palka

*Historical Dictionaries of Ancient Civilizations
and Historical Eras, No. 2*

The Scarecrow Press, Inc.
Lanham, Maryland, and London
2000

SCARECROW PRESS, INC.

Published in the United States of America
by Scarecrow Press, Inc.
4720 Boston Way, Lanham, Maryland 20706
http://www.scarecrowpress.com

4 Pleydell Gardens, Folkestone
Kent CT20 2DN, England

British Library Cataloguing in Publication Information Available

Library of Congress Cataloging-in-Publication Data

Palka, Joel W., 1962–
    Historical dictionary of Ancient Mesoamerica/Joel W. Palka.
        p. cm. — (Historical dictionaries of ancient civilizations and historical eras ;
    2) Includes bibliographical references.
    ISBN 0-8108-3715-3 (cloth : alk. paper)
    1. Indians of Central America—Antiquities—Dictionaries.   2. Indians of
Mexico—Antiquities—Dictionaries.   3. Central America—Antiquities—
Dictionaries.   4. Mexico—Antiquities—Dictionaries.   I. Title.   II. Historical
dictionaries of ancient civilizations and historical eras ; no. 2.

F1434.H57   2000
972'.00497'003—dc21
                                                                            99-087307

♾ ™The paper used in this publication meets the minimum requirements of
American National Standard for Information Sciences—Permanence of
Paper for Printed Library Materials, ANSI/NISO Z39.48–1992.
Manufactured in the United States of America.

*Dedicated to all past, present, and future researchers
of ancient Mesoamerica*

Contents

Series Editor's Foreword

Once overshadowed by the better researched civilizations of the Middle East and Asia, the great cultures of ancient Mesoamerica are becoming increasingly known and appreciated. Most familiar are the Olmec, Maya, and Aztec, but there are many more, including the Mixtec, Tarascan, Toltec, Zapotec, and others. This revival has not been easy, because many traces have been lost, almost obliterated in certain cases, since the Spanish conquest. The untiring efforts of archaeologists have elucidated some of the past while still leaving many gaps and mysteries. But the remains of magnificent temples and palaces, the splendid examples of arts and artifacts, the testimonies pressed into stone and gold bear witness to the erstwhile grandeur.

The *Historical Dictionary of Ancient Mesoamerica* is an excellent first step in discovering this fertile cradle of civilization. The dictionary includes entries on the many cultures—the better and lesser known, the more and less successful, the stronger and the weaker. Other entries present important places—once capitals and major cities, now often archaeological sites. The dictionary also includes entries on significant figures, including indigenous rulers, the Spanish conquistadores, and preconquest gods. Particularly intriguing are the entries describing the region's political, social, and economic activities as well as its religious rituals and worldview. The chronology charts the historical progression, and the introduction recounts the cultures that succeeded one another until the Spanish conquest put an end to their natural growth. But this book can only be a first step, and further steps can be sought through the many sources identified in the bibliography.

This volume was written by Joel W. Palka, who is both a teacher and an archaeologist. After teaching at Vanderbilt University, he became an assistant professor in anthropology and Latin American studies at the University of Illinois–Chicago. During this period he has also engaged in considerable field research, mainly in Guatemala, where he is presently director of the Lacandon Maya Archaeological Project. Although Dr. Palka's specialization is the Maya culture of Mexico and Central America, his interests include the entire Mesoamerican experience, on which he has lectured and written extensively. This background provides the base on which Dr. Palka has constructed a very solid historical dictionary.

Jon Woronoff
Series Editor

Preface

Ancient Mesoamerica has captured the attention of many archaeologists and has gained worldwide interest ever since the publication of photographs, drawings, and descriptions of exciting discoveries of ruined cities, carved stone monuments, beautiful artifacts, and exotic locations in Mexico and Central America during the 19th century. Initially, the images of and written details about majestic stone temples, portraits and hieroglyphs in stone, plus carved jade objects and brilliantly painted polychrome pottery, circulated among readers of travel literature and caused a tremendous stir in the scientific and anthropological communities. Many wanderers, archaeologists, and antiquarians rushed to Middle America, or Mesoamerica, to collect beautiful pieces and photographs from these ancient civilizations, and they published their findings in handsome and detailed volumes.

Ever since the publication of these early accounts, the cultures and archaeological sites of ancient Mesoamerica have been a major focus of intensive research, public and private funding, and lay interest. Today, a large cadre of archaeologists, ethnohistorians, and art historians dedicate their careers to examining and learning more about ancient Mesoamerican societies, and large numbers of university and high school students know at least as much about the Classic Maya and the Aztec civilizations as they do about many other archaeological cultures and areas. Ancient Mesoamerican cultures and their achievements continue to be extremely popular subjects for college courses, study groups, tourist attention, public lectures, and scholarly investigations.

This historical dictionary covers some of the major discoveries of the diverse investigations that have taken place throughout ancient Mesoamerica over the last 100 years. The results of previous and continuing research and explorations plus recent interpretations of ancient cultures and new work at archaeological sites in Mesoamerica are summarized here. While the amount of data concerning the cultures of ancient Mesoamerica could easily fill a large, multivolume reference set, this book concentrates only on the major points and findings regarding ancient Mesoamerica gleaned from more than a century of research. For the purpose of this historical dictionary, it was deemed preferable to include important details in a large number of entries as opposed to longer, more general discussions of fewer topics.

Included in this treatise are information and insights on archaeological sites, material culture, social and economic organization, religion and belief systems, and the social history of ancient Mesoamerica. The entries contain geographical, chronological, historical, and interpretive data that serve as a condensed and accessible resource on the past in Mesoamerica. Also presented here are entries on a select few historical personages of ancient times, including brief notes on their lives and accomplishments taken from hieroglyphic texts, painted books, or codices, and written documents and oral histories from the colonial period. The striking photographs for this volume were taken and prepared by Jean Pierre Courau, who has lived and researched in Mesoamerica for many years. I sincerely thank him and my other colleagues for sharing their information with me for this work. Rosa Cabrera kindly produced the map of Mesoamerican sites.

Because of the nature of my research concentrations and publications in conjunction with my specialties and experience, much of this historical dictionary covers the Maya area and southern Mesoamerica. However, since there are new discoveries and a growing interest in the archaeology of western and northern Mesoamerica, I have included information from these regions with the data from the more well-known areas and cultures to the south. Many future investigations of prehistoric cultures in these and other relatively "little-explored" areas in Mesoamerica will transform our thinking about history and society in this region and will necessitate the rewriting of reference and scholarly works. Still today these areas are sometimes viewed as peripheral to developments elsewhere in Mesoamerica, however, and are not always adequately covered in the literature.

This volume synthesizes vast amounts of historical and material evidence from all of the subregions of ancient Mesoamerica. The objective of this work is to provide descriptive information, a general background, and current theories and ideas on the topics at hand. Those who wish to know more will quickly realize that there is a wealth of published information, providing both general and detailed descriptions of results and interpretations of archaeological research programs in Mesoamerica, that can be accessed (a bibliography is provided at the end of the dictionary). Standard spellings found in most of the archaeology literature are followed here; in newer books and articles, where the orthography for indigenous terms are given, sounds and linguistic elements are represented by different letters. *Lacan-*

don becomes *Lakandon, Quiche* is now *Kich'e,* and so on. Thus the reader must be aware of these spelling shifts as well as the various spellings in different languages in the literature. As a last note, the words set in boldface type in the text of the dictionary represent cross-references to the major archaeological sites, people, materials, deities, concepts, and regions of ancient Mesoamerica that have been given entries here.

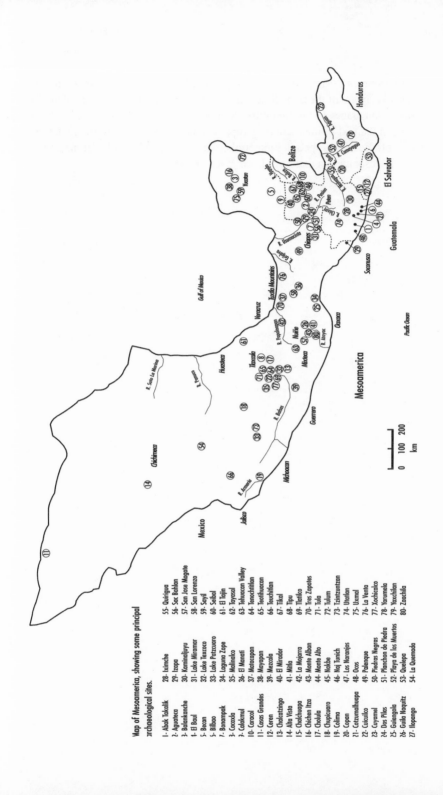

Map of Mesoamerica, showing some principal archaeological sites.

1- Abaj Takalik
2- Aguateca
3- Balamkanche
4- El Baul
5- Becan
6- Bilbao
7- Bonampak
8- Cacaxtla
9- Calakmul
10- Caracol
11- Casas Grandes
12- Ceren
13- Chalcatzingo
14- Alta Vista
15- Chalchuapa
16- Chichen Itza
17- Cholula
18- Chupicuaro
19- Colima
20- Copan
21- Cotzumalhuapa
22- Cuicuilco
23- Cuyamel
24- Dos Pilas
25- Guiengola
26- Guila Naquitz
27- Ilopango

28- Iximche
29- Izapa
30- Kaminaljuyu
31- Lake Miramar
32- Lake Texcoco
33- Lake Patzcuaro
34- Laguna Zope
35- Malinalco
36- El Manati
37- Matacapan
38- Mayapan
39- Mezcala
40- El Mirador
41- Mitla
42- La Mojarra
43- Monte Alban
44- Monte Alto
45- Nakbe
46- Naj Tunich
47- Los Naranjos
48- Ocos
49- Palenque
50- Piedras Negras
51- Planchon de Piedra
52- Playa de los Muertos
53- Quelepa
54- La Quemada

55- Quirigua
56- Sac Bahlan
57- San Jose Mogote
58- San Lorenzo
59- Soyil
60- Seibal
61- El Tajin
62- Tayasal
63- Tehuacan Valley
64- Tenochtitlan
65- Teotihuacan
66- Teuchitlan
67- Tikal
68- Tipu
69- Tlatilco
70- Tres Zapotes
71- Tula
72- Tulum
73- Tzintzuntzan
74- Utatlan
75- Uxmal
76- La Venta
77- Xochicalco
78- Yarumela
79- Yaxchilan
80- Zaachila

Chronology

10,000+ B.C.   Mobile big game hunters and gatherers; Paleo-Indian and Clovis cultures; Preceramic period.

8000+ B.C.   Archaic Period begins; small game hunters and gatherers; experimentation with plant and maize cultivation; seasonal campsites; more diverse stone tools.

5000 B.C.   Semisedentary camps; advances in agriculture; grinding stones for plant foods appear; populations rising.

3500 B.C.   Permanent villages evolving; increase in domesticated plants.

1800 B.C.   Early Formative Period begins; sedentary village life; early architecture and ceramics; agriculture, hunting, and gathering.

1200 B.C.   Rise of Olmec civilization; monumental architecture and art; interregional trade; social differentiation; early tombs; carved pottery.

1000 B.C.   Large villages and towns are common; trade and agriculture are important; regional chiefdoms.

600 B.C.   Middle Formative Period; Olmec culture wanes; rise of Maya civilization and complex cultures in Mexico.

500 B.C.   Writing emerging in Mexico; population growth; continued evolution of the state; warfare.

100 B.C.   Late Formative times; Early Teotihuacan culture; large sites and states present; interregional interaction heightens; fortifications; carved stone art is found in many regions.

A.D. 200   Start of Early Classic Period; largest public architecture; stone art is common; warfare and trade intensify; long count calendar.

A.D. 500   Influence of Teotihuacan grows; powerful Maya states; rise of Classic Mexican civilizations.

A.D. 600   Late Classic Period; proliferation of populations, architecture, and art throughout Mesoamerica.

A.D. 700	Teotihuacan falls; Classic Maya civilization; height of Classic Period cultures and populations.
A.D. 800	Classic Maya downfall occurring; changes in trade, politics, and religion; population decline and movements in Mesoamerica; Terminal/Epiclassic Period begins.
A.D. 900	Early Postclassic Period; rise of Toltec state; Maya florescence in Yucatan; highland Oaxaca cultures continue from Classic.
A.D. 1000	Toltec influence extends throughout region.
A.D. 1200	Aztecs enter Basin of Mexico; declining Maya states; Late Postclassic times begin.
A.D. 1400	Growth of states; large Aztec, Maya, Mixtec, and Zapotec polities and centers; alliances and trade.
A.D. 1500	Height of Aztec and Tarascan empires.
A.D. 1521	Spanish conquest of Aztecs; conquest and colonization of Mesoamerica begins.
A.D. 1524+	Spanish conquest of Maya area; Postclassic Period ending and beginning of Colonial Period.
A.D. 1697	Last independent Maya kingdom of the Itza falls.
A.D. 1800+	Little-contacted native settlements continue in rainforest; Spanish colonial period ending.

Introduction

Mesoamerica—the term and its defining characteristics were coined by anthropologist Paul Kirchoff in 1952—is a culture area that encompasses Mexico (including Yucatan), Guatemala, Western Honduras, and El Salvador. Some of the better known archaeological peoples of this region include the Olmecs (one of the first New World civilizations), the Maya (known for their temples, artworks, and hieroglyphic writing), the Aztecs (of whom we have vivid Spanish accounts of warfare, city life, sacrifice, and economic organization), the Toltecs, the Tarascans, the Mixtecs, and the Zapotecs. Mesoamerican cultural traits in general include the ball game; human sacrifice; stone and earth temple architecture; calendrics and astronomy; worship of the sun, moon, and heavens; writing; monumental stone art; clay figurine and polychrome ceramic making; jade and green stone working; state-level political organization; rain and sun deities; ancestor veneration; royal tombs; and maize agriculture, to name only a few.

This cluster of "cultural configurations" is what makes ancient Mesoamerican peoples collectively distinct from other New World cultures. Despite the fact that there existed general similarities among the ancient Mesoamerican cultures, there were also significant differences relating to material culture, religious beliefs, political organization, settlement patterns, and overall economic structure. For instance, high-quality jade crafts were at their height during the Olmec Formative Period, the Maya of the Classic Period recorded their histories and auto-sacrificial rituals in the longest and most numerous hieroglyphic texts, and Postclassic Mexican peoples specialized in metallurgy and sea trade.

Additionally, there were disparities in political structure and population density. Some societies like the Chichimecs and Lacandon consisted of small roaming bands, the Olmecs and west Mexican peoples were at the level of chiefdoms or incipient states, the Maya and Zapotec were organized into numerous small regional states, and the Aztecs and Tarascans had evolved into empires that controlled large areas and populations. The particulars of the religions, social organization, and general lifeways of the ancient Mesoamericans also differed greatly, but they were joined in similar histories, some general cultural traits, and geography.

However, there was also considerable diversity in environments and climates throughout Mesoamerica. For example, northern Mesoamerica was dry and desert-like, as it is today, with scrub forest and little plant cover. The central part of Mesoamerica surrounding the Basin of Mexico included some of the highest altitudes in the area, and it had abundant lake resources, mountains, and volcanoes. The coasts of the Gulf of Mexico and the Pacific Ocean were among the richest areas in this region since they were blessed with fertile alluvial and volcanic soils and large amounts of rainfall.

The mountainous region of southern Mexico and central Guatemala had lush forests, abundant rain, and constant cool temperatures. The rainforests of northern Guatemala and Chiapas, Mexico, were hot, humid lands with flat areas, low rolling hills, and snaking rivers. Finally, the flat limestone shelf of the Yucatan Peninsula was a drier climate than other parts of Mesoamerica, and its soils were thinner and surface water practically nonexistent. These different environments provided different materials, flora, fauna, and living conditions for their ancient human inhabitants. Furthermore, the diverse ecological zones did not determine a particular society's structure and cultural evolutionary trajectories but provided constraints and possibilities for social change and diversification.

The great Mesoamerican civilizations seen by the Spanish conquistadores in the 16th century had their roots in the early settled societies beginning around 2000 B.C., but archaeological cultures were present in this area from Paleo-Indian to Archaic times, from approximately 10,000–2000 B.C. The evolution of Mesoamerican culture is typically divided into distinct periods in much of the region; the most common of these chronological divisions (with estimated dates) are: Formative Period (1800 B.C. to A.D. 200), Classic Period (A.D. 200 to A.D. 900), and Postclassic Period (A.D. 900 to Spanish colonial times).

These major chronological divisions are usually subdivided into separate phases of "Early," "Middle," and "Late" within each period. Of course there are slight differences in time lines and chronological dates, depending on the region, known data, idiosyncratic local developments, amount of comparative information, and dating techniques. For example, some archaeologists argue that the Classic Period ended almost a century earlier in the western and southern Maya area.

There are many ancient Mexican and Central American cultures covered in this dictionary that cannot be described and summarized here. However, there are a few cultures that have received a lot of attention in research and writings and as a result are often recalled when one thinks of "Mesoamerica." One of the first civilizations of the region, often called the "Mother Culture," is the Olmec Formative Period culture, centered in the Gulf Coast area and well known for its colossal stone heads, three-dimensional stone sculptures, jade artifacts, and earthen mounds. This area was also the locus of Classic to Postclassic cultures, such as the Huastec Maya and Totonacs, known for the ball game and their distinctive sculpture and ceramics.

Teotihuacan, a huge metropolis in central Mexico, dating from Formative to Classic times, was an expansionistic state that was responsible for some of the largest stone architecture and most beautifully painted polychrome murals in the New World. There were contemporaneous precocious societies in west Mexico, such as the Teuchitlan tradition centered in Jalisco, that exhibited large centers, large tombs, elaborate ceramic figurines, and intensive agriculture.

Maya civilization of southern Mexico and upper Central America, which also had its beginnings during the Formative Period and persisted until the Spanish conquest, is known widely for its impressive cities of temples and palaces, stone sculptures, hieroglyphic inscriptions, and artwork. The neighboring cultures in the rugged mountainous region of Oaxaca, Mexico, the Zapotec and the Mixtec, mastered writing and painting in books and creating fine objects and ornaments out of gold. The Toltecs of central Mexico established the legacy of Postclassic Mexico with interregional trade and contacts, expansion through warfare, and royal bloodlines sought by later cultures.

Not to be forgotten are the mighty Aztecs who built cities in Postclassic central Mexico and an empire that encompassed much of central Mesoamerica and who are universally known as great warriors, sacrificers, traders, architects, and artisans. The Postclassic Tarascan kingdom of west Mexico needs to be mentioned here as one of the great Mesoamerican civilizations, because they controlled vast territories, successfully repelled Aztec intrusions, and produced excellent metal and fired-ceramic crafts.

These ancient cultures have drawn countless explorers and scholars since the middle of the 19th century. Some early accounts (in the early 1800s) of archaeological sites and finds in Mexico and Central America come from the Austrian Guillelmo Dupaix, the Guatemalan official Modesto Méndez, and German naturalist Alexander von Humboldt. The most famous travelers to visit Mesoamerican archaeological sites and report them to the world were John Lloyd Stephens, a New York lawyer, and Frederick Catherwood, an English architect and draftsman, who visited Yucatan and Central America around 1839–42.

Their popular publications surprised the world with their descriptions and dramatic drawings of exciting new ruins and artifacts. Following these reports of "lost cities," explorers and archaeologists trekked to Mesoamerica to investigate and record these ancient cultures. Between 1870 and 1905, men such as Claude-Joseph-Désiré Charnay, Alfred P. Maudslay, and Teobert Maler headed for Mexico and Central America to acquire more descriptions, drawings, and, more importantly, artifacts and photographs for publications and museum collections.

The work of this vanguard of explorers and researchers spurred archaeologists to scientifically investigate ancient Mesoamerican ruins and cultures. Early archaeology projects and studies were led by Edward Thompson, Sylvanus G. Morley, Herbert Spinden, Antonio and Carlos Villacorta, Mathew Stirling, Frans Blom, Anna Shepard, Alfred Tozzer, and J. Eric S. Thompson, to list only a few of the many who focused on finding and digging archaeological sites and objects throughout the region. These people performed some of the earliest studies of Mesoamerican artifacts, architecture, cultural histories, writing systems, and indigenous art. The results of their efforts inspired the next generation of scientists, historians, and archaeologists, including Ledyard Smith, Edwin Shook, Tatiana Proskouriakoff, Gordon Willey, William Sanders, Richard MacNeish, Michael Coe, Alberto Ruz Lhuillier, Kent Flannery, George Kubler, Floyd Lounsbury, Alfonso Caso, Doris Stone, Ignacio Bernal, and Adrian Recinos, to carry out anthropological and historical analyses of past Mesoamerican cultures and their settlement patterns, evolving societies, trade, religious beliefs, interregional interactions, diet, art and architecture, and social organization.

Today there is a flurry of research activity on myriad topics in Mesoamerica by numerous archaeologists, scientists, anthropologists, ethnohistorians, and their students. The current generation owes much to the pioneering research, preliminary studies, and cultural insights of the investigators of the last 150 years. Our knowledge of many Pre-Columbian cultures in Mexico and Central America continues to grow, and tremendous breakthroughs have been made over the last 50 years concerning our understanding of artifact production, architectural design, hieroglyphic texts, art and iconography, cultural evolution, and ceremonies and ritual. Although traditional studies of sites, structures, and artifacts are still found, significant research on gender, agriculture, disease, linguistics, belief systems, migration, social status, dress, and other highly specialized problems and issues is on the increase.

Because of the long history and diversity of area studies and because of the comparative approach that is prevalent in this field, there is an abundance of information and published research available. Many of the earlier—as well as current "cutting edge"—scholarly publications on Mesoamerican sites, material culture, and societies are listed in the bibliography of this historical dictionary. Scholars and students of Mesoamerican prehistory have at their fingertips a very large body of literature, and new exciting and important excavation reports and research syntheses reach the presses every month. This makes summarizing past Mesoamerican cultural achievements, and scientists' reports of them, a worthwhile, rich, and busy enterprise.

The Dictionary

A

ABAK TAKALIK. A large Formative Period site (ca. 1000 B.C. to A.D. 200) located in the foothills near rivers that run to the Pacific Coast of Guatemala. This site rests just south of the mountain chain that crosses Chiapas and Guatemala, and thus benefited from abundant resources and a favorable living and agricultural environment. Abak Takalik, found in the department of Retalhuleu, measures nearly six square kilometers and is almost entirely made up of earthen mounds and scattered stone sculpture.

The sculpture at this ruin is of purely Formative Period style, with its early representations of standing human figures wearing ceremonial attire. One monument may have been a recarved boulder sculpture that was once similar to **Olmec** Early Formative **colossal heads** found near the Gulf Coast of Veracruz. A large boulder sculpture of a crouching figure with a down-turned mouth found near the site also closely resembles Olmec art. Stone **stelae** carry early **calendar** dates that have numbered baktun 7 and 8 coefficients, or cycles, which place them between 100 B.C. and A.D. 100 (firmly Late Formative dates).

Both the architecture and monumental art of the site have general affinities with the contemporaneous ruins of **Izapa** in Chiapas and **Kaminaljuyu** in highland Guatemala. However, contact with the Early-Middle Formative Period Olmecs is also apparent in the iconography on its stone monuments. The earliest **ceramics** from the site date to the Early Formative and are similar to wares from the Pacific Coast. However, during the Middle Formative, stronger ties to local piedmont sites, such as **Bilbao** and **Monte Alto,** are more evident through similar ceramic styles. Recent excavations at Abak Takalik have been carried out by teams from the University of California and the Institute of Anthropology and History of Guatemala. These investigations involve the consolidation of stone monuments and earthen architectural features.

AGRICULTURE. *See* CACAO, CHINAMPA, DIET, MAGUEY, MAIZE, and MANO AND METATE

AGUATECA. An unusual archaeological site of the Classic **Maya** and in **Mesoamerica** as a whole, in that many of its structures have rich collections of artifacts still in situ on their floors. Aguateca, which is located near the site of **Dos Pilas** in southwestern **Peten,** Guatemala, was sacked during intensified **warfare** at the time of the Classic Maya downfall. Much of the site was burned, forcing the inhabitants to flee from their dwellings, leaving their possessions behind. Objects found on structure floors include shell pendants, carved bone, stone tools made of **obsidian** and **chert,** painted **ceramic** vessels, clay masks, and **manos and metates.** One elite palace structure was the home of a scribe, and many of the materials necessary for the **trade,** such as inkpots made of cut shell and grinding implements for the preparation of pigments, were recovered.

Aguateca is a beautiful site with large **temples** and stone **stelae** bearing portraits of Maya rulers and **hieroglyphics.** The site overlooks Lake Petexbatun from a defensive position on a high bluff. The site also has defensive walls and a deep chasm that protect it from attackers. According to hieroglyphic texts, Aguateca and Dos Pilas were ruled by the same dynasty, centered at Dos Pilas. At the time of the Maya collapse, the ruling elite and local populations appear to have moved to Aguateca because of its highly defensible position. Work that focuses on the excavation of the preserved floor artifact assemblages and seeks to elucidate the causes and effects of the Classic Period collapse continues at Aguateca.

AHAW (Ah-**how**). This is a word in many Mayan languages that can be glossed in English as "ruler," "noble," or "lord." It is also often spelled "ajau" and "ajaw." This term is written in **Maya hieroglyphs,** and it appears in the names and titles of Maya kings and elites. High-ranking **women** and scribes may also carry this title. Kings were often called *k'ul ahaw,* or "sacred ruler." *See also* TLATOANI

ALTAR. Altars in ancient **Mesoamerica** were in the form of rounded or squared stones, or also tables and benches made of wood (see photo). Altars were placed in **temple** rooms, before stairways leading to temples and residences, and in front of images of **deities,** ancestors, and rulers. Altars marked sacred and ceremonial space where important rituals were practiced or where offerings and sacred items were kept. Sometimes altars were simply makeshift constructions of wood and stones in houses, fields, and public areas that were dismantled or abandoned after their ceremonial use. Ceremonial caches, or offerings, containing painted **ceramics, jade,** shell, incense burners, and other objects, were often placed under altars.

Many large rounded stone altars were placed before carved stone **stelae** in Classic **Maya** sites. Although the majority of these altars are plain, or without carved designs, many of them have elaborate iconography and **hieroglyphs.** It is also commonly assumed that these altars served as places for leaving offerings or performing rites and **sacrifices.** However, some sculpted altars display clues that they may have been used as thrones or seats—their iconography depicts seated Maya nobles or the altar as a cushion or mat, the texts mention the "seating," or taking of the throne of Maya kings, and some hieroglyphic texts may describe the "altars" as thrones or seats.

ARCHITECTURE. *See* BALL COURT, TEMPLE, TOMB, and VAULTED ROOF

ASTRONOMY. Ancient peoples from **Mesoamerica** were great sky watchers, and they recorded the movements of the sun, moon, planets, and stars through observations with the naked eye that were put down in **hieroglyphic** and pictoral **codices.** Information from Spanish documents, ethnographies, and archaeology attests to the importance of the sky and its wandering celestial bodies and constellations to Mesoamerican societies. Astronomy was so important to these people that **calendars** and rituals were created around celestial observations. Additionally, religious beliefs strongly reflected this sky watching, and cities were built and aligned according to movements of the heavens. Importantly, a large number of Mesoamerican sites are arranged according to the cardinal directions determined by the path of the sun.

In the **Aztec** culture, the sun and the moon and their travels were closely watched, and they were associated with specific **deities.** Rituals and **sacrifices** were carried out for these deities in order to sustain them and preserve their predictable movements through the sky. For instance, Aztec "new fire" ceremonies and thousands of human sacrifices were performed to aid **Huitzilopochtli**—an aspect of the sun god—to arise each day after a treacherous journey through the dark **underworld.** The Aztec Moon Goddess was associated with the feminine earth and fertility deities and was often prayed to and given offerings. The cycles of the moon were—and still are in many areas—watched in order to time the calendar months and to track human gestation.

Much of what we know about ancient **Maya** astronomy comes from studies of hieroglyphic writing, iconography, and architecture. Information on the Maya calendar from carved stone **stelae** and panels, in addition to the codices, indicates that the Maya studied and predicted the cyclical movements of the sun, moon, **Venus,** and possibly other planets. The Maya also recorded and predicted lunar and solar eclipses. Maya astronomy was crucial in determining specific rituals, the naming of people and the determining of their destinies, and for other cultural practices.

The Maya chose times for war and for taking captives according to the position of Venus and the sun for religious reasons and to avoid disruptions in the agricultural cycle. Maya art also contains various symbols and representations of the sun, moon, Venus, stars, and constellations. The architectural features of Maya **temples,** mainly window alignments and horizon markers, were often used to sight the movements of the sun, moon, and stars. At the Classic Period center of **Tikal,** for instance, the impressive roofs of tall temples mark solstice and equinox sunrises and sunsets when viewing the sun from one structure to the next.

ATLATL. Nahuatl term for "spear thrower" that has been adopted in the archaeological and anthropological literature to name this device. The atlatl is usually a piece of rounded or flattened wood or branch, notched at one end in order to fit the end of a dart or spear shaft used for hunting or **warfare.** Atlatls often have attached rings that are used as finger holes for gripping and flinging the dart. The spear thrower is used as an extension of the power and thrust of the arm, which allows a person to accurately fling a spear further and at greater velocity.

A few examples of wooden atlatls from Pre-Columbian central Mexico are carved with elaborate designs, some of which depict richly attired warriors. In the **Maya** area, atlatls are shown in Classic Period art, but they appear to be more commonly depicted and were possibly used more often during Postclassic times with the **Toltec** and **Aztec** cultures. Nonetheless, these **weapons** may have been used most by the victorious armies in armed encounters. Atlatls, however, were probably invented and frequently used by **Clovis** and Archaic Period hunters for hunting big game, and they may have been used more often in central Mexico through time. Interestingly enough, the atlatl was still being used up until recently by the **Tarascan** peoples on the lakes of **west Mexico** to down water fowl.

AZTECS (As-tehks). General term for **Nahuatl** speaking peoples in Pre-Columbian central Mexico, which connotes "people from **Aztlan**." Today the word *Aztec* is typically used to refer to the Mexica people who resided in the island city of **Tenochtitlan** in Lake **Texcoco** in the **Basin of Mexico.** The Aztecs are widely recognized for their imperial political and economic structure; religious ideology that involves natural elements, ancestors, sacred landscapes, and human **sacrifice;** and for their monumental stone art and architecture, which is routinely uncovered during construction projects in contemporary Mexico City. The Mexica Aztecs had one of the most powerful states and one of the more splendid capital centers in all of ancient **Mesoamerica.**

Of the many **deities** important to the Aztecs, we know much about the widely revered **Huitzilopochtli, Quetzalcoatl, Tlaloc, Tezcatlipoca, Coatlique, Xipe Totec,** and **Coyolxauhqui,** which are often mentioned in sources that date to early colonial times. Aztec art is famous the world over for its monolithic stone carvings, including the **calendar stone** and the **chacmool,** portable objects carved from **jade,** feather work, and finely painted and modeled **ceramics.** They also created **codices,** or books, that contained painted images, but not many **hieroglyphs,** on bark paper or animal skin. The Aztec capital of Tenochtitlan was the home of thousands of inhabitants, towering **temples,** ornate palaces, **ball courts** for the bouncing **rubber** ball game, marketplaces, **tzompantli,** or skull racks, irrigated **chinampa** agricultural fields, and the residences of the **calpulli** "clans."

The Aztecs were newcomers to state politics in central Mexico during the 13th century when they wandered into the Valley of Mexico (or **Basin of Mexico**) while migrating from their original homeland. Here they became **tribute** paying vassals and mercenaries of local established states. Through political intrigue and much success in **warfare,** the Aztecs eventually gained their independence and their own tributary towns, agricultural plots, and land for their capital center. The Aztecs came to power in central Mexico and were able to expand to other parts of Mesoamerica through the military and political support of a "triple alliance" between the peoples of the towns of Tenochtitlan, Tetzcoco (Texcoco), and Tlacopan (Tacuba).

Aztec imperial expansion was driven by the need to acquire food, materials, and labor for the growing Aztec state and also to obtain the necessary sacrificial victims on the battlefield to feed the sun during its daily journey. The Aztecs would subjugate an area by means of military force, then set up rulership through local elites and allies and ensure their subordinates' allegiance and tribute payments with the threat of warfare and by political and marriage alliances.

The Aztec empire was at its peak and possibly facing drastic political and economic reform in order to continue making conquests, when the Spanish **conquistadores** under Hernan Cortes arrived in A.D. 1519. The Spaniards were greeted by the Mexica-Aztec ruler **Motecuhzoma,** who was trying to consolidate his realm and implement political and economic changes at the time. Because of military strategy and advanced weaponry, and, critically, through the help of thousands of indigenous allies (both former friends and enemies of the Aztecs), combined with the spread of deadly epidemic diseases that decimated native populations, the Spanish were able to sack Tenochtitlan, subdue the Aztecs and their last emperor, Cuauhtemoc, and appropriate their territories by A.D. 1521.

AZTLAN (Ahts-**lahn**). The mythical homeland from which the **Aztec** people are believed to have originated and subsequently left to migrate to central Mexico. From this original homeland they wandered through northern **Mesoamerica** until they reached Lake **Texcoco** (Tetzcoco) in central Mexico and founded the city of **Tenochtitlan.** *Aztlan* is **Nahuatl** for "Place of the Herons/Cranes" or "Place of Whiteness," and it is said to have been a habitable island in a beautiful lake. The word *Aztec* signifies "people from Aztlan," and this term has been applied to Nahuatl speakers of Postclassic central Mexico. The Aztecs of Tenochtitlan referred to themselves collectively as the "Mexica."

Anthropologists and historians have long tried to locate Aztlan, or the area in which the mythological place is based, either in central or **west Mexico** or in Veracruz, by studying Aztec myth and archaeological evidence. These areas have numerous lakes and water fowl as described in the Aztec myth of Aztlan. However, the true location of Aztlan, or the area that inspired the legend, may never be known. There are conflicting and vague details from the Aztec chronicles and a number of distinct places seem to be referred to in the histories. It is also possible that Aztlan is truly mythological and existed only in Aztec **religion** and beliefs. Also there are many sacred "Places of the Reeds," **(Tollan),** or additional sites of origin, in Mesoamerican lore (such as the centers of **Teotihuacan** and **Tula**), which further confuses the search for Aztlan. Even Aztec kings sent out parties in search of Aztlan, where it was believed communication with **deities** and ancestors was possible, but the place, or places, of these visits was never recorded or definitively identified.

Aztec legend states that their premigration ancestors lived on Aztlan, an island surrounded by reeds in the center of a large lagoon. The journey from Aztlan by the Aztecs, who may have been hunters, gatherers, and incipient farmers earlier on, was initiated and led by **Huitzilopochtli,** an important Aztec deity who may have been linked with a historical person and culture hero/leader.

The Mexica-Aztecs wandered many years throughout Mexico visiting sacred places, including **caves** and hills. They overcame obstacles and arduous tests by supernatural beings to eventually settle in Tenochtitlan, itself an island surrounded by reeds and herons, which may have helped shape Mexica-Aztec history, legends, and origin myths concerning "Aztlan" or "Tollan." Many Aztec **codices,** such as the Boturini and Mendoza, illustrate the Aztec migration from Aztlan and their travels and trials in search of a new homeland in Mexico. *See also* CODEX MENDOZA, PIPIL, and TLAXCALA

B

BAJOS. These are mostly natural (but sometimes human-constructed) depressions or low areas in the terrain of rainforests, particularly in the lowland jungles of the **Maya** region, where water and fine sediments collect. Some bajos were modified through the removal of sediments and organic material to enrich garden plots, or **chinampa** raised fields, or they were deepened so they could hold more water. At the Formative Period center of **Nakbe** in Guatemala, bajo soils were extracted to thicken and fertilize agricultural fields. Many Maya sites, such as **Tikal,** El **Mirador,** and **Dos Pilas,** are located near bajos, which were used as sources of water and as areas for hunting animals and collecting certain plants, including palms and **cacao.**

If it weren't for using the bajos as reservoirs, many central lowland Maya sites would have been without water during the dry season. Some archaeologists believe that the bajos were significant for the raising of fish and other aquatic foods in addition to being necessary for canoe transportation and defense against attackers. One theory on the collapse of Classic Maya civilization states that the silting and filling in of bajos from extensive overcropping and erosion may have cut off this crucial supply of water to the troubled, overcrowded cities. Recent research projects studying bajos near Tikal, Guatemala, have found abundant settlement and substantial use of the bajos throughout prehistoric times.

BALANKANCHE. An impressive **cave** that was recently opened near the ruins of **Chichen Itza** in **Yucatan,** Mexico. The cave is full of artifacts of the ancient **Maya,** who performed ceremonies and pilgrimages there. Subsequent archaeological, iconographic, and ethnographical research has shown the importance of caves in Maya ritual, belief systems, and settlement layout. Balankanche appears to be the locus of rituals principally dedicated to the **deities** of rain and agricultural fertility: **Chac, Tlaloc,** and the **Maize** god, which may have been aspects of the same deity or closely related supernatural beings.

Throughout the cave, **ceramic** vessels and **manos and metates** (used for grinding maize and other foods) in miniature were discovered intact. These artifacts were typically left in niches, near cave formations and stalagmites, and near underground pools of water. One immense cave formation of joining dripstones resembles the Maya sacred Ceiba, or world tree. Until recently, Maya shamans still visited this and other caves in the area to perform rituals and offer prayers to supernatural beings, **underworld** deities, and the ancestors.

BALL COURT. Formal ball court constructions are found throughout **Mesoamerica** (and the Southwest United States and Caribbean, which attests to interregional interaction), but the game was probably also played in streets and other open areas at both small and large settlements. Examples of ball courts can be seen at El **Tajin** (Veracruz), **Tula** (Hidalgo), Santa Quiteria precinct at Arenal (Jalisco) of the **Teuchitlan** tradition, **Copan** (Honduras), **Chichen Itza** (Yucatan), **Iximche** (Guatemala), and **Tikal** (Guatemala).

Ball courts can be easily spotted even before they are excavated, because they consist of two long parallel constructions with a narrow playing alley between them (see photo). These buildings are made of earth or stone masonry, and many of them have sloping benches flanking the alley to keep the bouncing **rubber** ball in play. Many courts also have "I"-shaped playing areas, or enclosed end zones that are perpendicular to the central playing alley (Iximche). Other courts may have vertical walls with stone rings or hoops set vertically into them (Chichen Itza), and still others may exhibit stone markers set into the sloping benches (Copan) and round sculptures or markers placed in the central playing alley (Copan). **Temples, altars,** storage areas, and spectator steps and seats might also be attached to the ball courts.

The ball game and players are commonly depicted in Mesoamerican painted **ceramics,** modeled ceramic figurines, stone sculpture, painted books (**codices**), and murals. Rubber balls molded to various sizes, knee and elbow pads, hand stones (*palmas*), and waist protectors (yokes/*yugos* and *hachas*) were used. Despite the rich information from archaeology and ethnohistoric accounts, relatively little is known about the development or rules of the ancient Mesoamerican ball game. The game probably had major political and ritual functions that were associated with **warfare, sacrifice, religion,** and elite competition. Ball courts are found near temples of the elite and central **plazas** in the largest centers, and the courts are aligned with the cardinal directions. This placement underscores their politico-religious function with the nobles.

Mesoamerican elites and rulers were highly regarded as ballplayers (Classic Maya *ah pitz'*), and their games were played for the highest stakes: sacrificial victims and the perpetuation of the cosmos. The occasion of the game probably determined who was to be sacrificed (winners, losers, all, or no one, depending on the outcome and/or **calendar** date). Points may have been scored by hitting markers with the ball, sending the ball into the end zone, or passing it through a ring. According to evidence from art and written documents, the ball was probably not touched with the hands, head, or feet. Professional players and betting (with **textiles** and clothes) were described by the Spanish. A version of the ball game is still being played by a growing number of teams in various parts of northwest Mexico. Today games often end in ties, and points can be subtracted for certain plays or mistakes.

BALL GAME. *See* BALL COURT

BARRA. The designated name of one of the earliest sedentary and **ceramic**-making societies known by archaeologists to date from the Early Formative Period in ancient **Mesoamerica.** The Barra peoples existed along the resource-abundant Pacific Coast, in mangrove swamps, and river deltas and valleys in Chiapas, Mexico, Guatemala, and El Salvador. This culture is similar to, but predates, the **Ocos** people, and we do not know if they were ancestors of the **Maya** who resided in this region much later.

Barra sites are easily identified by a few large earthen mounds and excellent examples of hard-fired and painted ceramics. Ceramics suddenly appear at this time as well-made and beautifully decorated bowls and storage jars called "tecomates." Fired clay figurines, which probably depict human females, were also initiated by this culture. These people subsisted by fishing and collecting along the coasts and rivers, and they supplemented their **diets** with plants, including **maize,** that they either gathered or cultivated.

Significant innovations in this area at this time were settled life, incipient agriculture, **trade,** and the invention of ceramics which could have been partially a result of interaction and borrowing from other societies, including peoples from lower Central America and South America. Barra settled life and material culture, including ceramics and grinding stones, appear rather suddenly in the archaeological record. Hence, they might possibly be attributed to contacts with other cultures or to the spread of technology and ideas from further west in Mexico or from South America. Exotic **obsidian** is also found at these sites, which points to interaction and trade with highland societies. Later Mesoamerican civilizations, such as the **Olmec, Zapotec,** and the Maya, built on some of the earlier technology, subsistence patterns, and cultural aspects of the coastal Barra people.

BASIN OF MEXICO. This area in central highland Mexico was, and still is, as witnessed by modern urban developments, a focal point of settlement and significant cultural achievements. The Basin of Mexico, or the Valley of Mexico, contained a large lake in antiquity (before it was filled in by the Spanish **conquistadores** and subsequent populations during the building of Mexico City) that was surrounded by hills and volcanoes. Archaeologists working in this region have discovered the earliest inhabitants of **Mesoamerica: Clovis**-related peoples who hunted mammoths and later archaic hunters who roamed the shores and environs of Lake **Texcoco** (Tetzcoco) gathering plant foods and hunting animals in this rich ecosystem. The Basin of Mexico has a long sequence of occupation that includes some of the greatest civilizations in ancient Mesoamerica because of its great variety of natural resources (food and construction materials) and hospitable climate.

The presence or influence of the **Olmecs** and related Early Formative cultures, whose artisans carved fine **jade** artifacts and made exquisite stone sculptures and unique **ceramics,** is found in the Basin of Mexico at several sites, including **Tlatilco.** Some of the first stone-faced **temple** architecture and large-scale centers, like **Cuicuilco,** are also located in this area. **Teotihuacan,** the huge Classic Period metropolis that was one of the largest cities in the Pre-Columbian New World, rose from the dense populations and rich resources of the central basin and nearby lake areas, including the **obsidian** mines in the hills.

Likewise, the empire of the **Aztecs** built on the grandeur and achievements of local Postclassic states to form one of the largest and most complex New World states. These people built their capital, **Tenochtitlan,** on an island in Lake Texcoco and eventually incorporated or allied themselves with adjacent city-states, including the Pre-Columbian center of Texcoco to the east. Upon their conquest of the Aztecs, the Spanish built the capital of their New World empire on Tenochtitlan not only because of the large available labor pool and its central location but because of the availability of water and resources and the agreeable climate of the highland basin.

BAUL (EL). Archaeological site of the **Cotzumalhuapa** culture and art style located in the piedmont area near the Pacific Coast of southern Guatemala. This ruin is also near **Bilbao,** another large Cotzumalhuapa-type site. Recent surveys and excavations at El Baul have explored the Classic to Terminal Classic Period occupations of the site and its unique carved stone artworks. Many elite and residential structures have been found and investigated, and the site is currently endangered by encroaching urban settlement. One large three-dimensional stone sculpture at the site depicts an aged male **deity.** A carved slab stone **stela** shows a standing human figure, and people still leave offerings of candles, flowers, and food in front of or on this monument. These sculptures are similar to other monuments and iconography in Veracruz, especially El **Tajin,** and other Mexican sites.

The people at El Baul probably interacted with people in Mexico and less with the **Maya,** or it is possible that El Baul was inhabited by immigrants, perhaps **Nahua** peoples who left Mexico much earlier. A Formative Period stela (Stela 1) that has one of the earliest **calendar** dates in its **hieroglyphic** inscription and the earliest date in the Maya geographic region was found in El Baul. The human figure on Stela 1, which carries a baton or possibly a torch, is richly attired in clothing and an ornate headdress. A face, which could be that of an ancestor or deity, gazes down at this figure from elaborate scrollwork. This monument attests to ties with **Izapa, Kaminaljuyu, Abak Takalik,** and early Maya centers to the north. Many of the sculptural pieces were taken to Berlin during the 19th century, and these carved stones, and others that have been recently uncovered, are currently being documented.

BECAN. A **Maya** site in Campeche, in the state of **Yucatan,** Mexico, made famous and particularly intriguing by the discovery of a deep defensive ditch and impressive rampart system that surrounds the site core. This discovery at Becan has led to debates on the nature of Maya **warfare** in state formation and sociopolitical interaction. Becan had a sizeable resident population by Middle Preclassic times, but it was most extensively in-habited during the Classic Period. The defensive works were begun dur-ing the Late Formative Period and added onto and maintained during Classic times.

There may have been a connection between Becan and **Teotihuacan** in the Early Classic Period, because green **obsidian** from Central Mexico and Teotihuacan-style **ceramics** were found in excavations at the site. This site is a small-to-medium-sized center with a small number of large **temple** constructions and **plazas,** but few stone carvings or **stelae.** Becan is well known for its mosaic sculptural facades on palace-like structures known as the Chenes and Rio Bec regional architectural style. These sculpture mosaics contain scrolling, geometric patterns, and a giant earth monster face. *See also* AGUATECA, DOS PILAS, and TIKAL

BILBAO. A major Classic to Terminal Classic Period **Cotzumalhuapa** cul-ture site found near the south coast of Guatemala that was centered in the hilly piedmont zone. Bilbao is situated near the modern town of Santa Lu-cia Cotzumalhuapa, and the monumental stone artworks and architecture of this site are surrounded by coffee and sugarcane plantations. Many sculpted stone **stelae** and other freestanding monuments of human figures and **jaguars** have been removed from the site. However, low relief carv-ings in immovable boulders that depict people, supernatural beings, the ball game, and the rain **deity, Tlaloc,** still remain.

Only small-scale excavations have been done at Bilbao, but many large mounds with stone and adobe architecture that surround courtyards and an extensive ancient settlement await exploration. The art and material culture associated with this site and cultural-historical traditions point to possible connections or more extensive interaction with Mexican cultures than with the ancient **Maya.** The people who lived at Bilbao may have been related to the **Nahuatl**-speaking **Pipil** populations who migrated to Central America from central Mexico in antiquity. *See also* BAUL (EL)

BONAMPAK (Bohn-ahm-**pak**). A Classic **Maya** site in the **Usumacinta River** region in lowland Chiapas, Mexico, that became well known after a 1946 expedition report indicated that a standing structure still contain-ing vibrant polychrome mural paintings in three rooms had been discov-ered (see photo). Bonampak is a medium-sized Maya center that has about 10 known carved monuments in low relief that are scattered around a large central ceremonial **plaza.** It also has a large acropolis area that is built on a natural hill, which is common in the Classic Maya sites of lowland Chiapas, such as **Palenque. Hieroglyphic** texts from the murals, monuments, and nearby sites indicate that the elites from Bonampak interacted with nobles from the Usumacinta region sites of **Yaxchilan, Piedras Negras,** and Lacanha. This site was abandoned at the end of the Late Classic Period, perhaps because of local endemic **warfare,** as portrayed in the murals.

Structure 1 of Bonampak contains well-preserved multicolored wall paintings in the three rooms, and each of the doorways to these rooms has a carved stone lintel above it that depicts battle scenes involving local elites. The murals in Room 1 show a gathering of Maya nobles dressed in full ceremonial splendor as they meet and dance in front of the Bonampak nobles and future heir to the throne. In a highly unusual scene in Maya art, a band plays trumpets, drums, rattles, and other musical instruments before the important gathering of nobles.

Room 2 depicts the fury of a pitched battle between two Maya armies, the victorious one led by the Bonampak ruler "Chan-Muan." Besides warfare, this mural also shows the presentation of near-naked captives to the ruler and his warriors at a stepped and terraced building. The Room 3 paintings display a scene of ritual, music, and dance that took place after the **sacrifice** of the war captives. Maya nobles dance to trumpets with banners while wearing elaborate costumes and headdresses, and the royal family performs a bloodletting ceremony. New infrared photography of the murals has discovered interesting details, such as cloth bundles that are labeled with the **hieroglyph** for **cacao** (*cacaw*) that may mark the quantities of chocolate beans presented for **tribute.** *See also* CACAXTLA

C

CACAO. The word for cacao, or chocolate, comes from its **Maya** name, *cacaw*. Cacao beans grow in pods on the trunks of small trees (*Theobroma cacao*) that are found in areas of rich and moist soil of the tropics. Cacao beans were used in **Mesoamerica** as currency and for exchange even until the 19th century. New evidence from infrared imagery taken of **Bonampak** murals suggests that the Classic Maya paid **tribute** with or brought as gifts bundles of cacao beans. Cacao beans and pods are often depicted in **ceramics** and stone sculptures.

The cacao beans were ground up and mixed with water—and sometimes with ground **maize**—and then frothed to make a chocolate drink. This drink was a standard refreshment in Maya elite feasts. Classic Period

Maya ceramic cylindrical vases have in their **hieroglyphic** rim texts, "his/her/their drinking vessel for cacaw," and a carved stone panel at the site of **Piedras Negras** in Guatemala states that Maya kings became drunk on a cacao drink that was presumably fermented. Soon after the Spanish conquest, cacao was taken back to Europe, where it was mixed with milk and sugar to make various foods and drinks. *See also* DIET

CACAXTLA (Kah-**kash**-lah). Hilltop site with palace complexes, residences, and **temples** dating to around A.D. 700–850 near the border of Puebla and **Tlaxcala,** Central Mexico, where excellently preserved and brilliantly painted murals were discovered during looting in the early 1970s. Some murals, with astonishing detail of ancient life, **religion,** and **warfare,** and perhaps other paintings that still await to be uncovered, are done in a hybrid **Maya**-Mexican style that is seen in East Mexico and the Maya area during the Terminal Classic and Early Postclassic Periods. Many of the designs are Maya, but the **hieroglyphic** writing system, consisting of day signs and possibly personal names, is Mexican.

This site was probably situated along **trade** and interaction routes between Central Mexico and the Maya area. The term *cacaxtli* means "backpack frame or bundle" or "merchant," and one of the murals actually depicts the Maya merchant god resting near his traveling pack of goods. Was this center important for ancient Mesoamerican merchants, and does it retain its original place name? Another section of murals depicts an ongoing battle between ferocious **jaguar** warriors (indigenous Mexicans?) and a losing cadre of downed eagle knights (Maya peoples?). Each group, and possibly distinct ethnic peoples, are drawn differently. The defeated people in eagle regalia may be **Putun** Maya from the plains of Tabasco and Campeche found to the east, but more than likely they were **Huastec** Maya from adjacent Veracruz. *See also* BONAMPAK

CAKCHIQUEL. A **Maya** people of highland Guatemala who are located near the **Quiche** Maya, with whom they are related culturally, linguistically, and historically. The Cakchiquel are known for their beautifully woven **textiles,** their hilltop fortress capital called **Iximche,** or "Tree of Maize" (the **Ramon** tree), and their military conflicts with the Quiche and Spanish **conquistadores** in Late Postclassic and Early Colonial times. Today much anthropological research is being conducted on Cakchiquel culture, linguistics, and clothing styles.

The Cakchiquel allied themselves with the Spanish under their commander, Pedro de Alvarado, who was sent by Hernan Cortes to subjugate the Maya lands in Guatemala. The Cakchiquel helped defeat the Quiche in battle in 1524 and take their capital of **Utatlan.** Iximche then became the first colonial capital of Guatemala, until the Cakchiquel rebelled against their Spanish overlords and the town was partially destroyed and soon abandoned. Recent archaeological investigations in the Cakchiquel area have uncovered **obsidian** mines and workshops, plus numerous ruined centers and carved stone monuments dating from the Formative to Postclassic Periods.

CALAKMUL. One of the largest known Classic **Maya** sites, which is on par with **Tikal** and El **Mirador** (impressive ancient Maya sites just to the south) in **temple** construction and settlement size. Calakmul is found in the state of Campeche in southern **Yucatan,** Mexico. This site also claims the honor of having the highest number of carved stone **stelae:** 113. Unfortunately, most of the site's stone monuments are eroded or have been destroyed by looters. Calakmul is more than likely "Site Q"—an enigmatic Maya center referred to in many looted **hieroglyphic** texts with the "Snake Head" place name and emblem glyph. Teams of Mexican and U.S. archaeologists are working at the site and on its inscriptions.

The center of Calakmul contains large temples, palace structures, stone stelae, and many residences. Some of the elite palaces are enclosed by high walls that probably served a defensive function. The tallest construction at the site, Structure II, may have been started in the Late Formative Period, because it contains the typical triadic arrangement of temple superstructures from this period in the lowlands. El Mirador and **Nakbe,** other Formative-era sites found just across the border in Guatemala, contain temples with this tri-superstructure arrangement.

A small platform, Structure III, near the tallest buildings at the site core yielded a rich Early Classic **tomb** that contained many **jade** beads, ear ornaments, and three mosaic jade masks. The site also has a **ball court** for the ball game and many large, open **plazas.** Although a rarity in the Maya area, Calakmul has an example of a sculpted rock outcrop that depicts seven bound human captives. Nearby rivers and **bajos** provided water to the ancient inhabitants, and raised fields, or **chinampa**-like gardens, were created in the swamplands near the river.

According to hieroglyphic texts from throughout the Maya area, including **Caracol,** Tikal, **Palenque, Copan, Seibal, Dos Pilas,** and many other sites, Calakmul was one of the most powerful Maya states in the Classic Period, and it may have controlled a large territory and held sway over a number of Maya centers. Many Maya lords, both near and far, were subordinate to, or allied with, Calakmul kings. The ruling elite of distant Dos Pilas were strong allies of Calakmul. The Calakmul dynasty also waged war on other major Maya sites, like Tikal, with the help of its subordinates, including Dos Pilas. Calakmul kings also visited other Maya sites, such as Seibal, for rituals and royal accessions. Calakmul had ties with the area around El Mirador as well, attested to by the fact that many **ceramic** sherds of polychrome "**codex**-style" vases made farther south in this area were found in excavations at Calakmul.

CALENDAR. Across **Mesoamerica** a cyclical calendar of counted days was, and in some places still is, in use. For the ancient cultures, a "Calendar or Sacred Round" or "Almanac Year" (**Aztec** *tonalpohualli;* Maya *tzolkin*) of 20 named days combined with a number from 1 to 13, intermeshing with a monthly calendar ("vague year") with a combination of 18 named months of 20 days each and a final month of five days with "unlucky" auspices, was important for cyclical time reckoning. The count of the days, or calendar round, results in 260, which may have stemmed from observations of agricultural, solar, lunar, or human gestation cycles, and the monthly calculation totaling 365 days was a vague tropical solar year. These calendars also were used to record history, time and events, and agricultural cycles.

The beginning of the calendar round and its specific day and month signs and corresponding numbers is reached every 52 years. Evidence from Formative Period art suggests that the calendar round was used by the **Olmec** and highland Oaxaca peoples by 800 B.C. and perhaps much earlier. This calendar was important in the concepts of completion, renewal, and rejuvenation, and it was also used in naming practices, divination, religious ceremonies, recording events, and **astronomy**.

The Long Count, or linear, calendar was used by the Maya and other cultures, such as the Isthmian peoples, to link events with and to tie into the cyclical calendar round. The Long Count began at the creation of the current era, in terms or events unknown to us (August 13, 3114 B.C. in the Gregorian calendar, calculated by correlations of Mesoamerican and Spanish reckonings taken from historical documents), and it is calculated by multiplying a certain number by five different periods: *baktun,* or 400 years (360 days), *katun,* or 20 years, *tun,* or a year, *uinal,* or a month (20 days), and *kin,* or a day. The number two in front of the katun sign would signify 40 Maya years in **hieroglyphic** texts.

Hence, a Maya Long Count and combined calendar round date written as 9.15.6.4.16 (in order of *baktun, katun, tun, uinal, kin*) and 6 *Cimi* 4 *Tzec* is approximately May 3, A.D. 738 in the Christian/Gregorian calendar. The Long Count was also important for ritual purposes and for marking significant historical events. The Long Count was sometimes abbreviated by the Maya—especially in the Postclassic—when they listed just the number of 20-year periods (the *katun*).

The appearance of the Mesoamerican calendar in elite monuments and books indicates its importance as a political and religious tool and makes it a distinguishing trait of this culture area. Today, computer programs are widely available for calculating dates and obtaining calendrical and as-tronomical data. The current calendar era and baktun count will end (com-plete the final and 13th cycle of baktuns, or 400 years) toward the end of the month of December A.D. 2012, and we can expect to experience in-teresting prophetic observations and predictions in Mesoamerica and throughout the world at that time. *See also* CALENDAR STONE (AZTEC) and TRES ZAPOTES

CALENDAR STONE (AZTEC). Not actually a "**calendar,**" but a carving commemorating the five mythical creations of the world as believed by the **Aztecs.** This round sculpture is part of a larger monument that was once perhaps an **altar** or throne that was broken up and interred beneath the **plaza** floor of the Aztec capital of **Tenochtitlan.** Featured in the carv-ing of the center of the stone is what appears to be the sun god, or the **de-ity** that presides over the current world (see photo).

The **hieroglyph** 13 Reed is located directly above the face of the sun god, and this calendar date marks the beginning of the present creation and the year that Itzcoatl ("**Obsidian** Snake" in **Nahuatl),** the king who presumably commissioned this monument, rose to power. This nicely il-lustrates how Aztec elites, and **Mesoamerican** elites as a whole, used the calendar and **religion** to legitimize their rule and positions in society while connecting themselves to the cosmos.

In four square spaces immediately surrounding the face of the sun god are the signs 4 **Jaguar,** 4 Wind, 4 Rain, and 4 Water, which are dates from when the four previous creations, or "suns," began. These were four dis-tinct creations of life, people, landscapes, and the cosmos. The 20-day names from the Aztec calendar also appear in a band around the central sun face and four creation dates. These, if combined with numbers from one to 13, would make up the Aztec Calendar Round cycle. Around the outside edge or border of the stone is the head, body, and tail of the fire serpent deity, which is connected to Aztec elites, the ancestors, and the cosmos.

CALPULLI. The **Nahuatl** name of the traditional and basic social, economic, and political unit in ancient **Aztec** society. The calpulli (plural *calpultin*) was the center of Aztec life in that it was the main residential, lineage, and landholding social unit. The calpulli has been described as a conical "clan-like" system, with its landowning kinship organization. In this type of organization lineages made up the calpulli and these family groupings were internally ranked and endogamous units. Therefore, marriages were not outside of the larger lineage group.

Families of the calpulli owned, used, and inherited land within their lineages, and some calpulli organizations had occupational specializations, such as craft production or trading enterprises. **Chinampas,** or raised fields among canals, were owned and maintained by Aztec calpultin. Each of the calpulli territorial divisions, or wards, had their own **schools** and **temples,** and they often worshiped and fought together in wars for the Aztec state.

CANEK. Canek is a name of elite **Maya** men in Postclassic **Yucatan** and **Peten,** Guatemala. It is also the name of the king who ruled the **Itza** Maya and a confederation of kingdoms at the time of the Spanish conquest of Peten in the 17th century. This name also appears in Yucatan, which demonstrates the historical and linguistic connection between the Itza and the Yucatec Maya. Ah Canek was the last ruler at **Tayasal,** or Noh Peten, the island capital of the Itza, located in Lake Chaltunha, or Peten Itza. Canek and the Itza were repeatedly visited by Spanish friars and **conquistadores** and asked to surrender peacefully, but the ruler and the people of Peten resisted, and their towns were taken by force and by assault from the lake in boats manufactured on the shores by the Spanish.

A manuscript (maybe a fake, or written in Spanish by a **priest**—possibly a Yucatec Maya) that tells of a visit to Peten, and describes the settlements and certain aspects of Itza culture was recently found in Mexico City. But, more importantly, it provides a long discussion of the king Canek, his person, power, behavior, and even clothing. Hence, this manuscript, which had to be photographed in infrared light in order to read it, was dubbed the "Canek manuscript." An exciting discovery within this manuscript is that the **hieroglyphs** for the name *Canek* are rendered as a snake (*kan*) and a star (*ek*).

CARACOL. An important **Maya** site near the Maya **Mountains** in western Belize, Central America. This ruin has many monumental **temples** and carved stone **stelae** that have portraits of rulers and finely incised **hieroglyphics.** The finding of a glyphic stone **altar,** or perhaps a marker for the ball game in the **ball court,** and its decipherment seems to indicate that Caracol defeated the ruler of **Tikal,** Guatemala, in battle at the beginning of the Late Classic Period. This may explain a "hiatus" in the Tikal dynastic sequence, stela commemoration, and building programs at this time that has been recognized by archaeologists for many years. According to textual evidence, Caracol may also have had interaction with nobles from the Maya site of **Calakmul** and possibly engaged in **warfare** with nearby **Naranjo** and the capture of their king.

A large project concentrating on mapping and excavation at Caracol discovered numerous causeways, or **sacbe,** radiating out from the site's core to outlying residential groups. Many of these connected sites have **tombs** filled with human skeletons, **ceramic** vessels, worked **jade,** hieroglyphic texts, and other fine offerings. Many tombs contained multiple remains, as if they were family or lineage mausoleums. A significant implication of these findings is that there was a growing "middle class" in Maya society during the Classic Period fluorescence. Extensive terrace systems have been reported at the site, and they await further investigation that would look into Maya agricultural practices.

CASAS GRANDES. A large site in Chihuahua, Mexico, just south of the border with New Mexico that dates from Early to Late Postclassic times. The site, also called Paquime, is located in a fertile river valley and was founded around A.D. 1250. This important center provides key evidence of **Mesoamerican**/Southwest United States interaction in Pre-Columbian times: Southwest United States pueblo-like apartment complexes, many of which were multistoried, housed the populace who traded in shell and Mesoamerican parrot and macaw feathers for U.S. turquoise.

Also discovered were quarters for craftspersons, workers, and jewelers and market places. In addition, pens specifically used for containing tropical birds, a Mesoamerican style I-shaped **ball court** for the ball game and **temples,** and Mexican feathered serpent imagery were found at the site. Effigy mounds and central **plaza** areas are also evident at this impressive manufacturing and trading center. Casas Grandes fell around A.D. 1450 during a period of intense **warfare.** *See also* CHALCHIHUITES and TRADE

CAVE. A feature of the landscape that has critical symbolic and ritual functions for ancient and contemporary Mesoamericans. For the most part natural, but some human-formed, caves are associated with archaeological sites, and many structures are placed over them or oriented toward their entrances. The Pyramid of the Sun at **Teotihuacan** rests over an expanded cave that had cloverleaf-like chambers carved out of rock to make it resemble the lobed cave, Chicomoztoc, or womb of the **mountain** Culhuacan, of **Aztec** origin myths. Caves were seen as places of birth and emergence, and they also were believed to be portals into the **underworld.**

The largest ceremonial buildings of the Classic **Maya** site of **Dos Pilas** also have caves that run underneath them. Caves throughout **Mesoamerica** were also ceremonial locales where people were **sacrificed** or buried, where incense was burned, and where offerings, especially **ceramic** vessels and food, were left. Pilgrimages were made to significant cave sites, such as **Balankanche** and **Naj Tunich,** where rituals were performed and offerings made to **deities.** The Maya also removed stone formations from caves and took them back to their cities, as witnessed by a carved stalactite at **Yaxchilan** and rocks in building fill at Dos Pilas. Archaeological projects in caves in the Maya area have uncovered large quantities of broken and whole ceramic vessels, stone tools made of **chert** and **obsidian,** and human burials throughout the cave passages.

CEHACH (Kay-**hahch**). Name in Yucatec **Maya** meaning "people of the deer" or "deer people." This Maya group, which spoke a dialect of Yucatec, lived in northwestern Guatemala, in southern Campeche, **Yucatan,** and in southern Tabasco, and they were the traditional enemies of the **Itza, Lacandon,** and other lowland Postclassic Maya peoples. Spanish **conquistadores** and friars described Cehach **warfare,** settlements, and economics from the 16th to the 18th centuries.

The Spaniards also mention that these people "worshiped" deer and did not hunt them. The Spanish, on the other hand, found deer easy to kill here, because there were many animals and they didn't fear people. Many Cehach settlements were located near lakes and swamps, and they had defensive walls of stone, tree trunks, and spiny plants surrounding them. Only a small amount of archaeological and ethnohistorical research has been carried out with the little-understood Cehach Maya.

CENOTE (Sen-**oh**-tey). Sinkhole in limestone topography often found in the **Maya** lowlands—particularly in **Yucatan,** Mexico, and **Peten,** Guatemala—wherein water is found. Many times a cenote is the only place where fresh water is to be had, especially in the driest regions of Yucatan and in the jungles where there are few streams or rivers. Cenotes may even be present at the end of deep **caves** in the lowlands, such as **Balankanche** in Yucatan. The Spanish term *cenote* is taken from the Yucatec Maya *dzonot,* which labels this topographic feature.

Cenotes were not only important to the Maya for water, they were crucial for religious ritual as well. The sacred cenote at **Chichen Itza,** for instance, was discovered to contain a large quantity of offerings, including **jade,** victims of human **sacrifice, ceramics,** incense, wooden and metal artifacts, and **textiles.** Offerings were often made to the rain and water **deities,** including **Chac,** who were believed to be the denizens of cenotes, and sacrificial victims were also used to communicate with them. Underground **caves** may connect with cenotes, and Maya sites are often clustered around cenotes and buildings are oriented toward them. The Postclassic site of Tulum, Yucatan, has a cenote with a building placed over it, and painted murals in a principal structure at the ruin portray deities such as Chac and the **maize** god involved in ritual around a cenote in a cave.

CERAMICS. Fired clay ceramics were used all over **Mesoamerica** for the preparation and storage of food. Ceramics were also used to hold offerings and were buried along with the dead. Plates contained paper, blood, and other **sacrificial** offerings for burning, and ceramic vessels with exterior "spikes" or modeled **deity** faces served as incense, or **copal,** burners. Broken and whole ceramic vessels are found everywhere on archaeological sites, including **temples,** residences, middens, or trash dumps, dedicatory caches in buildings, and even in **caves.** Ceramics are of primary importance to archaeologists, because they provide clues to chronological sequences, **trade,** economic organization, technology, and religious beliefs (see photos).

Ceramic vessels were formed from prepared clays and then fired in open sites or in kilns. Mesoamerican ceramics are painted or have carved designs on them that depict people, animals, supernatural creatures, and important deities. **Maya** ceramics with hieroglyphic texts are often "name tagged," or contain **hieroglyphs** that describe the vessel shape, its intended contents, and the name of the owner of the vessel. Tall cylindrical vessels were used to drink **cacao** beverages, for instance. Cylindrical vessels made at the Maya **Ik site,** possibly the site of Motul de San Jose in **Peten,** Guatemala, are some of the finest painted polychrome ceramics of the Classic Period and were traded or given to nobles throughout the Maya area. *See also* BARRA, COLIMA, FINE PASTE CERAMICS, PLUMBATE POTTERY, REMOJADAS, and USULUTAN

CEREN (JOYA DE). This site is one of the most exciting finds of **Mesoamerican** archaeology in the Zapotitan Valley, which is near a highly active volcanic region in west-central El Salvador. While constructing grain silos, workers encountered earthen and thatched-roof houses buried under several meters of volcanic ash. Subsequent excavations proved that these structures were more ancient than initially posited; the **ceramics** recovered, radiocarbon dates from building materials and associated burned wood, and geological data indicate that the site was abandoned in the Classic Period (ca. A.D. 600), following an eruption of Loma Caldera.

Ceren is an archaeologist's dream site, because it was covered fairly rapidly, but the occupants were able to flee with some of their possessions. The village site of Ceren is special for many reasons: the pre-Hispanic buildings are extremely well preserved; it is one of the few areas in Mesoamerica that has standing domestic architecture of perishable materials; many artifacts and goods were still left in situ by the inhabitants escaping the eruption; and the fine ash covered nearby fields and gardens, allowing for the examination of agricultural techniques and plants through plaster molds made of the spaces where they decayed.

The land around Ceren is extremely fertile because of continuous ash deposits from the volcanoes. Young **maize** plants were growing in field furrows near Ceren when Loma Caldera erupted. Maize, the thorny **maguey** plant used for needles, food, and the alcoholic beverage **pulque,** and root crops were growing near the houses. Storage areas were identified by the presence of large ceramic vessels filled with maize, beans, and other foods and by collections of artifacts and domestic materials. It was also discovered that the residents secured many of their goods in the roofs, particularly sharp **obsidian** blades, and placed many items along the edges of their houses outside under the roofs.

Houses were commonly constructed of wood and cane with mud packed around it. The domestic structures contain porches, terraces, benches, interior niches, steps, columns, multiple rooms, and additions. Inside and outside the residences and in activity areas, grinding stones, chipped stone (obsidian and **chert**) knives and flakes, worked bone, ceramic vessels, stucco-covered gourds, and baskets were found. Based on architectural features and construction plus the associated artifact assemblages, other specific buildings were found to include kitchens, a communal structure, a sweat house for **sweat baths,** and a ceremonial structure. The ethnicity of the Ceren people is not known, but the architecture and artifacts show affinity or contact with Maya peoples.

CHAC (Chahk). An important and primarily benevolent **deity** of the **Maya** that is named in Classic Period **hieroglyphic** inscriptions and was central to the belief systems of the Postclassic Maya of **Yucatan.** *Chac-Xib-Chac* occurs frequently on Classic Maya painted **ceramic** vessels, where the deity is shown performing **sacrifices.** Chac, or God B in the literature, is a rain god that is frequently depicted in the Postclassic iconography of Yucatan, where it is drier than other parts of the Maya area. This long-nosed deity, which is associated with water, clouds, storms, the sky, and rayn, decorates the sculptural facades of palaces and **temples** here, like at **Chichen Itza,** and is represented in the Maya **codices,** which were probably created in Yucatan just before the conquest.

The codices give the offerings and rituals associated with Chac and rain. Even today, the contemporary Yucatec Maya perform rituals to Chac and leave the deity food and other offerings during a dry spell to request rain. Chac is also believed to dwell in **caves, cenotes,** and in clouds, where the deity makes rain and thunder. Four Chacs of different colors were linked with the cardinal directions and different parts of the cosmos: East with red, North with white, West with black, and South with yellow. The Chacs were honored and given offerings during certain months of the year in precolonial Yucatan and were consulted for the planning of ceremonies and planting. *See also* CHALCHIUHTLICUE and TLALOC

CHACMOOL. Term employed from the 19th century to the present to describe three-dimensional reclined stone human figures found at **Tenochtitlan, Tula, Chichen Itza,** and other **Mesoamerican** sites that date from the Terminal Classic to the Postclassic Periods. The Chacmool is a monolithic stone sculpture that depicts a seated, and perhaps a fallen, man or warrior. These figures were fashioned with the knees and torso in a raised position and with the face turned away from the front of the body. Chacmool figures hold an offering bowl on their midsections, where presumably hearts and other ceremonial items were placed.

It is believed Chacmools might represent fallen and wounded warriors because of the posture shown in the sculpture and because the figures wear helmet-like headgear and **chert** knives strapped to their arms. An example of this type of monument at the **Aztec** capital of Tenochtitlan is still painted red, blue, and white over its entire surface. Although Chacmools are found throughout central Mexico and even in **west Mexico** with the **Tarascan** culture, they may have appeared early on in the **Maya** area at **Quirigua** and Chichen Itza.

CHALCATZINGO (Chal-kaht-**sing**-goh). **Olmec** site in Morelos, Mexico, that is noteworthy for its considerable distance from the Gulf Coast "heartland" of the Olmec civilization. It is also a special site because of its location near huge pillars of volcanic rock, its importance as a **trade** and political center, and for its pure expression of Olmec art in cliff carvings, **ceramic** vessels, a stone block **altar** or throne, and other artifacts. **Colossal heads** and large pyramidal structures are absent, however. Nonetheless, this site was highly influenced by distant Olmec centers, and it may have been colonized by elites and artists through elite contacts and marriage alliances.

The carvings in the cliff walls are significant for their unusual depiction of **women,** rituals, and the supernatural. Chalcatzingo was an important node in the communication and trade network between the Gulf Coast area and central and **west Mexico.** It was more than likely one of many sacred ceremonial and pilgrimage centers for Formative Period **Mesoamerica.** Archaeology here has focused on the development and daily life at this site and has shown the importance of local cultural evolution and inputs in the rise and florescence of Olmec civilization.

CHALCHIHUITES. The region of northwestern Zacatecas, Mexico, where several large archaeological sites whose inhabitants interacted with the cultures of the Southwest United States and lower **Mesoamerica** are found. This region lies near the northern limit of Mesoamerica and the southern extension of the southwestern Pueblo cultures. Some of the larger centers in this region, ones that contain monumental architecture, **temples, ball courts,** sunken **plazas,** and polychrome **ceramics,** are Alta Vista, Cerro Moctezuma, and Cerro de los Bueyes. Populations grew here during the Classic Period after the decline of the important regional power of **Teotihuacan** in central Mexico and following an increase in local and regional **trade.**

It appears that the Chalchihuites centers specialized in the mining of pigments such as hematite and cinnabar, plus they extracted **chert** for the making of stone tools. Additionally, turquoise from northern Zacatecas and New Mexico was worked and exchanged and possibly taken to central Mexico to the south. Portions of the local population also produced and traded painted pottery between the centers. Many of the designs on the Chalchihuites ceramic vessels closely resemble the geometric forms and animal shapes seen in the Southwest United States. *See also* CASAS GRANDES and QUEMADA (LA)

CHALCHIUHTLICUE (Chal-chee-uuht-**lee**-kay). **Nahuatl** name of the **Aztec deity** with female attributes who was associated with the worship of water on the earth's surface. Chalchiuhtlicue can be glossed as "She of the **Jade** Skirt"; jade, a hard green stone held sacred by ancient **Mesoamerican** peoples, was connected to water because of the luster and wet appearance it has when polished and its dark green hue. Chalchiuhtlicue was worshiped near springs, lakes, streams, and rivers where shrines, offerings, and **sacrifices** were to be found.

Children were sometimes dressed in green skirts and drowned as offerings to help sustain this deity. These beliefs were connected to the earth (**Tonantzin**), fertility, agriculture, and nature. This goddess may have been seen as a sibling, female counterpart, or relative of **Tlaloc,** the Aztec rain god. Representations of Chalchiuhtlicue in Aztec art show the deity in human female form, wearing a skirt adorned with symbols of green jade.

CHALCHUAPA. A highland region in western El Salvador that includes the large archaeological site called Tazumal or also Chalchuapa. Archaeology at Chalchuapa demonstrates a continuous occupation from the Early Formative (about 1200 B.C.) to the Postclassic Period. The largest zones of habitation, however, date from the Middle or Late Formative to the Classic Periods. The earliest cultures here had ties with adjacent Pacific coastal cultures, and their **ceramics** resemble those of the Guatemalan and Chiapas **Ocos** peoples. Ceramic and sculpture forms also closely resemble those of the **Olmec** of the Gulf Coast area, including monumental art and portable **jade** carvings. Later on in the Formative Period, material culture and architecture at Chalchuapa had affinities with **Kaminaljuyu** in the Guatemalan highlands. These distant highland peoples may have been interested in obtaining **cacao,** hematite, or **obsidian,** or simply interacted socially and politically with the growing center of Chalchuapa.

At Chalchuapa, contact was maintained with sites in El Salvador and nearby Honduras, beginning in the Formative Period and leading to Classic times. Similar ceramics, including **Usulutan** wares from El Salvador, are found in large quantities here. Architectural construction styles at the site also resemble forms from other sites in western El Salvador and Honduras, which points to extensive interaction between these areas. However, the sculptural style and **hieroglyphs** on Monument 1 of the El Trapiche group bear closer affinities to other Late Formative monuments at Kaminaljuyu and El **Mirador,** farther to the northwest. This script is different from the later Classic **Maya** hieroglyphs, and it may be more closely related to the Isthmian script seen on the La **Mojarra stela.** The eruption of the Mount **Ilopango** volcano cut the growing occupation of Formative Chalchuapa short with its extensive ash and pumice covering the area.

By the Late Classic Period, Chalchuapa was once again a thriving region of **trade** and habitation. Artifacts attest to interaction with sites in Honduras and in the distant Maya lowlands. Polychrome Copador ceramics from **Copan** are present, as are types from the **Peten** lowlands sites, such as **Tikal.** However, the markers of Classic Maya civilization, such as hieroglyphic monuments, stone sculpture and stelae, and finely painted pottery, were not present. This suggests that Chalchuapa worked within its own local sphere of influence and interacted to a greater extent with peoples in Honduras and El Salvador. *See also* CEREN (JOYA DE) and QUELEPA

CHERT. Common stone used by ancient Mesoamerican peoples for the manufacture of tools such as scrapers, knives, blades, projectile points, and adzes. Chert was also shaped into disks, animals, people, and other forms for ceremonial usage and prestige items. Eccentric cherts or flints in the shapes of people and animals have been uncovered at the **Maya** sites of **Copan,** Honduras, **Dos Pilas,** Guatemala, **Quirigua** in the **Motagua River** region in Guatemala, and many other Maya sites.

This easily mined and workable stone occurs as nodules in limestone, which is found throughout **Mesoamerica,** and is quarried or gathered near stream cuts or gullies. Chert working was popular in nearly all Mesoamerican cultures, and chert workshops have been found at the Maya sites of Dos Pilas, Colha (Belize; one of the largest known workshops in the Maya area), Xunantunich (Belize), and near Rio Azul (Guatemala). Many of the chert workshops produced tools for local **trade** and consumption, but cherts from Colha were distributed throughout the eastern Maya region. Chert blades and waste flakes also cover many elite Maya **tombs.**

Chert can be worked in its natural state, or it can be heated in a hot fire to achieve easier and better fracturing and flaking. In tool making the chert cores are reduced and prepared by removing large flakes, and then the tool shapes are formed by careful flaking and chipping at the core and the flakes. Chert is not as easily worked or as sharp as **obsidian,** but it is readily available, more durable, and less brittle. Chert knives, lance heads, and ceremonial eccentrics are frequently portrayed in Mesoamerican art.

The **Lacandon** Maya of **Peten,** Guatemala, and Chiapas, Mexico, made exquisite chert arrowheads until very recently, and today they manufacture crude projectile points for bow and arrow sets sold to tourists in Chiapas. *See also* ECCENTRIC FLINT

CHICHEN ITZA (Chee-**chen** Eet-**sah**). A large Terminal Classic to Early Postclassic **Maya** city (covering at least five square kilometers) in central **Yucatan** that is famous for its impressive **temples,** carved stone, large **ball court,** and well of **sacrifice.** The name *Chichen Itza* means "opening of the wells of the **Itza**," who were the people that ruled here and in central **Peten,** Guatemala. This site is one of the most famous ruins in the world and is visited by thousands of people each year. Contemporary Yucatec Maya work as guides, vendors, and tour operators in the ruins.

The art and architecture at Chichen Itza exhibits influence from or evidence of interaction with central Mexico, particularly with the **Toltec** site of **Tula.** The interaction may have traveled both ways, but the central Mexican myth of **Quetzalcoatl** suggests migrations from Tula to Chichen Itza. However, recent work in chronology and iconography hints that Chichen Itza may have been the source from which the influence spread. Chichen Itza was the capital of a large and powerful Terminal-Postclassic state that ruled much of Yucatan before it collapsed and was later replaced by the Late Postclassic center of **Mayapan.** Some of the main buildings at Chichen Itza were excavated and restored in the 1920s to the 1940s by a project sponsored by the Carnegie Institute of Washington.

The El Castillo temple structure dominates the main **plaza** at the northern end of Chichen Itza. This monumental structure has nine terraces (possibly indicating a funerary structure like at the Maya sites of **Palenque** and **Tikal**), a temple superstructure, and a stairway on each of the four sides of the building. The widest north door is framed by stone feathered serpent columns. The north and south stairways each point in the general direction of a large **cenote,** or sink hole with water, and the stairways have stone serpent heads at their bases. Interestingly, the sun at its zenith during the equinox casts a shadow on the side of the north stairway that resembles the undulating body of a snake. An earlier temple was found inside this building, and it contains a stone **jaguar** throne that is painted red and decorated with green stone inlays.

The Temple of the Warriors at Chichen Itza is strikingly similar to the main temple at Tula. It has interior stone columns that supported a roof of perishable materials and rows of exterior square stone columns to the front and south sides that have portrayals of warriors, captives, and

Chichen Itza elites carved into them. This building also has large serpent columns flanking the entrance to the temple and a reclining **chacmool** figure in stone. The Temple of the Warriors is in the vicinity of three regular ball courts, a **sweat bath** structure, and "the market" structure and flanks two large plaza areas.

The Great Ball Court, measuring roughly 170 meters long by 70 meters wide, is the largest in **Mesoamerica.** This construction incorporates the Temple of the Jaguars, which contains sculptures and painted murals depicting **warfare,** important people, and Maya towns. This ball court has two end zones, one each at its north and south sides, a low-sloping bank on the playing alley, and two flanking vertical walls that reach several meters in height. The lower sloping walls of the court contain carvings that depict ballplayers and the decapitation of one of the players. The middles of the upper walls have tenoned vertical stone rings through which the players would pass the ball to score.

The Sacred Well or Well of Sacrifice (the great cenote at the site) is found to the north of the El Castillo structure and the Great Ball Court. A raised causeway, or the "Sacred Way," leads from the north plaza to the Sacred Well. A small structure is found on the edge of the large cenote just to the east of the causeway. Processions began in the main plaza and ended at the cenote, where ceremonies and **sacrifices** were performed. Offerings and human sacrifices were presented to the rain gods below, and dredging of the cenote yielded objects of **jade,** wood, shell, cloth, and bone, in addition to quantities of human bone and skulls.

On the south side of the main group of ruins and near a large cenote are found the structure that contains the High **Priest**'s Grave, the Caracol, and the Nunnery Group. Archaeologists discovered a richly stocked **tomb** of a noble in the building of The High Priest's Grave. The Caracol structure, named "shell" for its round shape and interior spiral staircase, may have been used for the worship of Quetzalcoatl—as were some round structures in central Mexico. This building was possibly an ancient observatory used for **astronomy** or the tracking of the movements of the sun and moon, since windows are aligned with the setting of these heavenly bodies at certain times of the year.

The Nunnery Group contains palace-like structures with **Puuc** style buildings and their ornate sculptural facades. Like the Temple of the Warriors, these buildings have stone depictions of the rain deity **Chac** in the full round on the exterior walls and corners. Many of the site's **hieroglyphic** texts are found on rectangular stone lintels of these structures as well. Many of the decorated stone facades and carved stone art probably date to the Terminal Classic Period.

Recent epigraphic data from hieroglyphic texts at Chichen Itza suggests that the center was jointly ruled by elites from different families whose names appear in colonial Maya documents, one of them being *Cocom* and another *Itza*. More archaeological research is needed at this important Maya site to sort out its chronology and occupational history, study the ethnicity of the city's inhabitants, and to learn more about its crucial role in the history of the northern Maya lowlands and the interaction with central Mexican peoples. *See also* TOLLAN

CHICHIMECS. Generic name for the peoples that migrated into the Valley of Mexico during Postclassic times. The Chichimecs were also one of the earliest major immigrant groups to enter central Mexico who eventually settled and created local city-states. The Chichimecs are often depicted in Mexican **codices** in their wanderings, wearing animal hides and carrying bows, arrows, and spears. These people were believed to have been wandering bands of great hunters and desert dwellers from northern Mexico.

However, the original Chichimec homeland(s) and sites have not been found. These people apparently were a semisedentary society of gatherers and part-time cultivators who lacked a state-level government and economic system. Many later peoples of Postclassic central Mexico, including the **Aztecs,** claimed descent or cultural inheritors from the Chichimecs.

CHINAMPA. Form of raised field agriculture that was prevalent in the **Basin of Mexico** during **Aztec** times, from which this name was taken. Chinampas are large garden and orchard plots near lakes and slow-moving rivers where earth and mud were piled between stakes and trees. Canals were dug around chinampas to extract fertilizing silts from them, to provide water for the plants, for canoe travel, and for fish farming. Chinampas are thus typically square or rectangular, and were mistakenly called "floating gardens" initially by the Spanish, because they were surrounded by water.

Maize, fruit trees, and vegetables were grown year-round on the sustainable chinampas. These agricultural plots were crucial for feeding the large populations in central Mexico, particularly in **Tenochtitlan,** and they were owned and inherited by Aztec **calpulli.** Large-scale chinampa plots are also known in **west Mexico** with the **Teuchitlan** tradition during the Classic Period and are found also in the **Maya** area but on a smaller scale. Archaeological evidence from the Maya area suggests that this type of agriculture may have had an early start during the Formative

Period and become more wide spread during the Classic Period. *See also* BAJOS and DIET

CHOLULA. This pre-Hispanic center in Puebla, Mexico, separated from the **Basin of Mexico** by a chain of **mountain**s and volcano peaks, is home to one of the most massive buildings in the New World. Spanish **conquistadores** described rituals on this huge **temple,** and eventually a church was built on the summit of the structure, which today is often mistaken for a natural hill. Parts of the temple substructure have been restored by archaeologists, and excavations revealed a long sequence of constructions in the building's interior. Archaeological work is documenting the lengthy chronology and associated artifacts of this center. Historically, Cholula and its pyramid are associated with frog, flower, and water imagery.

According to the archaeological evidence and historical sources, the city of Cholula has been occupied from the Formative Period to the present, and it was an important pilgrimage center. Additionally, the occupants of the city have come from central Mexico, Veracruz, and **Tlaxcala** at different times during the city's history. Specific architectural elements and artifactual styles link the site to **Teotihuacan,** El **Tajin,** and the **Toltecs.** An earlier, unique mural found at the site contains drunken revelers participating in a ritual. Also, biconical ceramic figures with loop handles, which were commonly used by Postclassic Mexican peoples, appear to have been made in or near Cholula. Many nobles and people were killed by Spanish conquistadores at Cholula when they tried to ambush the intruders who were en route to the **Aztec** capital of **Tenochtitlan.** *See also* TOLLAN

CHULTUN (Chul-**tuhn**). Underground chambers excavated in limestone bedrock with lids of limestone slabs to seal them. These single-chamber probable storage areas are found primarily near **Maya** archaeological sites in **Peten,** Guatemala, and are quite numerous in **Yucatan.** In these human-made features, a vertical shaft connects to an adjoining chamber up to two meters high and wide. These chultunes may have been used to store foods, such as **maize,** breadnut, or **ramon** nuts, and dried beans. However, in Yucatan where water is scarce at times, archaeologists have demonstrated that water was drained and stored in chultunes by individual households for their consumption. Often these underground storage areas were later used for depositing trash or for burying the dead. Chultunes are commonly found at **Tikal** and Uaxactun in Peten, Guatemala, and at **Sayil** in Yucatan.

CHUPICUARO (Chuh-**pee**-quah-roh). Culture and art style that probably dates to the Formative and Early Classic Periods of the Lerma River drainage in southern Guanajato and near lakes in northern Michoacan, Mexico. Although comparatively little archaeological survey and excavation have been carried out in this area and although much of what we know about these peoples comes from looted materials, it seems that the Chupicuaro culture was centered on lacustrine environments and resources.

This culture is recognized for its **ceramic** anthropomorphic figurines representing **women** and ceramics invariably with geometric and step-fret or scroll designs. The importance of female figurines in Chupicuaro culture suggests that the belief in a creator earth goddess in **west Mexico** was an ancient one and possibly of prime importance to women's rituals. Some figures also show ballplayers and **deities.** A cemetery of nearly 400 burials was found near the ancient village of Chupicuaro in Guanajato that were richly stocked with ceramic vessels and figurines. Decapitated humans, skulls, and dogs had also been interred. However, few signs of architecture, mainly some stone alignments and burned earth floors, were found.

CLOVIS. A type of projectile point commonly found in North America but only in a few isolated finds in central Mexico, the Guatemalan highlands, and central Belize. They are also found in lower Central America and are more commonly recovered in the southern and western parts of the United States. These points are easily recognized by their diagnostic leaf shape and fluting, or the removal of a single, long and thin flake from the base of the point to its middle. Clovis points were made of **chert** and **obsidian** from about 12,000 to 9,000 years ago. These tools were used by small bands of early **Mesoamerican** hunters and gatherers to kill large game and perhaps as **weapons** against other bands of humans. The points were hafted on straight sticks and used as spears or throwing darts from an **atlatl.**

COATLIQUE (Koh-at-**lee**-kay). The **Aztec** earth goddess who gave birth to the patron **deity Huitzilopochtli** in Aztec beliefs (see photo). Coatlique lived on Coatepetl (serpent **mountain**) when she was attacked by her daughter **Coyolxauhqui** and her other offspring, the "Four Hundred Huiztnaua" beings. Upon their assault, Huitzilopochtli was instantaneously and miraculously born from Coatlique with **weapons** to defeat his aggressive siblings and save his mother.

The **Templo Mayor** at the Aztec capital of **Tenochtitlan** symbolizes the mountain Coatepetl and the events of this ancient myth. Coatlique means "serpent skirt," and this deity has serpents for a head, arms, and legs, which are entwined in her skirt when she appears in Aztec art. Serpents represented the streams of blood offerings made to the earth for its regeneration. A large three-dimensional stone sculpture found below Mexico City may depict Coatlique, who has serpents for her appendages, large clawed feet, and sacrificial human hearts and hands for a necklace.

CODEX (CODICES). These very unusual and rare written book or books were once abundant in **Mesoamerica** both before and after the conquest. Many of these codices were originally part of the libraries or collections of nobles and **priests.** These books were made of strips of soaked and beaten bark paper (*amate*) covered with stucco and then painted, as was common in the **Maya** area, or painted on deerskin, as was often the practice in central Mexico. The indigenous codices may have been spread out on the interior floors or tacked to the walls of **temples** for the priests and onlookers to view and read the images and texts while performing ceremonies or recounting histories.

The books are often accordion-like with screen-fold pages of the same size that are bound and covered, or just sheets of animal hide. In Classic Maya art, the codices are shown as being screen-fold books covered with **jaguar** skin. No known Classic Period codices (or earlier ones) are believed to have survived time and the Spanish conquest, but some may appear in caves or **tombs** someday. The extant Postclassic and colonial codices were appropriated by Spanish **conquistadores** and priests and sent to Europe or kept in Mexico. The pre-Hispanic codices are filled with brilliant, multicolored picture drawings, depictions of **deities** and people and their actions, symbols, and **hieroglyphic** writing.

Codices were written by scribes and other elites to record native histories, rituals, religious beliefs, and calendrical observations and dates. These books were frequently used by elites and priests in public ceremony and were reminders or mnemonic devices in oral presentations of myth and history. The Classic Maya also produced codex-style **ceramic** vessels that exhibited book-like scenes of humans, deities, and animals with accompanying hieroglyphic texts flanking the images.

Some well-known and studied codices of the Maya area include the **Dresden Codex** and the Codex Paris (where they were discovered and housed in libraries) and the central Mexican codices, Borgia and Mendoza. The **Codex Nuttall** is a famous **Mixtec** book from Oaxaca that contains important cultural and historical data on these people. Many of the surviving codices were created by the Postclassic **Aztec,** Maya, and Mixtec people. Many hundreds of indigenous Mesoamerican codices were burned by priests during colonial inquisitions because they felt that the books were the makings and teachings of the devil and responsible for the natives' relapses to paganism.

CODEX MENDOZA. This book is a crucial source of cultural information on the preconquest **Aztecs** of central Mexico. Although this **codex** was produced in the mid-16th century and after the Spanish conquest and colonization of Aztec territory, the images and texts within relate to precontact Aztec **warfare** and conquests, customs, social organization, economic structure, and material culture. The Codex Mendoza was destined for Spain as part of the documentation of the peoples, lands, local histories, and holdings under the control of the expanding Spanish empire in the New World. The manuscript changed hands over the years, and today it is kept at the Bodleian Library at Oxford University.

The multicolored painted images on the folios of European paper were created by native Aztec scribes commissioned by the Spanish to record the highlights of Aztec culture and history. Spanish notations and descriptions of the images were placed right on the manuscript at the time of its production. The first section of the codex contains an outline of Aztec history from the founding of their capital at **Tenochtitlan** to the conquests of the rulers of the empire. This section contains indigenous **calendar** dates, images of people and their name **hieroglyphs,** and ancient place names and cities of central **Mesoamerica.**

The **tribute** rolls of the conquered polities and territories make up the second portion of the book. This part has several pages depicting in vibrant colors the actual tribute items, such as **jade** beads, **jaguar** skins, **ceramic** vessels, **quetzal** and other bird feathers, cotton cloaks, foods, and clothing and their quantities that were delivered to Tenochtitlan. The last section contains painted scenes from Aztec everyday life, including punishments of their children, duties of apprentices, marriage ceremonies, occupations, and captive taking. The combination of the rich imagery created by native scribes, the Spanish commentary accompanying the designs, and the topics recorded in the Codex Mendoza make it an invaluable source for the study of ancient Mesoamerica and the Aztecs. *See also* CODEX NUTTALL and DRESDEN CODEX

CODEX NUTTALL. The **Codex** Nuttall is the name given to a Postclassic **Mixtec** manuscript originally from Oaxaca. This indigenous book is decorated with beautifully painted drawings of human figures, **deities,** structures, ceremonies, and native material culture. This codex mainly contains historical information regarding Mixtec family histories and genealogy, plus it provides some information on religious ritual, mythology, and divination. The famous Early Postclassic Mixtec ruler named **Eight Deer** is also depicted in the Codex Nuttall in the sections that treat Mixtec history and ritual.

COLIMA. A state in **west Mexico** where early **Mesoamerican** cultures, villages, and **ceramics** are found. Some of the earliest ceramics (ranging from the Early to Late Formative Periods) from this area include "Capacha" ceramics (from a site of that name), which are found at many archaeological sites, middens, and shaft **tombs**—a typical tomb style of Formative Period west Mexico where a vertical shaft leads to a funerary chamber filled with human remains and artifacts. Many of these tombs contain whole vessels and large anthropomorphic figurines. Many of these ceramic types and figurines are seen in other parts of west Mexico, as in the states of Jalisco, Nayarit, and Michoacan. The ceramics are frequently monochrome, being painted in brown, black, red, or orange.

The ceramic forms are very distinctive with some vessels having wider openings and narrowed at the middle or waists, while others have globular bases with tall, narrow necks. Some very unique pottery styles include the "stirrup spout," where two narrow necks emerge from the sides of the vessel and then meet in a single tube or opening at the top. Some vessels have two main bodies, one on top of the other, that are connected by three stirrup tubes. This form of pottery appears earlier in South America, and it may have been borrowed from there if it was not invented independently.

Other ceramics are realistic copies of gourds, pumpkins, squashes, and other plants. Large hollow figurines in the shape of humans and animals, including warrior and dog effigies, are also common to the Colima ceramic assemblage. *See also* BARRA and OCOS

COLOSSAL HEADS. Large sculptures of volcanic stone (basalt) heads found in certain **Olmec** sites on the hot and humid plains of Tabasco and Veracruz in southern Mexico (see photo). These sculptures are several feet tall and wide, and they weigh several tons. They were first discovered and excavated by outside explorers and archaeologists in the first half of the 20th century, which started off scientific investigations of the Olmec civilization. Olmec colossal heads and basalt sculptures continuously surface in archaeological projects at large Olmec sites. These portrait sculptures have been found at **San Lorenzo,** La **Venta,** and **Tres Zapotes,** and they probably existed at other sites in the Gulf Coast region, such as Laguna de los Cerros, and possibly in highland Guatemala at **Abak Takalik.**

Colossal heads are early portraits of people that were carved in the full round and placed near monumental architecture and platforms from about 1200 to 500 B.C. during the Early to Middle Formative Periods. These sculptures are more than likely portraits of Olmec rulers, ancestors, elites, or possibly ballplayers or **deities,** because of the location of these heads in the cores of ceremonial centers and the great efforts and expense used in acquiring and making them. The stone blocks were brought in to the Olmec centers from the distant **Tuxtla Mountains** in Veracruz, possibly on rafts and log rollers, and then carved on site or in nearby workshops by specialists supported by elites.

Recently, a stone monument workshop site, called Llano del Jicaro was found near Laguna de los Cerros in Veracruz. Many unfinished monuments with recognizable iconography are visible at this site. The colossal portraits have helmets or headgear, and distinctive facial features that show that these sculptures may represent particular historical personages. Colossal heads were often broken, damaged by drilling, buried, or re-carved, presumably after the ruler or noble person died or left the Olmec sites in order to remove the power from the stone. A new theory is that the colossal heads were ancestral portraits carved from stone **altars,** or thrones of the rulers, after the Olmec rulers died. *See also* STELA

CONQUISTADORES. The accounts and descriptions of native Mesoamerican societies by early European explorers, soldiers, and **priests** are crucial for understanding the way of life and history of the indigenous peoples of this region. Spanish conquistadores arrived in **Mesoamerica** in the early 16th century, and by the 1600s many indigenous people, including the **Aztecs, Maya, Mixtec, Tarascans, Totonacs,** and **Zapotecs,** had been subjugated and their lands colonized by them. Some of the more well-known conquistadores are Hernan Cortes, who defeated the Aztecs, Pedro de Alvarado, conqueror of the Aztecs, Maya, and **Pipil,** Francisco de Montejo, who conquered the Maya and colonized **Yucatan,** and Martin de Ursua, who defeated the last independent Mesoamerican kingdom of the **Itza** Maya in lowland Guatemala. Notable European priests who wrote extensively on the indigenous peoples and cultures are Diego de Landa (Yucatec Maya), Bernardino de Sahagun (Aztecs), Thomas Gage (highland Maya), Francisco Ximenez (highland Maya), Bartolome de las Casas (Maya and Aztec), Antonio de Remesal (highland Maya), Juan de Villagutierre Soto-Mayor (lowland Maya), Geronimo de Acala (Tarascans), Diego Duran (Aztecs), and Francisco de Burgoa (Mixtec), among many others.

COPAL (Koh-**pahl**). Term for a type of incense from the resin of a particular species of tree (*Bursera*) found in the **Mesoamerican** lowland tropical areas. The word *copal* is derived from the **Nahuatl** *copalli*. The term for this type of incense or resin in many Mayan languages is *pom*. The dried tree resin was burned during ancient rituals in incense burners, or *incensarios,* and today this substance is still being used as it was in the past. It is also prized for its abundant smoke, sweet aroma, and long storage life.

Copal was an important **trade** and **tribute** item from the jungle lowlands, and it is still being bound and shipped to market in cornhusks to be sold. Mesoamerican peoples also held this incense as sacred and an important ritual offering, because they described it as "sacrificial blood" (the resin) from organisms central to their world and the cosmos (the trees). In a section written in the **Popol Vuh** of the **Quiche Maya,** copal resin is even substituted for human blood and a heart by the **underworld** lords.

COPAN (Koh-**pahn**). Copan is one of the more beautiful and most important of the archaeological sites of the Classic **Maya** in the southern lowlands of **Mesoamerica.** The site core of Copan is situated along the banks of the Copan River, a tributary of the **Motagua River,** in a fertile alluvial valley in western Honduras. This ruin is located in the eastern foothills of the **mountain** chain that runs through Guatemala, thus the climate is somewhat cooler and the vegetation differs from that of the hot, humid lowland rainforests. For instance, there are many pine trees in this area, especially in the surrounding hills. Copan receives abundant rainfall in the winter, has much prime agricultural land and water in the river valley, is surrounded by abundant natural resources, and is located along a route of ancient travel, all making this an optimal place for a large Maya center.

The ruins at Copan are concentrated in the site core where a considerable number of large **temples** and elite residences and **tombs** are clustered near the river. These monumental buildings are interdispersed among several ample courtyards and **plazas**. Within these courtyards, stone monuments and sculpture are placed on the floors and near the structures. The main plaza at Copan is very large and rectangular and is demarcated by stone steps where people can enter the plaza or remain seated to rest and watch the rituals, **dances,** and **markets.** The main plaza also contains many carved monuments, a small pyramid with stairways on all four of its sides, and a **ball court** toward its southern end. Some of the most elaborate and largest stone artworks and buildings are found here.

Copan is famous for its monumental architecture made of stone blocks and earthen fill, and its exquisitely carved stone sculpture. The architects and sculptors at the site used a local green volcanic stone, of which large quantities were quarried from nearby cliffs. It is easily carved, and the rock hardens after prolonged exposure to the air and sun. There are many large temples and palaces at Copan, and they are adorned with beautiful stone sculpture mosaics or sculpture carved in the round, or in three-dimensional form. Some of the most impressive monumental stone artworks at the site are the ornately carved **stelae** and **altars** in the main plaza.

The stelae consist of monolithic portraits of past rulers in their ritual finery that symbolizes their high rank and status, and the monuments are covered with **hieroglyphic** texts that record the names and titles of the kings and important events and ceremonies in their lives like on Stela A of "18 Rabbit." In many Copan stela texts, the name of the monument is given along with the action or ritual of "planting or setting up" (*ts'apah*) a wide banner stone, or stone stela (*lakam tun*), such as on Stela C of "18 Rabbit." The stelae hieroglyphic texts also contain calendrical information, the dates on which ceremonies were performed or when events in the lives of the rulers took place, and other information regarding Classic Maya elites and belief systems.

The so-called altars at Copan are often flat and rounded monolithic carvings with images and hieroglyphic writing on them. Some of these monuments are large three-dimensional stone zoomorphs consisting of bicephalic sky serpents and an earth turtle complete with lifelike legs for support. Another rounded stone altar resembles a **rubber** ball, which has a rope tied around it and grooves for sacrificial blood and other liquid offerings to flow down its sides. Altars are often found in front of or near the carved stone stelae. These monuments may have not only served as altars for ceremonies and places to leave offerings for elites and their ancestors, but they may have functioned as seats for the nobles as well, such as Altar Q of the king "Yax Pasah." The iconography and the glyphic texts on the altars at Copan suggest that they were used as thrones or places to sit during ceremonies, visitations, or coronations.

One of the most impressive temples at Copan, and in the Maya area in general, is the Hieroglyphic Stairway (Str. 10L-26), which is located in the southern end of the main plaza near the large ball court. The Hieroglyphic Stairway is the largest in the Maya area, and it is one of the longest known aboriginal texts in the New World. The 63 risers on the stairway are decorated with finely carved hieroglyphs that number approximately 2,200. From these steps are visible some of the most beautiful versions of the Copan "emblem glyph," of which the main sign is a bat's head (read as *Xukpi?*).

The Hieroglyphic Stairway is embellished with full-round stone portraits of ancestors of previous kings seated in the center, and it is flanked by richly carved balustrades that have designs that resemble owls, fans, and scrolls. The building also exhibited a temple superstructure that was adorned with stone sculpture and hieroglyphs, but this ornate construction toppled over in antiquity. The Hieroglyphic Stairway was completed just after the middle of the 8th century A.D. by the 15th king of Copan, "Smoke-Shell" (*Butz' Yipi*), whose portrait stela is in front of the structure. The hieroglyphs and iconography of this building are a tribute to the importance and grandiosity of the Copan dynasty, and several earlier constructions and tombs of previous nobles were found during tunneling operations within the construction fill.

Another large building, Str. 10L-22, faces an enclosed inner courtyard and may have been the residence of later Copan kings. Hieroglyphic texts in this structure and chronological evidence from different phases of this building's construction indicate that Str. 10L-22 may have been commissioned by the 13th king of Copan, known as "18 Rabbit" or *Uaxaclahun U Bah K'awil*. Str. 10L-22 is a multiroom palace structure that has a large mouth of an earth creature framing its entrance and a "sky band," complete with clouds, reptilian sky monsters, holders of the earth (*bacab*), and hieroglyphs in the interior doorway of the building.

The Copan ball court is one of the finest and largest of the buildings of this sort for the ball game in Mesoamerica. It was one of the first examples of architecture to be completely excavated and then restored at the site. This ball court is I-shaped with a narrow central playing alley and perpendicular end zone areas. Two multiroomed constructions with **vaulted roofs** contain sloped banks that run parallel to one another so that the bouncing rubber ball stays in play during the game.

Beautifully fashioned large tenoned stone macaw heads were placed at the tops of the sloped banks, presumably to deflect the ball or to be hit to score points. The facades of the vaulted superstructures of the ball court supported mosaic stone sculptures of full macaws with outstretched wings and open beaks, which may have symbolized the sun or messengers from the **underworld** lords. The floor of the ball court was paved with flat stone blocks that had three carved markers or sculptures set into them. These markers show ball games and players, including "18 Rabbit," in underworld scenes. Steps found on the north end of the court allowed people to watch the game, or were used to roll bound sacrificial victims down like a ball.

Extensive excavations in the acropolis at Copan have uncovered earlier buried structures, tombs, caches, and sculptures inside the monumental architecture. Some of the interred structures carry carved and painted stucco facades depicting Maya **deities** and ancestors. The tombs of the Maya elites that have been located contain whole painted ceramic vessels and **jade** artifacts. Cached offerings buried during building dedications and destruction include exquisitely made **eccentric flints** with translucent human faces and headdresses. These caches sometimes contain worked jade artifacts that have been burned and shattered. The early monuments are important finds, because they contain significant historical information.

Much of the hinterland surrounding the site core of Copan has been mapped and excavated. This residential area supported a large population, estimated at 20,000 to 30,000 people, that stretched several kilometers beyond the site. Domestic buildings of different sizes and shapes are associated with people of various socioeconomic rank and status. The Sepulturas area, located about one kilometer to the north of the site core, has been extensively excavated and reconstructed. Stone masonry buildings of various sizes were discovered, and the largest buildings contained sculpture facades. This residential zone has an occupation that dates from Middle Formative times to the Terminal Classic Period.

A range-type palace structure (Str. 9N-82) in the Sepulturas area has stone portraits of ancestors on the outside walls and a hieroglyphic bench in its central room. The bench text gives the names and titles of the subordinate lord of one of the last kings, named "Yax Pasah," who resided in the palace-like structure. In the central plaza area of this palace compound is where evidence for the earliest occupation and burials at the site, which date to the Early to Middle Formative Period, are found. The burials in this area contain **ceramics,** such as globular, long-necked bottles and small bowls with **Olmec**-affiliated designs on them, that are similar to wares found at **Tlatilco** and **Cuyamel caves.** Later iconographic styles link Copan to other sites in the Maya lowlands and its Classic Period Copador pottery was widely traded to other parts of Honduras and western El Salvador.

Research in the residential area in the peripheries of Copan suggest that the downfall came gradually, with elites abandoning the site first and people of lower socioeconomic standing leaving the area later. The collapse at Copan may have been brought on by ecological degradation or drastic economic transformations. Excavations are further exploring the downfall and some of the final occupants at Early Postclassic Copan who lived in small platforms scattered about the site.

Decipherments of hieroglyphic texts at Copan and **Quirigua** found in the nearby Motagua River region demonstrate close ties and interaction between the two sites. Earlier Copan kings are mentioned in Quirigua inscriptions: the father of "18 Rabbit," "Smoke Imix God K" (*Butz' Imix K'awil*), visited Quirigua during the coronation of its king, and later "18 Rabbit" was captured and killed by the Quirigua ruler "Cauac Sky" in A.D. 738. Texts carved at a later date indicate that the mother of one of the last kings at Copan, "Yax Pasah," was from **Palenque,** Chiapas, and that his brothers held important offices and positions in the Copan civil-religious structure. Some of the earliest inscriptions at the site, some found in recent tunneling excavations, suggest that one of the first Copan kings, Yax K'uk' Mo, may be related to elites at **Teotihuacan** or **Kaminaljuyu** and that he arrived at Copan to rule.

COTZUMALHUAPA (Kohts-uuh-mahl-**wah**-pah). A distinctive art style and archaeological culture of the southeast Pacific Coast of Guatemala and western El Salvador. The iconography, material culture, and settlements of this comparatively little-studied culture differ substantially from those of the **Maya** of the surrounding areas. Cotzumalhuapa art appears on large boulders and large volcanic stone **stelae,** and the iconographic style and content more closely resemble those of El **Tajin** in Veracruz, **Izapa** in Chiapas, and other sites in southern and central Mexico.

The sculpture of Cotzumalhuapa depicts **Tlaloc,** a Mexican rain **deity,** and human **sacrifice.** Tenoned sculptured portrait heads carved in the full round and human figures, whose costumes, bodies, and facial features resemble people shown in the ancient art of Mexico, are also present. Additionally, ball game equipment, such as stone yokes, *palmas,* and *hachas* are commonly found at Cotzumalhuapa sites. While some archaeologists have argued that Cotzumalhuapa art and society were highly influenced by Mexican societies, many other anthropologists believe that Mexican peoples actually migrated and lived in this area.

A few of the largest "type sites" of the Cotzumalhuapa culture include **Bilbao** and El **Baul** in Guatemala, and Cara Sucia in El Salvador. This region is one of the hottest and most humid areas in **Mesoamerica,** but it is also one of the most ecologically rich regions because of the environment and the fertile soils and ash from adjacent volcanoes. In ancient times, tropical flora and fauna flourished here and supported large indigenous populations before the area was logged and cleared for farming in recent times.

There is some debate on the dating of the Cotzumalhuapa culture. Some archaeologists believe that this particular society dates to the Terminal to Early Postclassic Period (ca. A.D. 900–1100) when **Nahua**-speaking **Pipil** peoples migrated into the area. However, it is generally held that the culture dates to the Middle and Late Classic Periods (ca. A.D. 400–800). Thus, it is possible that if the culture is intrusive to the area, the people may have migrated from Veracruz or other parts of Mexico at this time. Also, contact with central Mexico and the Pacific Coast of Guatemala (**Soconusco**) was important from the time of the rise of **Teotihuacan** up until the Spanish conquest.

Research on the Cotzumalhuapa culture of Guatemala is documenting new sculptures and studying stone monuments that were taken to Germany, and comparisons are being made between this art style and the iconography of other Mesoamerican groups—especially those of Mexico. Surveys and excavations are also showing that the archaeological sites and ancient populations of this particular culture were more extensive than earlier assumed. It is also found that even Cotzumalhuapa bridges, or maybe dams, were constructed in this region. More excavations and working of the **ceramic** chronology is planned to help deal with the dating, iconographic, and migration problems with this enigmatic civilization.

COYOLXAUHQUI (Koh-yohl-shah-kee). The name of the sister of the **Aztec** patron **deity Huitzilopochtli** and the daughter of the earth goddess **Coatlique.** In the migration myth of the Aztec people, Coyolxauhqui was decapitated and dismembered by a miraculously born Huitzilopochtli while she attempted to kill their mother for being dishonorably pregnant with Huitzilopochtli. The disarticulated dead body of this warrior **woman** is depicted on a large carved stone **altar** at the base of the Aztec **Templo Mayor** in **Tenochtitlan.** The Coyolxauhqui stone shows the fallen woman topless and with serpents representing streams of blood flowing from her severed limbs. This sculpture commemorates the mythical event where Coyolxauhqui is killed by Huitzilopochtli and toppled down the **mountain** home of their mother, Coatlique.

CUICUILCO (Kwee-**kwil**-koh). This archaeological site is one of the first large ceremonial centers with monumental stone architecture known in the central **Basin of Mexico.** During the Late Formative Period at about

400 B.C., this center is estimated to have held approximately 20,000 people, and one of the main structures is a large round **temple** pyramid that is faced with stone masonry. Two stone and earth ramps conducted worshipers to double **altars** at the temple's summit. The exact extent of the construction of Cuicuilco cannot be discerned at this time, since most of the site was covered by an ancient volcanic eruption and lava flows. However, mounds, or the remains of ruined structures, appear almost a kilometer to the east of the main pyramid, making this quite an impressive Formative center in **Mesoamerica** at the time.

CUYAMEL. The name of an undisturbed **cave** site in eastern Honduras that contains many human burials and whole **ceramic** vessels that apparently date from the Early to the Middle Formative Periods (ca. 1200–600 B.C.). Ceramic vessel forms include long-necked bottles with globular bases, gadrooned gourd-shaped vessels, double bottles, and flat-bottomed bowls with flaring walls. These vessels are similar in form and date to material found at **Copan** and **Playa de los Muertos** in Honduras, **Tlatilco** in central Mexico, and the **Colima** ceramics in **west Mexico.** One bowl bears incised designs that are **Olmec** in style, which demonstrates contact between eastern Honduras and this Formative-era civilization to the west. Interestingly enough, few sites have been located in the area that produce similar ceramic material. One exception is an early cemetery ("Las Sepulturas") discovered at Copan.

D

DANCE. Dance figured prominently in the ceremonies of indigenous New World peoples. In ancient **Mesoamerica,** dance was often performed in the **plazas** near the main **temples** of the cities. This activity was a central part of important rituals to **deities** and for gatherings of the nobility; dance was a main form of communication with the supernatural and the ancestors. For example, **Aztec priests** imitating the deity **Xipe Totec** danced in skins of victims who had been **sacrificed,** and Classic **Maya** nobles danced during feasts, religious rituals, and heir designation rites.

In Mesoamerican dance and ritual, for the most part, men and **women** danced separately and at different points in the ceremony. People typically wore their finest garments and were adorned with **jade** jewelry, feathers, banners, and animal skins. Classic Maya **hieroglyphic** inscriptions frequently mention dance (*ahk'ot*) alongside imagery showing richly clad nobles with their arms, legs, and costumes that appear to be rendered in motion. The objects that the Maya elites are dancing with are also mentioned, such as certain staffs and snakes, together with how and when they are dancing, in one case as "ballplayers." *See also* DANZANTE

DANZANTE. A sculptural style found at Formative to Classic Period sites in Oaxaca, Mexico, including **San Jose Mogote** and **Monte Alban.** The stone slab monuments are set into walls or masonry structures (see photo). These sculptures show human figures poised with arms raised and legs bent as if in motion, or **dance.** Subsequent research on this art form and comparative studies with similar stone carvings on the Peruvian coast of South America and in the **Maya** area has shown that the "danzantes," or "dancers," are more than likely **sacrificed** victims and war captives, and rarely dancing nobles and shamans. These figures are sometimes accompanied by their names and titles to show their rank and importance, which exalts the captor.

DEATH. Illness and death were significant preoccupations of ancient Mesoamerican groups, and their prevention and the beliefs associated with them were an important part of religious ritual. Death was often viewed as being the result of evildoing or through the actions of malevolent **deities.** Death was seen as a change of status and physical being for an individual; a person went to another world to begin a new existence, but the living could still communicate with important ancestors during certain ceremonies.

To have life, there had to be death, thus people had to die and some had to be **sacrificed** to perpetuate human existence and the entire cosmos. The deceased were often buried in **tombs** or burials that included possessions of the person, prized jewelry and artifacts, and **ceramic** vessels, some of which contained food and drink for the afterlife. The Day of the Dead in contemporary Mexico with its food offerings, presentation of items cherished by the deceased, and elaborate ceremony has deep Pre-Columbian roots. This ceremony was perpetuated by similar European beliefs and practices introduced after the conquest.

Death can be equivalent to soul loss, where the wandering soul moves to the supernatural realm to be recycled in the future only after it regains strength. The destiny of the deceased depended on their social status and the means by which they died. For instance, drowning victims remained in a watery paradise with the rain and fertility gods. Dogs, or other animals, and human attendants sometimes helped the dead on their way into the **underworld** and afterlife. The deceased may travel to the underworld, where they are given trials by the underworld gods, as seen in the **Popol Vuh.** Usually the dead elites were able to overcome these tests to rise into the heavens as visible entities. The bodies of people were laid to rest in the ground because they were believed to have come from the earth and to be nurtured by it, and in turn must sustain the earth.

Deities associated with death and the underworld are very common in the art of ancient **Mesoamerica.** Death gods are rendered as skeletons, or they are connected with rotting flesh, owls, and **jaguars,** which hunt at night. The underworld lords received the dead and sacrificial victims. The death dates of **Maya** lords and verbs for death are mentioned in many Maya **hieroglyphic** texts.

DEITIES. The gods of ancient **Mesoamerica** are numerous and varied from culture to culture. However, there are some very salient similarities in Mesoamerican beliefs of the supernatural and with some of the aspects of important deities worshiped. For instance, the worship of deities is directly tied to nature, the ancestors, life itself, the cosmos, the place of humans in the universe.

Mesoamerican gods are multifaceted and interconnected; many deities share features, behaviors, and significance. The **Aztec** deity **Tlaloc,** for example, represents rain, water, and **warfare** and is associated with groundwater, **mountains,** and clouds. The Aztec deities **Quetzalcoatl** and **Ehecatl** share attributes and are both linked to wind, storms, and the sky. The ritual occasion, **calendar** date, or the specific ceremonies to a deity or deities help determine the role, utility, and aspects of the gods at any particular time.

A short list of some deities found across this culture area contains gods representing the sun, earth, **underworld, death, maize,** rain, moon, and wind. Although many different deities existed in the belief systems of Mesoamerican peoples, theirs was not a true pantheon of separate supernatural beings. Instead, the gods were all part of the cosmos or same "life force"; the Mesoamerican world and supernatural universe consisted of an all-encompassing energy and collection of things, whether they be the earth, sun, plants, people, animals, or the deities. These religious views are still apparent with contemporary peoples of Mexico and Central America. However, today deities are still sustained by the **sacrifice** of animals and objects, but not with people and their blood as in the past. *See also* CHAC, COATLIQUE, COYOLXAUHQUI, HUITZILOPOCHTLI, IXCHEL, TEZCATLIPOCA, TONANTZIN, TONATIUH, and XIPE TOTEC

DIET. For general "textbook" descriptions of the ancient **Mesoamerican** diet, the "trinity" of **maize,** beans, and squash is traditionally invoked. These staples were also supplemented by meat from wild animals (peccaries, deer, rodents, birds) and fruits and plants (palms, **ramon** nuts, roots) gathered in the forests. However, time-honored information from ethnographic sources, studies of ethnohistoric documents, and, more recently, from physical evidence from carbonized remains in the archaeological record demonstrates that their diet was much more complex and varied. A mosaic of root crops, fruits, nuts, leaves, plus the Mesoamerican "staples" of corn, squash, and beans constituted the ancient diet. Some important foods that were prepared in Mesoamerican cuisine were tamales, or maize cakes, stuffed with beans, chile, and meat, and drinks were made of maize gruel and **cacao** mixed with water. Written sources also indicate that the **Aztecs** even ate cakes of lake algae and insects.

Many indigenous groups planted a great variety of plants near their settlements. Also their gardens, orchards, and fields mimicked the diversity and quantity of plants that occur naturally in the local tropical forests. A Maya maize field could also have been used to plant root crops, pineapple, fruit trees, and tobacco besides beans and squash. More studies of ancient carbonized plant remains, preserved pollens, and other physical evidence of plants and their use are needed to complete the list of past Mesoamerican cultigens.

Turkeys, fish, deer, parrots, monkeys, and peccaries probably were widely kept near homes or semidomesticated to be raised for food. The domestic dog was also an important food source with many of these cultures. Today, archaeological projects are relying more upon the recovery of carbonized food remains, chemical analysis of human and animal bone, and data from early written sources to better comprehend the extent of the foods eaten by past societies. *See also* CHINAMPA, MANO and METATE, and MILPA

DOS PILAS. This is an important Classic Maya site located near the lake and river named "Petexbatun" between the **Usumacinta** and Pasion Rivers in **Peten,** Guatemala. Dos Pilas has many monumental buildings, range-type palace structures, high-quality carved monuments, **stelae,** and **hieroglyphic** stairways, and more than 300 residential structures. Although Dos Pilas was known and visited earlier by local hunters, chicle gatherers, loggers, and **Lacandon Maya** Indians, the site was not brought to the attention of the outside world until it was "discovered" by explorers and archaeologists in the early 1960s. Dos Pilas is being intensely studied by mappers, archaeologists, spelunkers, epigraphers, geographers, and paleobotanists to learn more about the lives of the people at this regional capital and about how the Classic Maya civilization collapsed.

Dos Pilas was settled during the Late Classic Period possibly by an off-shoot or exiled lineage from the great center of **Tikal,** Guatemala, according to hieroglyphic and archaeological evidence. The emblem hieroglyph for Dos Pilas is the same as that of Tikal: the tied hair sign (Mutul?). The city was built on higher ground just to the south of a natural spring and swampy area. At its height, Dos Pilas was the home of approximately 5,000 to 7,000 people, and its rulers controlled much of the Pasion River region politically and economically through **warfare** and alliances.

A **tomb,** possibly of the second of these powerful rulers, containing worked **jade,** painted **ceramics,** and a well-preserved skeleton of an older male, was discovered in investigations at the site. Other important discoveries include hieroglyphic pottery and jade in burials on nonelites, an intricately carved stone panel depicting a sacrificial bloodletting rite of a royal Maya youth, and an additional hieroglyphic stairway.

The collapse and abandonment of Dos Pilas was more than likely because of intensified competition and warfare between a growing number of elites. Dos Pilas fought battles with the sites of **Seibal,** Tikal, the **Ik site, Yaxchilan,** and others. Ruler 4 of Dos Pilas, who went on a raiding spree toward the end of his reign, may have lost a battle and was captured by the king of the nearby site of Tamarindito around A.D. 761. During the time of war and collapse, defensive walls were constructed over and around monumental architecture and **plaza** areas to enclose and protect them and the residents from outside attack.

Nonetheless, these defenses were to no avail, because the site was largely abandoned toward the end of the Late Classic (when many other sites were being abandoned throughout the Maya area) and much of the population went to peripheral areas or to other Maya sites. *See also* AGUATECA

DRESDEN CODEX. A **Maya** pictographic book, or **codex,** made of painted, stucco-covered paper that may have been brought to the Old World by Spanish **conquistadores** or priests. It was eventually found in Vienna then bought and placed in the Dresden Library in 1739. It is believed that this codex was probably made in **Yucatan** during Post-classic times, because of its artistic style, the **deity** images portrayed, and the Yucatec elements in the **hieroglyphic** texts contained within it. Its organization and layout suggest that it had sections or "chapters."

The Maya Paris and Madrid codices are also similar in form and content.

This screen-fold book has pages that are divided up into panels with black and red lines. These panels contain images of deities and offerings detailed in black, red, and blue, and the hieroglphic texts above the figures at the top of each panel are executed in black paint. The Dresden Codex contains abundant and crucial information on Maya society, **religion, astronomy,** the **calendar,** and material culture. The book contains calendrical calculations, divinations, and deities with offerings to be given to them. It was the combination of images and syllabic texts in the Dresden Codex that ultimately resulted in the deciphering of the ancient Maya written script. *See also* CODEX NUTTALL

E

ECCENTRIC FLINT. An artifact actually made from **chert** (the similar flint, a mineral of chalk deposits, is scarce in the limestone and volcanic lands of **Mesoamerica**) that is flaked and chipped into a variety of unusual forms. Some "eccentrics" are made of **obsidian** as well, and both materials are difficult to reduce into complex shapes. Instead of projectile points and cutting tools, the chert object is fashioned into elaborate three-dimensional shapes with appendages, such as human figures, animals, insects, and abstract forms. Specific examples of eccentric flints include ancestor figures, scorpions, star shapes, circles with perforated centers (which are difficult to execute), pointed trilobed scepters, and dogs.

Some of the most elaborate eccentric cherts were made in the **Maya** area during the Classic Period. Eccentrics are often recovered from elite households, dedication caches in monumental architecture, or elite burials. Recently at **Copan,** Honduras, exquisitely crafted eccentric chert artifacts, depicting humans wearing elaborate headdresses and holding objects, were found in excavations within buried buildings. These eccentrics, which are translucent in many places and took many days to complete, were offerings of the ruling elites for constructing or burying **temples**.

EHECATL (Eh-**hey**-cotl). The **Nahuatl** name of an important aspect of the **Aztec deity** called **Quetzalcoatl:** the "Quetzal feathered serpent." The name of this deity signifies "wind"—the wind that swept the way for **Tlaloc,** the central Mexican god of rain and lightning. This deity was also an important cultural hero in that he helped create the present race of humankind by rescuing their bones and essence from the **underworld.** Ehecatl is usually depicted in stone sculpture and painted **codices,** or books, in human form with a long beak for a mouth and wearing jewelry made of cut and worked shell. **Temples** for this deity were circular and were topped with a conical roof.

EIGHT DEER. Well-known **Mixtec** ruler who was brought into the realm of history through study and interpretations of **codices,** or pre-Hispanic books, from Postclassic Oaxaca. "Eight Deer **Jaguar** Claw" was most praised for conquering several Mixtec centers and for attempting to unite the different polities into a kingdom that could survive his death. He may have lived around A.D. 900–1000, and he had several wives and a brother with whom he coruled some kingdoms. His richly adorned relatives and the participation of Eight Deer in several rituals are portrayed on the painted pages. The codices also show how he went to **Toltec Tula** to receive his turquoise nose plug as a sign of his high office and rulership. It is reported that Eight Deer was eventually sacrificed for attempting to go beyond lineage-governing practices to try to create an empire. The **Codex Nuttall** contains drawings and paintings of Eight Deer in his ceremonial dress, performing rituals, in **warfare,** and playing the ball game in a **ball court**.

F

FINE PASTE CERAMICS. These special pottery types are unlike other **Mesoamerican ceramics** in that they are generally thinner and without visible clay temper. When this type of ceramic is examined through cross-sectioning through the vessel wall, its fine pastes typically do not exhibit dark gritty cores or color changes, because of the temper-less clay and consistent firing temperatures during their manufacture. Some fine ceramics are made of clay tempered with volcanic ash or a very fine grit of sand or calcite, but true fine wares consist principally of refined clay.

Fine ceramics are common during the end of the Late Classic Period and into the Postclassic, especially in the **Maya** region. At **Dos Pilas,** three different types of Fine Orange pottery from **Yucatan,** the **Usumacinta River,** and local Pasion River, and two types of Fine Grey wares from Yucatan and the Usumacinta River were recovered. These sources of ceramics and probable **trade** contact were determined by analyzing local clays and the clay composition of the ceramics themselves. Another widely dispersed fine ceramic type is Thin Orange, which was made and distributed throughout central and eastern Mexico, during the height of **Teotihuacan** in the Early to Middle Classic Period. *See also* CHICHEN ITZA and SEIBAL

FIRE. Fire was believed to have been created by ancient **Mesoamerican deities** and then later it was given to people. Besides its use in cooking, fire was important for religious rituals, such as the burning of incense, or **copal,** or other offerings. Fire was also used to destroy **temples** during military conquests. In **Aztec** society, the new **calendar** round was commemorated with the extinguishing of all fires, and new flames were ceremoniously made with a fire drill in the chest cavity of a sacrificial victim. This "new fire," which was then taken to relight fires everywhere, rejuvenated the sun, world, human populations, and a new era. Ancient Mexican deities associated with fire are **Tezcatlipoca** ("Smoking Mirror"), Xiuhcoatl ("Fire Serpent"), Xiuhtecuhtli ("god of terrestrial fire"), and Huehueteotl ("Old, Old God"), who was the aged deity of fire and hearths.

As with the Aztecs and other ancient Mesoamerican peoples, fire was an important element in rituals, like with the Classic **Maya.** The Maya and other cultures burned incense in **ceramic** and stone braziers as offerings to their deities and ancestors who received it through the sweet smoke that was produced. Sacred fires were also lit with fire drills, and this action is depicted in **codices,** or painted books, and a Classic Period carved stone panel. The Maya also burned blood-soaked paper from **sacrifices** and objects (including animals, bundles of sticks, and hearts) in fires so that the deities could directly receive the offerings through the rising smoke. Fire was also important in **cave** ceremonies; torches and burned bowls and offerings are being recovered in ongoing archaeological excavations at cave sites.

FIVE SUNS. The "five suns" refer to the creation of the five eras, or worlds, as clearly witnessed in the creation myths and **calendar stone** of the **Aztecs.** The fifth sun is the current sun of the present world, and the four previous ones are associated with their own particular gods, races of people, and worlds. The signs for the four previous suns, or creations, are the day signs and numbers in the year when the suns began, and these surround the representation of the current sun on the Aztec **Calendar,** or Sun Stone. The four earlier suns in **Nahuatl** are *Nahui Ocelotl* (4 **Jaguar**), *Nahui Ehecatl* (4 Wind), *Nahui Quiahuitl* (4 Rain), and *Nahui Atl* (4 Water); the current era is *Nahui Ollin* (4 Motion).

FLINT. *See* CHERT

FLOWERS. Flowers were symbols of beauty in ancient **Mesoamerican** cultures and often were connected with elites and ritual. The **Aztec deity** *Xochipilli* was directly associated with flowers, beauty, pleasure, and the arts. Flowers were often given as offerings to deities, as they still are today at many shrines and churches. Marigolds, or *cempoalxochitl,* are part of **altars** to the dead in Mexico. In Mesoamerican art, especially in murals at **Teotihuacan,** flowers and people adorned with flowers are depicted.

In Classic **Maya** society, flowers were important symbols of rank and lineage. Sons were seen as metaphorical "flowers," or *nik,* that sprouted or grew from their fathers. A title or name of Maya kings, *hanab,* may be a type of flower found in the lowlands, and the **hieroglyph** for this term strongly resembles an opened flower. Flowers with wide pedals and extended pistils are also represented in Maya **jade** ear flares and other jewelry. For the Maya, flowers were also essential offerings for deities and used in rituals. The **conquistador** Hernan Cortes' lame and abandoned horse, which was perceived as an other-worldly/supernatural being by the **Itza** Maya, was presented with flowers as offerings and food.

G

GODS. *See* DEITIES

GOLD. Gold work and jewelry were prized in many societies of later preconquest (Postclassic) **Mesoamerica.** The Postclassic Period **Aztecs, Toltecs, Mixtec,** and **Maya** all used gold objects and personal adornments (see photo). Gold was perceived as a product of the sun and the supernatural, and the **Nahuatl** term for gold, *Teocuitlatl,* meant "excrement of the gods." Gold- and metalworking were invented in South America long before this metal and technology came to Mesoamerica, and gold objects were widespread in this continent by 800–600 B.C. Some of the earliest appearance of gold ornaments is in the 8th and 9th centuries in the Maya area, Oaxaca, and lower Central America.

Goldsmiths had high status in Aztec society. Mixtec gold workers were held in the highest esteem in Mesoamerica for their delicate filigree and lost-wax casting techniques that produced high-quality objects with fine detail. A Mixtec **tomb** discovered at **Monte Alban** was filled with fine gold objects (see photo). A cached offering for a stone **stela** at the Maya center of **Copan,** Honduras, contained a gold bell. Gold bells and artifacts were also recovered from the sacred **cenote** well at the Maya site of **Chichen Itza.** A necklace of gold **jaguar** heads was recovered from a burial of an elite personage at the highland Guatemalan site of **Iximche.** Much of the Mesoamerican gold and gold jewelry taken by the Spanish **conquistadores** from the Aztecs and Mixtecs to be shipped back to Europe was melted down for bars and coinage. *See also* METALLURGY

GUIENGOLA. A unique center today found in **Zapotec** territory in the hills near the Pacific Coast of Oaxaca, Mexico. In late Pre-Columbian times, the Zapotec joined forces with the **Mixtec** to defeat the conquering **Aztec** during an epoch of intense conquest **warfare.** They resided in the impressive Zapotec fortified center of Guiengola on a hilltop as a base and redoubt for this military campaign and resistance to the Aztec presence.

The site is encircled by several kilometers of tall stone defensive walls, and it has only one central access point in the form of a long stairway. The site core contains a few large **temples,** residences, elite palaces, a tower-like construction, and a **ball court** for playing the ball game. Guiengola also has wells and catchment basins made for collecting rain and runoff water. Archaeological evidence and ethnohistoric sources indicate that this site was only used for short periods during outbreaks of war. *See also* AGUATECA

GUILA NAQUITZ. A **cave** site near the Oaxaca Valley in the highlands of Oaxaca, Mexico, that contains crucial evidence of early occupations and plant use in ancient **Mesoamerica.** The cave site was used by archaic peoples (ca. 8000–6000 B.C.) who left behind stone tools and plant remains. Some of the earliest evidence for the use and cultivation of bottle gourds and **maize** is found at Guila Naquitz. Also dried remains of acorns, maguey, prickly pear, and other plants that were recovered in excavations, along with the remains of small mammals, provide insights on the **diet** of the first semisedentary and settled peoples of Mesoamerica. *See also* TEHUACAN

H

HIEROGLYPHS. Term coined in describing ancient Old World scripts, including Egyptian and Greek writing systems, that means "sacred signs/writings," which was subsequently employed to describe Meso-american writing. Hieroglyphs, or signs representing words, names, or concepts in ancient **Mesoamerica,** are found on stone monuments, such as **stelae, altars,** panels, and lintels, **codices, ceramics,** murals, and on arti-facts made of **jade,** bone, and shell. Hieroglyphs can be abstract signs, di-rect representations of the things referred to, or phonetic syllables.

In Oaxaca, early hieroglyphs appear on stone sculptures and later in **Mixtec** codices (painted books), and in Postclassic central Mexico, **Aztec** "glyphs" that usually represent names or **calendar** dates occur mainly in codices and on stone monuments. **Maya** hieroglyphic writing, on the other hand, is found in the widest variety of media and contexts.

The earliest known hieroglyphic writing in Mesoamerica is demon-strated for Formative societies in Oaxaca. Stone monuments dating to about 800 to 500 B.C. contain hieroglyphs that name people and calendar dates. These people, who may have been the ancestors of the **Zapotecs,** probably invented writing for religious purposes and for recording dy-nastic information. In the writing system of the Classic Zapotec sites in Oaxaca, some personal name signs, numbers, and calendar glyphs have been deciphered.

The **Olmec** of southeastern Mexico may have had an earlier system of writing, but convincing evidence of true hieroglyphs in secure archaeo-logical contexts is currently lacking. Another writing system, the Isth-mian script of Veracruz, was coeval with the earliest Maya writing of the Late Formative, but much more complex at the time. This script, along with the Oaxacan writing systems, has yet to be completely deciphered.

By far the most elaborate writing in ancient Mesoamerica was devel-oped by the Classic Maya. The largest corpus of texts, the most highly varied media that exhibit hieroglyphs, and the longest inscriptions be-long to these people. Maya hieroglyphic texts appear on stone stelae, al-tars, stairways, lintels, and panels, on artifacts such as ceramic vessels, jade jewelry, bone and shell items, codices, and on painted wall and **tomb** murals.

Maya writing contains some ideographs, or signs representing actual things, such as a **jaguar**'s head for "jaguar" and an eyeball for "see," for example. However, Maya texts mainly consist of logographs, which are signs that represent words, ideas, or syllables (a vulture head or the clus-ter of syllables *ah-ha-wa* for **ahaw,** or "ruler"), and phonetic signs that signify a consonant/vowel combination such as "bi" or "ka." Much of the Maya writing contains calendrical information and describes events in the lives of the ruling nobles. A common class of Maya hieroglyphic signs are called "emblem glyphs," which are site-specific glyphs or emblems of Maya centers or lineages. *See also* MOJARRA (LA)

HUASTEC (Wahs-teck). The Huastec (sometimes spelled "Huaxtec") are Mayan-speaking people who inhabit the Huasteca, or region of northern Veracruz and eastern San Luis Potosi in eastern Mexico. The Huastecs are separated from other **Maya** to the south by the Isthmus of Tehuantepec and many different groups of non-Mayan speakers. According to linguistic analyses, the Huastec split off into their own language, culture, and territory from about 2500 to 2000 B.C. This was an important time for the establishment of agriculture, sedentary life, and migrations and contact throughout **Mesoamerica.** The Huastecs may have been separated or driven north from their Maya neighbors by the development of early **Nahua, Totonac,** or **Olmec** cultures.

Large archaeological sites, stone carvings, and artifacts are abundant in the Huastec area, but relatively few large-scale scientific excavations have been conducted in this region. The later Huastec people interacted heavily with the cultures from central Mexico, particularly **Teotihuacan** and **Tula,** and the local site of El **Tajin,** as seen in **ceramic** styles, **trade** items, architecture, and art works. Because of their location and development, the Huastecs may have been in contact with societies of the southern United States. After A.D. 900 Huastec culture flourished; populations, monumental art, and site construction were at their greatest extent. Huastec Maya may be depicted as defeated warriors by the Terminal Classic Period site of **Cacaxtla** in the adjacent state of **Tlaxcala.**

Many ancient Huastec sites have a large number of round structures. Some buildings have unique asphalt floor coverings. The stone portrait **stelae** depict full figure humans, and in one case a richly dressed noble, or possibly a **priest,** runs a branch through his tongue in a bloodletting **sacrifice.** Huastec ceramics have distinctive black and white designs and pouring spouts. An intriguing discovery concerning the Huastecs is that they produced ceramic "toys" or figurines that have functioning ceramic wheels with wooden axles on their feet. It would appear that Mesoamericans had wheel technology, but chose to rely on human labor for transportation because of topographic and cultural considerations.

HUITZILOPOCHTLI (Wheat-zeel-oh-**pohch**-tlee). **Nahuatl** name for a principal **deity** of the **Aztecs,** which is glossed as "hummingbird on the left/south." This deity was associated with **warfare, sacrifice,** the sun, and elite rulership and lineage in ancient central Mexico. There is much speculation as to why "hummingbird" and "to the left" were so important to the Aztecs. For instance, it is known that hummingbirds fiercely defend their nests and "the left" had connotations of malevolence and "unnaturalness." However, the importance of this deity, the etymology of its name, and the historical specifics of the god's attributes are deeply rooted in Aztec history, myth, and culture. Thus, we will never truly thoroughly understand Huitzilopochtli and when and why he came to be.

The Aztecs believed that Huitzilopochtli led them from their island home of **Aztlan** to the **Basin of Mexico** to establish their empire in the capital city of **Tenochtitlan,** which he predicted would be founded on an island where an eagle was perched on a cactus. Hence, this deity could even be a creation from an important historical figure in Aztec history, a mythological ancestor, and religious belief combined.

After the Aztecs conquered and freed themselves from the rule of their masters, the Tepanecs, they elevated the role of their deity Huitzilopochtli to that of a principal deity whose cult was to be spread throughout Mexico. The **Templo Mayor,** or main **temple**—one of the largest pyramids at Tenochtitlan and central Mexico at the time of the conquest—had a shrine to Huitzilopochtli on its summit, and next to this shrine was a temple to **Tlaloc,** the rain god.

According to the Aztecs, Huitzilopochtli was born just as his sister, **Coyolxauhqui,** was plotting to kill their mother, **Coatlique.** Huitzilopochtli immediately came forth from his wounded mother armed with **weapons,** shield, and the **fire** serpent to slay his sister and his many aggressive half-brothers. The warrior god Huitzilopochtli was crucial to the continuance of the world and life itself, because he helped the sun battle the **underworld** forces and travel daily through the sky.

However, to do that, this god needed the blood and essence of human sacrificial victims taken from Aztec warfare and from **women** who died in childbirth. In this manner, the Aztecs propagated the belief and cult of Huitzilopochtli in Pre-Hispanic Mexico, and this helps explain how they were able to grow as one of the largest **Mesoamerican** empires and expand out of central Mexico.

Although Huitzilopochtli is depicted in Aztec books, representations of this deity are rarely seen in sculpture; it is possible that most of the carvings were made of wood or plaster. However, many of the sculptures of Huitzilopochtli were either hidden from or destroyed by the Spanish conquerors in the early 16th century. The deity is often painted wearing hummingbird feathers and beak, lances and shield, a mirror, and the fire serpent. *See also* TONATIUH

HUNTERS AND GATHERERS. *See* CHICHIMECS, CLOVIS, GUILA NAQUITZ, and TEHUACAN

I

IK SITE. Classic **Maya** center famous for its beautifully painted polychrome **ceramic** vessels, which flooded the art market and are found in elite burials in the southern Maya lowlands. The vessels, mostly cylindrical vases for drinking **cacao,** are recognized by their artistic style, the historical personages depicted and named on the vessels, and the "Ik" place name, or toponym, in their **hieroglyphic** texts. The vessels were more than likely made at one center and then distributed throughout the southern lowlands.

The site responsible for the manufacture of these vessels has not been securely matched with a known Maya ruin. But compositional analysis of the ceramics and of clays from around Maya sites suggests that they were made at a central **Peten** center. This center may be Motul de San Jose, which is located just to the south of the impressive center of **Tikal,** since a stone monument at Motul de San Jose has an "Ik" place name. Additionally, ceramic sherds at the site have a similar chemical composition to already analyzed Ik site vessels. The copious amount of Ik site pottery known to be on the art market, and the fact that some of these vessels were also found in burials at **Dos Pilas** and other Maya sites, suggests that these ceramics were manufactured for use in elite rituals, feasts, **trade,** and gift giving. New excavations at Motul de San Jose will uncover important information regarding pottery manufacture and Maya ethnicity at this important center.

ILOPANGO. A volcano in central El Salvador that experienced a violent eruption around A.D. 200–250 that left a deep, lake-filled depression and a massive ash and pumice deposit in a 100-kilometer radius. The ash fall buried many settlements and agricultural fields, such as seen later at **Ceren,** and led to rapid depopulation of the area. Archaeological and geological evidence suggests that the ancient cultures of El Salvador were often plagued with volcanic eruptions and ash falls that forced them to abandon their villages and cultivated areas over and over.

The ash covering from the Ilopango eruption would initially sterilize the soil, making it difficult for plant cultivation, but would allow for extremely rich soils, nonetheless, in a couple of centuries. The eruption may also have blocked out the sun and caused extensive rainfalls, which also would have forced people to move elsewhere. It has been hypothesized that people from central El Salvador may have migrated farther north into Honduras and the **Maya** lowlands bringing items and their local crafts, such as **Usulutan ceramics,** with them.

INCENSE. *See* COPAL

ITZA. Commonly known as the later-despised rulers of Early Postclassic **Yucatan** who were centered at their grandiose capital: **Chichen Itza.** **Maya** lore has it that the Itza were Mexicanized Maya from a foreign land to the southwest who entered Yucatan to subjugate and rule the territory and people. After the Itza were expelled from Yucatan by other local Maya elites, they headed to the island and peninsula center of **Tayasal** (*Ta Itza*) on Lake **Peten** ("island" in the Yucatec and Itza Mayan languages) Itza in northern Guatemala. Here the Itza set up a kingdom and local political alliance network that became the last Maya frontier before it was finally conquered by the Spanish in 1697.

Recent epigraphic work identified the title "Itza" in the inscriptions at Chichen Itza, but a more interesting and important finding was the discovery of this epithet in Classic Maya texts at Motul de San Jose (the **Ik Site**), an important Maya site near Lake Peten Itza, and on looted **ceramic** vessels. It would seem that the Itza had their beginnings in the Southern Maya lowlands and then traveled back and forth from Yucatan and Lake Peten Itza according to the prevailing political climate and kinship ties.

IXCHEL. Maya deity with female attributes that was described by Spanish **conquistadores** and who was a prominent being in the ideology of the Yucatec peoples during the Late Postclassic Period. Her name can be translated as "Lady Rainbow," which may point to a connection with the sky or ancient astronomical observations. She does not appear to be directly related to the moon or earth. Ixchel was the goddess of weaving, fertility, midwives, and childbirth and was usually depicted as an aged woman. This deity was connected to **sweat baths** and the birthing rituals within them, as seen in the iconography and inscriptions in Maya monuments and **ceramics. Women** made pilgrimages to Cozumel and Isla de Mujeres off the east coast of **Yucatan** to give offerings and conduct rituals for continued human fertility and safe births.

IXIMCHE. The name, which means "tree of **maize**" or **ramon**/breadnut tree, of the Postclassic center of the **Cakchiquel Maya** kingdom of the highlands of Guatemala. The Cakchiquel Maya rebelled against their **Quiche** Maya overlords around A.D. 1470 and established an independent kingdom centered at Iximche. The Spanish **conquistadores** commanded by Pedro de Alvarado conquered the Cakchiquel and set up the first capital of the new Spanish province of Guatemala in A.D. 1524.

Iximche is a relatively small center located on a hill in the highland Guatemalan pine forest that is surrounded by steep ravines on all sides but one. At the approachable side a moat was dug and defensive walls placed so that the city would be highly defensible against attack. An excellent lookout vantage point is provided by the site's location, and the setting makes for one of the more beautiful panoramic views of all of the Maya centers.

The site has many imposing **temples,** public **plazas,** palaces, and large residences, but no monumental stone art is evident. The ball game was played here in several capital I-shaped ball courts that were sunken into the ground. Excavation and restoration of temples and a **ball court** have been carried out at the site core, and settlement surveys and excavations in the areas surrounding the hilltop center are planned for the near future. Several indigenous burials were found at Iximche, and one royal burial contained a necklace of **gold jaguar** heads. *See also* UTATLAN

IZAPA. An archaeological site in Chiapas, Mexico, near the Guatemalan border that exhibits a distinctive iconographic style on sculpted stone **stelae** of Formative times. Izapa was a large and important center mainly during the final centuries of the Formative era (ca. 200 B.C. to A.D. 200) in **Mesoamerica,** much like El **Mirador, Kaminaljuyu,** and **Teotihuacan.** This ruin is situated in the hilly piedmont area just north of the Pacific Coast of southern Chiapas. The site is made up of an extensive settlement that to date includes about 160 large mounds spread over approximately two square kilometers. The architecture at Izapa is made of an earthen core held by an exterior of unshaped river cobbles and dried clay. Two main clusters of mounds exist at the site that have **temples, plazas,** and **ball courts** for the ball game.

The people at Izapa may have interacted with populations on the south coast and with the **Olmec, Maya,** and other Formative Period cultures. Cultural remains at Izapa date from the Classic Period all the way back to the Early Formative, and similar artifacts and iconography are shared between Izapa and southern Mesoamerica throughout this chronological sequence. It is hypothesized that the Mesoamerican 260-day sacred **calendar** was developed at or near Izapa, because at this latitude (14.8 degrees north) the sun travels from its overhead position to the south and then back to zenith again in 260 days. Apparently, the sun also rises behind a local volcano at summer solstice (June 22).

Roughly 100 monumental stone carvings are known to exist at Izapa, many of these being standing stone stelae. Some of the stone **altar**-like sculptures were discovered to have magnetic properties. The sculptures do not contain **hieroglyphic** texts or calendar dates, but stylistically they can be dated to Late Formative times, and associated **ceramic** material support this chronology. One stela may depict the Maya rain deity **Chac,** who is fishing with baskets. Many of these monuments depict historical figures, probably nobles or **priests** from the site, and some are actually shown performing ceremonies or in the company of other elites.

A few scenes record human **sacrifice,** while others show individuals in ritual dress. Another figure floats in a boat, while still another monument has a person being carried in a palanquin. The Izapa monuments may also represent some of the earliest scenes from the ancient history of the Maya recorded in the **Popol Vuh** of the **Quiche** Maya. Two figures, possibly the Maya hero twins, who were famous hunters, artists, and ballplayers, flank a descending alligator on one stone and a falling bird figure on another.

J

JADE. Precious greenstone or jadeite for jewelry and portable art was highly prized throughout **Mesoamerica.** Jade was used by elites and people of high rank and status in necklaces, bracelets, pendants, pectorals, anklets, and ear flares. A jade bead was often placed in the mouth of the dead person at burial, and jade beads are found around the skeletons of the buried elite. Its hardness, scarcity, and sacred green color, which symbolized water, vegetation, and life, are what made this stone so precious (see photo).

A source of jade is located near the **Motagua River** in eastern Guatemala, which is preferred for its light and dark apple green jade that is still used today in local jewelry making. There are also additional sources of jade in Costa Rica, the highlands of Guatemala, and apparently in Guerrero, Mexico. Jade was worked with hard stone tools, drills, strings, and strong abrasives. Jade jewelry is depicted in iconography in much of Mesoamerica, demonstrating its importance as a prestige item for these people.

Jade was highly sought after by the **Aztecs** who were paid **tribute** of jade (*chalchihuitl* or "precious green stones") by some of their subject provinces. The **Maya** craftspersons carved jade (*tup*, or "jewelry," in Classic Maya **hieroglyphic** texts) into round and tubular beads, worked it into celts and bars with low relief carvings of figures and hieroglyphs, and shaped it into large ornate ear ornaments that had to be held into place with counterweights. The largest piece of carved jade, depicting the Maya Sun God and weighing 9.7 pounds, was found at Altun Ha, Belize. The Maya also threw pieces of worked and partially worked jade into fires as offerings, where the heat caused the jade to fragment and explode.

The **Olmec** were master carvers of jade, and they chose light green and a bluish jade; generally, the largest and most beautiful jade artifacts are found at Olmec sites. These three-dimensional carvings are superbly executed, highly naturalistic, smoothly polished, and often are almost perfectly symmetrical. Many Olmec jades depict **deities** or the so-called were-**jaguar,** which is an anthropomorphic being with jaguar facial features. Portrait or burial masks were also manufactured from this material. Recently, several Olmec jade celts were uncovered at the waterlogged site of El **Manati,** and jade figurines and jewelry were found at the major Olmec center of La **Venta.** *See also* CHALCHIUHTLICUE and MEZCALA.

JAGUAR. The largest feline in the New World that is found in the jungles of Mexico, Central America, and South America. The black spotted, tawny colored hide of the jaguar (*Panthera onca*), or *ocelotl* in **Nahautl,** was cherished by many ancient Mesoamerican cultures through time. Jaguar pelts, for instance, are frequently depicted on **Maya** monuments and painted **ceramics** and were symbols of the nobility. Jaguars are frequently depicted in stone and murals, and stone jaguar thrones are found at **Chichen Itza, Uxmal,** and in other sites in **Yucatan.** Jaguar skins were placed in **tombs** of the Maya elite, where their claws and phalanges, which were left on the skins, have been recovered. Not surprisingly, "jaguar," or *balam,* was a common Maya title or name bestowed on the ruling elite and **deities,** and some gods have jaguar ears, tails, faces, or claws.

Not only sought for its beauty, the jaguar pelt represented supernatural and personal power, strength, cunning, and "nobility," because this animal was the mightiest predator known to these people. These fearsome animals were often animal companions, or a "co-essence" of Mesoamerican elites and warriors. The **Aztecs** even had the high warrior rank of Jaguar Knight. Jaguars were also associated with **death** and the **underworld** since they are extremely dangerous and fond of hunting at night. Jaguars were also captured and kept in ancient Mesoamerican societies. At **Copan,** the Maya sacrificed jaguars for an **altar** dedication and enthronement of a ruler, and the Aztecs appear to have held jaguars in zoos. Jaguars are currently in danger of extinction in **Mesoamerica,** and hunting them and the possession of their skins leads to severe punishment.

K

KAMINALJUYU (Kah-me-nahl-hoo-**yu**). An impressive and essentially Late Formative to Early Classic center that is now almost entirely covered by buildings and cement in Guatemala City. This important site once had over 200 mounds on about five square kilometers and some of the largest ruined structures, which are still visible in scattered locales in the modern urban landscape. Kaminaljuyu, or "Place of the Ancient Ones," is surrounded by **mountains** and volcanoes in a fertile valley with streams located in the central Guatemalan highlands. Because of the local volcanic ash and alluvial deposits, this site rests near prime agricultural land, and this provides a rich area for human occupation and population growth.

The people at Kaminaljuyu also had access to **obsidian, jade,** and volcanic stone sources from nearby eastern Guatemala as well. Extensive excavations have been done at the site, and digging today continues in city parks that were created to preserve parts of this important center. Excavations have encountered extensive canals and ditches that probably served for drainage, water dispersal, or crop irrigation.

The earliest occupants of Kaminaljuyu probably came from smaller settlements in the surrounding area and from the Pacific Coast region during the Early Formative Period. By Middle to Late Formative times the site was a large center that had several carved stone monuments and it held sway over several smaller satellite settlements. Sociopolitical and economic organization was quite complex at the time, as witnessed by the control of labor and resources, plus the extensive **trade** and contacts managed with **Izapa, Abak Takalik,** El **Mirador,** and other scattered Formative Period centers in southern **Mesoamerica.** At Kaminaljuyu and other early highland centers, many three-dimensional mushroom stones are present, signifying a connection to hallucinogenic drugs or a phallic, fertility cult. Many **ball courts** for the bouncing **rubber** ball game are also found in the area.

The power and richness at Kaminaljuyu peaked during the Late Formative "Miraflores" culture when the majority of the structures and stone sculptures were commissioned. It was the locus of one of the most important polities in Mesoamerica at this time. The stone monuments include **stelae,** whose designs are reminiscent of Izapa art, and iconography, from the **Maya** area. One stone stela contains an unread **hieroglyphic** text that resembles early texts from Veracruz and the Maya lowlands, and one human figure on the monument wears a mask and carries an **eccentric flint**.

Temples were constructed with frontal stairways and platforms that contain **tombs** that are well stocked with riches and **ceramics.** The tombs of Formative Period chiefs contain many whole pottery vessels, jade, carved shell, pyrite mirrors, stuccoed gourds, stone bowls, bone artifacts, and **sacrificed** or accompanying attendants. Some building dedicatory caches had decapitated human heads on ceramic plates. One tomb contained an elaborately carved trophy human skull.

An especially important finding at Kaminaljuyu is that there was extensive contact (direct and/or indirect), social interaction, or trade ties with the central Mexican metropolis of **Teotihuacan** during Early Classic times. It is also possible that Kaminaljuyu was part of a "web of interaction" of Formative to Early Classic Period cultures throughout much of Mesoamerica that made it indirectly tied to regional developments and societies.

Whatever may explain the interaction with and knowledge of distant cultures at this site, Kaminaljuyu during the Early Classic exhibits Teotihuacan style talud-tablero buildings, thin orange ceramics and green obsidian from central Mexico, and stuccoed and brightly painted pottery with iconography with Teotihuacan affinities (the **deity Tlaloc** and humans with speech scrolls, for instance). Similar interaction and the presence of material culture and architecture is seen at the Maya sites of **Tikal** and **Copan,** at **Monte Alban** in Oaxaca, and in many other centers in southern Guatemala, Veracruz, and **west Mexico.** Kaminaljuyu began to fall as other coeval centers like Teotihuacan, Izapa, and El Mirador also waned, but while the Classic Maya reached florescence in the lowlands.

L

LACANDON. The name generally applied to the **Maya** peoples residing near the upper **Usumacinta River** in the lowland jungles of Chiapas,

Mexico, and western **Peten,** Guatemala, since colonial times. The word *Lacandon* is a Spanish corruption of the Maya *lakam tun,* or "wide stone." This was a place name for a pre-Hispanic site on a limestone island in Lake **Miramar** and a limestone shelf (Planchon de Piedra) on the River Lacantun (another Spanish version of the word!), both in Chiapas. It is also possible that Lacandon was taken from the Maya term *acantun,* or "he/they of the sacred stone," which refers to the carving and placing of stone **stelae** by the lowland Maya. *Lakam tun* also appears as a place name in Classic Maya texts of the Usumacinta River region, thus it is an ancient toponym used in the area.

Until the mid-1700s the name Lacandon or Lacandones was given to Chol Maya speakers who were enemies of the **Itza** Maya of Central Peten and raiders of villages of the Spanish colonials. Numerous attempts at conquest by the Spanish of the Chol-Lacandon at their fortified site in Lake Miramar forced these indigenous people off the island and into the bush. The Chol-Lacandon Maya were eventually conquered in 1695 and then congregated in their native center of **Sac Bahlan** near savanna and forestlands in southern lowland Chiapas. Soon after colonization, most of these people were assimilated or exterminated by disease in Spanish towns in the cooler Guatemalan highlands.

Today Lacandon refers to a small number of Maya that speak a dialect of Yucatec who live in lowland Chiapas after fleeing conquest and colonization in **Yucatan** and then intermarrying with other Maya groups in the region. Isolated 19th-century archaeological sites of the Yucatec-Lacandon Maya are currently being excavated in Peten, Guatemala, to study cross-cultural interaction and indigenous culture change. The term *Lacandon* is now even used to name the general area of lowland Chiapas, the rainforest of Chiapas, and a range of hills (sierras) on the Guatemalan side to the east of the Usumacinta River.

LAGUNA ZOPE. This early archaeological site is located in a riverine and estuary setting near the Pacific Coast in the Isthmus of Tehuantepec in the state of Oaxaca. Inhabitants at Laguna Zope during the Early Formative manufactured **ceramics** similar to the hemispherical bowls of the **Barra** and **Ocos** cultures farther southeast on the coast of Chiapas and Guatemala. These cultures shared analogous environments and subsistence strategies, thus it is probable that they were in contact with one another. Laguna Zope is found near plenty of fresh water, rich alluvial soil, marine resources, and forest products, making it an attractive location for early settlers. By Middle Formative times (ca. 800–400 B.C.), the site was one of the largest in the area.

Other artifacts found at the ancient settlement include an abundance of **obsidian** chips, which it is hypothesized were used to grate manioc, but more than likely were used as general cutting tools. Quantities of shell, and quartz tools possibly used to work shell, recovered at Laguna Zope suggest that workshops for shell artifacts were present. The shell may have been used for **trade** to the Oaxaca highlands and the **Maya** area to the south. Ceramics from the Maya area and **Usulatan** wares from El Salvador are known from Laguna Zope during Late Formative times. Populations began to decline at the site at the beginning of the Classic Period, which may be related to shifting trade and the reliance on agriculture in local inland and highland centers.

M

MAGUEY. A cactus-like plant with long sword-like leaves with thorns on their edges that is found mainly in the drier climates of west and central Mexico and **Yucatan.** Maguey was additionally found around residences preserved under volcanic ash at **Ceren** in El Salvador, thus it may have been more widespread than previously thought. Maguey (species of Agave) was exploited for the rope and cloth that could be made from the tough fibers of its leaves, the curved thorns used for needles and bloodletters, but most of all, it was important for the drink **pulque,** which was a fermented alcoholic beverage (today tequila is distilled from it) made from the sweet maguey sap and used in rituals or often imbibed only by the elderly or **priests.**

Maguey products were important **tribute** items paid to the **Aztecs** and other central Mexican states, and today is an important crop for many indigenous peoples, particularly the Otomi of central and eastern Mexico. Hedges of the large and thorny maguey also provided an effective defensive perimeter for settlements and houses. Maguey plants and leaves are usually depicted in the art of pre-Hispanic central Mexican cultures, like at **Teotihuacan,** along with the drink pulque and pulque **deities.** In central Mexico and with the **Mixtec** peoples of Oaxaca, maguey was personified as a young goddess much like the youthful male **maize** god of the **Maya**.

MAIZE. The staple crop of Mesoamerican civilizations that had, and still has today, tremendous religious significance. *Zea mays,* indigenous maize, or corn of the Americas, has been a principal food source for settled communities since Early Formative times, except for parts of eastern and central Honduras where root crops were important, and in northern Mexico where the climate is drier. Maize is still central to the **diets** and economies of many current Latin American populations and countries. In fact maize is a mainstay in the diets of people and livestock throughout the world today.

Maize is a highly nutritious food, especially when soaked in lime water (completing the *nixtamal* process) to release essential proteins and then eaten with beans. Maize plants yield large quantities of food per acre through a relatively small labor investment, and they produce a great amount of storable surpluses that are also easily transported. Green maize can be consumed on a roasted cob or made into dough for tamales. Ripe maize kernels are treated and cooked in lime and are ground with **mano and metate** stones or in a mortar and pestle to be used in tamales (sometimes stuffed with meats, beans, or chiles), maize cakes and gruels, and tortillas. Maize was grown in **Milpa** fields, household garden plots, **chinampas** or raised fields, and on terraced slopes.

The earliest domesticated maize, consisting of small dried cobs and kernels, appears in the archaeological record at **cave** sites in the **Tehuacan** Valley, Puebla, Mexico, at about 3500 B.C. However, some investigators believe that maize was first domesticated in the highlands of nearby Oaxaca or Chiapas, Mexico, or western Guatemala at an earlier date, because of the great varieties of maize, early communities, and small carbonized cobs in these areas. Others propose an earlier South American origin for this important plant. Larger varieties of maize are found throughout **Mesoamerica** by Late Formative times, and modern maize varieties are commonly found in digs at Classic **Maya** and central and west Mexican sites.

Some paleobotanists believe that domesticated maize is descended from a related wild grass called *teosinte* (*Zea mexicana*), which is derived from the **Nahuatl** term meaning "god/sacred (*teo*) corn (*cintli*)." Nonetheless, another version of the domestication process of maize holds that maize, *teosinte,* and another related grass, *Tripsacum,* are hybrids of an early wild, hard kernel popcorn, which was the real progenitor of maize. This kind of hard corn, which other researchers claim is actually a kind of *teosinte,* however, is found at 5000 B.C. in the Tehuacan Valley. Although this is sufficiently early to be an ancestor of maize, the debates on maize origins and pedigree continue.

The importance of maize to Mesoamerican peoples is reflected in their religious beliefs, ritual, and iconography. Depictions of maize are seen in early **Olmec** and Maya art and were found throughout Mesoamerica at the time of the conquest. A maize **deity** appears in Olmec art as a corncob "**jaguar** baby," and representations of the Maize God were commonplace by Classic times. The Classic Maya created the Maize God in their sculpture and **ceramics** as a youthful male with maize foliage and a corncob issuing from his head. A central Mexican goddess often holds ears of maize in her hands in Postclassic figurines and sculpture. Mesoamerican myth recounts the creation of people from maize and their sacred connection and dependence upon this plant. Maya art and the murals at **Cacaxtla** that show human faces on ears of maize, plus the widespread nature of similar mythology, indicate that these beliefs are ancient ones.

Also currently, as well as in past societies in Mesoamerica, maize plays an important role in rituals pertaining to **sacrifice** and the perpetuation of life and the cosmos, ceremonies involving birth, **death,** and renewal, and rites related to kinship, marriage, and food sharing. Here, maize is prepared for ceremonial foods and drink, left as offerings, and used as the surface on which to cut umbilical cords or on which blood is dripped. Indeed the physical and ceremonial significance of maize is witnessed with contemporary Mesoamerican peoples who feel that no meal is complete, their bodies, vitality, and souls are not sustained, and ancestors and deities are neglected, if maize is not consumed.

MALINALCO. This picturesque site was occupied by the **Aztecs** in the territory of the Matlazinca people who were subjected militarily to Aztec rule. Malinalco is found southwest of Mexico City and on top of a forested hill with steep slopes that overlooks the **Basin of Mexico.** The town was easily defended, and it was an important religious and political center for the Aztec empire. Besides being a strategic place for Aztec expansion and regional governance, the **mountain** on which Malinalco rests was a sacred place associated with **deities** and important ancestors.

Today, Malinalco is one of the few major Aztec sites and religious centers left standing after the Spanish conquest of Mexico and through centuries of rebuilding over other native sites. Malinalco is best known for its **temples** and sculptures carved right out of the hill's natural bedrock. This made the site a permanent fixture of Aztec rule, but it also directly connected it to the earth, the deities, and the ancestors found within the hill. The site has been excavated and restored, and visitors can appreciate the stairways, rounded temple chambers, and the benches in the form of large eagles and **jaguars** sculpted from the bedrock. This site was an important ritual center, where the Aztecs communicated with their gods, but also where leaders could confer with each other and maintain alliances. The temple created in the bedrock was seen as a human-made **cave,** or supernatural place in the earth, and offerings of hearts and blood from victims of **sacrifice** were placed in a hole in the floor of the main chamber.

MANATI (EL). Recently, farmers and villagers eager to make a fishpond and divert the flow of water from a natural spring (from which the site gets its name) stumbled upon this archaeological site of the **Olmec** culture. The unsuspecting excavators uncovered carved wooden Olmec statues, **jade** celts and axe heads. This is extremely significant, because wooden sculptures are rare in **Mesoamerican** archaeology, because of their poor preservation in the tropics and from their destruction by Spanish **conquistadores.** However, the El Manati specimens are perfectly preserved, because they were placed in a bog. The fine clay soils and the consistent temperature and humidity helped to conserve them over the centuries.

El Manati is about 15 kilometers southeast from the Early Formative major Olmec center of **San Lorenzo** in Veracruz. Some signs of occupation and residences (but no **temples**) have been found near the site, however, most of what has been learned comes from excavations in the bog area. It appears that the Olmec occasionally arrived at this bog site to place offerings and **sacrifices** for the nearby spring. Archaeologists have found caches of several wooden statues, worked jade celts, skeletons of children, seeds, and the only known pre-Hispanic **rubber** balls for the ball game (but no **ball courts**) placed in groupings in the waterlogged earth. The wooden statues are limb-less anthropomorphic busts, representing Olmec **deities,** ancestors, or perhaps sacrificial victims. The rites here may have been performed for agricultural fertility, the ancestors, and the continuation of the cosmos.

MANO AND METATE. Quintessential grinding stones of ancient **Mesoamerican** peoples; food was prepared by grinding it on a large flat stone with the use of a flat or round hand stone. Grinding stones were also used to prepare ceremonial pigments and paints. These artifacts are found in large numbers at most archaeological sites near residences and **temples.** The metate is a stone carved flat or as a concave basin, where **maize** and other foods or pigments were placed to be ground. The mano was an elongated stone that was rounded or squared. Manos were manipulated, usually by **women** for food preparation, for grinding on the accompanying metate.

Manos and metates usually come in sets and are manufactured from limestone, quartzite, or volcanic stone. Many of these grinding stones in the **Maya** lowlands were made from limestone, but volcanic stone implements were traded from the highland centers, where they were quite common. Manos and metates are still used and sold in markets today throughout Middle America, and many people believe that food is properly prepared or tastes better only if these traditional stone tools are employed. *See also* DIET

MARKETS. Open markets were probably common at many large centers in ancient **Mesoamerica.** Markets were described by Spanish **conquistadores** on their treks through Mexico and Central America during 16th-century conquests. Tlatelolco was a main market in the **Basin of Mexico** and was located on the island of the **Aztec** capital of **Tenochtitlan.** Thousands of people gathered in the marketplace daily to buy, sell, and **trade** their materials and wares, which included **cacao,** large quantities of various foods, stone tools of **obsidian** and **chert, manos and metates,** feathers, **jade** ornaments, shell artifacts, **ceramics, textiles,** baskets, slaves, **gold** and silver, plants, and animals, to name a few. Materials and products were grouped together in segregated spaces in the market, which facilitated purchases and cost comparison.

Merchants (Aztec **pochteca**), soldiers, and judges were also available to mediate disputes and to help keep order and regulate prices. The marketplace was, and still is today, an important locus for social interaction and religious ceremonies. Earlier markets were probably held in the **plazas** of many ancient Mesoamerican centers. The plazas and large open structures in Classic **Maya** sites would have been excellent locations for public markets where trade materials, crafts, utilitarian items, and prestige goods could be obtained. However, archaeological evidence for a market function of ancient plazas is currently lacking or inconclusive. Markets are popular today in Mesoamerica, because in them, local populations and visitors have myriad goods, services, and information at their fingertips.

MATACAPAN. Located in the **Tuxtla Mountains** in southern Veracruz, Mexico, this site grew in size during the onset of the Classic Period, when it had established ties with **Teotihuacan** in central Mexico. This contact and interaction was materialized in local art styles and witnessed through the **trade** of **ceramics** and **obsidian.**

Matacapan was a center of ceramic vessel manufacture in the area that was organized and managed by local administrative elites. Its nucleated specialized workshops and many domestic groups participating in ceramic manufacturing were discovered in excavations in the 1980s. The ceramic vessels were not only used locally but were found in other regions in southern and central Mexico during the Middle Classic Period. At its peak, Matacapan is characterized as having a dendritic political economy in which ceramics were made specifically for export to other centers.

MAYA. Name for a people of related languages (of which there are only about 33 today) and ethnicity who are found in **Yucatan,** Chiapas, Mexico, Guatemala, Belize, and western Honduras and El Salvador. The ancient Maya (the term *Mayan* is used only when referring to the languages) are famous for their ruined cities with stone **temples** and palaces, carved stone **stelae** with portraits of rulers and **hieroglyphic** writing, and finely made portable art. Some well-known and often visited and investigated Maya archaeological sites include **Calakmul, Caracol, Chichen Itza, Copan, Dos Pilas, Mayapan,** El **Mirador, Nakbe, Palenque, Piedras Negras, Tikal, Uxmal,** and **Yaxchilan.**

Ancient Maya material culture includes **eccentric flints,** polished **jade,** polychrome **ceramics** with high-quality designs, worked shell, **chert** knives, bone implements, **manos and metates, obsidian** blades, and ceramic figurines. They also used feathers, palm mats, or *petates,* **textiles,** and **codices,** or paper and animal skin books, but little information concerning these items has been preserved in the archaeological record. The Maya are also recognized for their fine masonry architecture, royal **tombs,** residential burials, hieroglyphic writing and the **calendar,** painted murals, impressive **ball courts** for the ball game, **warfare** and human **sacrifice,** and large cities.

The Maya **diet** included **maize,** beans, squash, root crops, pineapples, avocados, **cacao,** and other fruits and vegetables grown in **milpa,** or slash-and-burn swidden fields, raised fields (**chinampas**) in **bajos,** and kitchen gardens. Some Maya **deities** were **Chac,** the rain god, *K'awil,* the god of kings and possibly smoke, fire, or tobacco, **underworld** deities, and gods associated with the heavens. The Maya worshiped their deities and ancestors at temples, **caves, mountains,** and **altars.**

Ancient Maya culture has roots in the Early and Middle Formative of **Mesoamerica** (ca. 1000–400 B.C.). At this time, the Maya interacted with other Mesoamerican peoples, while their lowland rainforest cities and highland centers grew. By Late Formative times (ca. 400 B.C.-A.D. 200), settlements were found throughout the Maya area, and some of the largest

Maya centers ever, such as El Mirador, were built. However, large populations, frequent **trade** and **warfare,** competing centers, and a great expression in material culture occurred during the subsequent Late Classic Period (ca. A.D. 200–800). This is the period that the majority of archaeological sites and material culture dates to.

Depopulation of many of the Maya centers and the decrease in monumental art, architecture, and hieroglyphic writing, which is often termed the "Classic Maya collapse," took place at the end of the Classic, or Terminal Classic, Period (ca. A.D. 775–875) throughout the Maya area. This may have been caused by shifting trade routes, intensified warfare, environmental disruption, or changing culture and ideology.

Postclassic and preconquest Maya culture was then more evident in the highlands of Guatemala (**Quiche** and **Cakchiquel**), central **Peten,** Tabasco (the **Putun** Maya), and in Yucatan, where they were eventually subjugated by the Spanish **conquistadores.** One of the last Maya kingdoms to fall to the Spanish was that of the **Itza,** located at **Tayasal** in central Peten. The **Lacandon** Maya are a society that had more limited contact with outsiders and retained more cultural autonomy until the 20th century.

MAYAPAN. This Late Postclassic **Maya** city in west-central **Yucatan** was founded by the **Itza** people around A.D. 1300 after the fall of **Chichen Itza** and other local states. A glance at the map of the ruins at Mayapan shows that the settlement at this center was very densely packed, covering about 6.5 square kilometers. This clustering of residences and **temples** was mainly done for defensive purposes, which is also attested to by a stone defensive wall that encircles the site.

Mayapan was created at a time of regional strife and political consolidation and competition by the ruling elites demanded their protection from their enemies and foreign invaders. This center was the seat of power for close to two centuries in Yucatan, but was destroyed during intensified **warfare** and revolts by internal factions.

Excavation at Mayapan revealed much cut stone architecture with many shrines and copies of monumental architecture from Chichen Itza (its prominent "El Castillo" pyramid in particular). Most of the range-type palace structures and temples, and a **cenote** well, are found near the center of the site with residences surrounding them. Although many structures are grouped around small **plazas,** there was little spatial order and few lands for fields were set aside in the placement of residential structures. Colonial documents and Maya histories suggest that Mayapan was supplied by **tribute** payments from external settlements and towns.

Among the ruined structures, large hollow **ceramic** figurines were discovered, and many of these were brightly painted incense, or **copal,** burners that were modeled into **deities** such as **Chac,** the rain god, and *Ek Chuah,* the Maya merchant god. Stone **stelae** were also recorded at the site, some of which had some **hieroglyphic** texts along with images of people and gods in low relief. Artifact types, particularly ceramic forms and **Fine Paste ceramics,** hint to **trade** ties and interaction with Gulf Coast societies in Tabasco. In general, the architecture, stone sculpture, and artifacts at Mayapan are not as finely made as those of earlier Maya sites.

MESOAMERICA. Term used generally in the anthropological literature to refer to the culture area encompassing Mexico and Central America, or "Middle America." Mesoamerica thus refers to the region spanning from northern Mexico to western Honduras and El Salvador. Distinct, impermeable boundaries did not exist for Mesoamerican peoples in ancient or modern times, because much interaction and cultural similarities were shared with societies in the Southwest and Southeast United States and in Nicaragua and Costa Rica.

This vast region has tremendous geographical and cultural diversity. Different ecozones include desert, tropical rainforest, coastal areas, highlands, and piedmont areas, to name a few, which are scattered throughout this area. Societies found here range from small egalitarian hunting bands to hierarchical conquest states with complexly organized economic and political structures located in various environments and through time. Major linguistic and cultural groups include the **Maya, Mixe-Zoque, Mixtec, Nahua,** or **Aztecs** (Uto-Aztecan language family), **Tarascan,** and **Zapotec.** Mesoamerica had some of the greatest cultural diversity and largest populations in the Aboriginal New World.

Besides general geographical parameters, cultural traits have also been provided to categorize "Mesoamerican" societies. However, not all of these traits are found in each and every Mesoamerican society, and some of the practices, customs, and cultural conditions are found in other cultures outside of this area. These major features include: the **ball courts;** human **sacrifice;** pictographic, or **hieroglyphic,** writing; **maize,** bean, and squash agriculture; **temple** construction; hierarchical, sedentary societies; use of **jade** and other greenstone; ceramic figurine art; carved stone monuments and **stelae;** brightly painted **ceramics;** and a pantheon of **deities,** such as rain, sun, war, and **underworld** gods.

METALLURGY. Ancient Mesoamerican cultures did not widely manufacture ornaments and utilitarian items of metal until late in their history. Metal came into more widespread use only during the Postclassic Period (ca. A.D. 900–1000) with the **Aztec, Maya, Mixtec, Tarascan,** and **Toltec** peoples, despite the fact that metallurgy was commonplace in South American civilizations almost one thousand years earlier (about A.D. 200–300). The most common techniques of metallurgy in **Mesoamerica** include the melting, casting, forming, and pounding of soft metals like **gold,** silver, and copper; hard tempered and cast metals such as steel and iron were not used in pre-Hispanic times. Most items were made in molds, some of which were hollow and filled with wax before the pouring of the molten metal.

Gold and silver were later used widely in Mesoamerica for jewelry and prestige items. Gold and silver sheeting and gilding for covering wood and other materials were also common. Tumbaga, or a mixture of silver, gold, and copper, was commonly used for the manufacture of ornaments in Mexico, because it was easier to cast finer details in such artifacts. A gold, or possibly tumbaga, bell was found in a Classic Maya cache under a **stela** at **Copan,** Honduras, but it was more than likely acquired through **trade** from lower Central America and not made locally.

The Postclassic Tarascan empire of **west Mexico** was renowned for its crafts and tools made of copper. Some of the tools in west Mexico are bronze, or items made of copper and tin alloy. Copper bells and gold and tumbaga beads and ornaments are some of the most commonly found metal artifacts in Mesoamerican archaeology. Many copper bells and gold items were found in the Well of **Sacrifice,** or **cenote,** at the Postclassic Maya site of **Chichen Itza** in **Yucatan.**

MEXICA (Mesh-**ee**-kah). *See* AZTECS

MEZCALA. Unique art style found near the Mezcala River in Guerrero, **west Mexico,** that consists mainly of small abstract and angular representations of humans and ancient buildings, probably **temples,** with steps and columns carved from pieces of a **jade**-like greenstone. Many of these items are simple in design, but they are well made, completely symmetrical, and very aesthetically pleasing. Many of these portable objects are in the art **market,** and they come from looted cemeteries, house burials, and structures from local village sites. Research points to a Late Formative date for this little-known culture and artistic expression. The greenstone used in the manufacture of these beautiful artifacts is more than likely of a local, yet still unknown source. More excavations are desperately needed to study the production and distribution of artifacts of the Mezcala style and to learn more about the enigmatic people who created them.

MILPA. Contemporary term for the slash-and-burn, or swidden, **maize** fields still found throughout the jungles of Mexico and Central and South America, and in other tropical areas of the world. Milpas are a practical and efficient means of agriculture in the thin tropical soils of the rainforest. Fertile soils are thin and cannot be plowed, because the rich humus would be covered with sterile clay. In this type of agriculture, the vegetation of the forest is cut, and after it has dried it is burned so that the nutrients held in the plants are returned to the soil. Just before the rainy season begins, plots of slashed and burned land are sown by hand with a digging stick and kernels of maize.

Milpa agriculture in ancient **Mesoamerica** was possibly quite unlike what is seen today. Instead of extensive fields of primarily crops of maize intermixed with beans and squash plants, ancient Mesoamerican fields may have mimicked the diversity of plant life in the rainforest. In this case, the all-important maize could have been grown alongside fruits, root crops, tobacco, trees, and many vegetables for the ancient Mesoamerican **diet.** In this manner, a greater array of plant foods was available, and less soil depletion and erosion meant little environmental destruction and dietary stress. Also, extensive milpa fields could have coexisted with raised fields and canals in swamps, or **chinampas,** and intensive kitchen gardening.

The milpa held great importance in the belief system and mythology of the ancient **Maya.** They believed that the milpa's crops sprouted from the back of a large earth crocodile. People were formed from maize dough, and Maya elites were thought to control the fertility and bounty of the milpa. In the stories of the **Popol Vuh** of the **Quiche** Maya, the milpa is a stage for tests by the **underworld** lords for the hero twins. In one instance, the milpa is destroyed by animals and then it is miraculously regenerated by the twin brothers. In Maya mythology and in practice, **sacrifices** and offerings were also provided to the milpas to ensure bountiful harvests. *See also* DIET

MIRADOR (EL). El Mirador is an impressive **Maya** site in northern Guatemala that possesses some of the largest monumental architecture in all of ancient **Mesoamerica.** Bush pilots even have mistaken the forest-covered **temples** for hills. This ruined Maya metropolis is located near extensive **bajos,** or swamps, in the remote rainforests of **Peten** just to the north of the Classic Period Maya site of **Tikal.** Only a few short projects have been undertaken at this remote location, and only large, well financed, and long-term investigations will be able to uncover the mysteries of the rise, florescence, and fall of this ancient Maya city.

One especially intriguing detail regarding El Mirador is that the immense pyramids and most of the huge center itself were built in the Late Formative Period (200 B.C. to A.D. 200)—much before the numerous cities and splendor of the Classic Period. A portion of the central ceremonial precinct of the site has been mapped, but comparatively little archaeological work has been carried out in the two-square-kilometer area of the site core. The settlement extends for kilometers, and raised roads, or **sacbe,** radiate outward to nearby sites such as **Nakbe.**

The massive buildings of El Mirador are constructed of large limestone blocks that were covered with stucco and painted bright red. Monumental buildings are adorned with huge modeled stucco masks of Maya **deities,** which are some of the largest works of art in Mesoamerica. The gods depicted may be the sun god and a bird deity. The pyramids at El Mirador are topped with temples of a triadic arrangement where the temple superstructure facing the central stairway is flanked by a structure on each side.

The Danta structure is the loftiest building at the site reaching some 80 meters in height. The Tigre pyramid measures about 60 meters tall, which make the El Mirador structures even taller than the soaring temples of Tikal. Much more impressive are the buildings' widths at their bases, which dwarf the lengths of structures at Classic Maya sites sixfold. Some Classic Period architecture is found at El Mirador, but these small constructions only overlay the massive Formative buildings. It is a distinct possibility that much earlier constructions will be found within the Late Formative constructions at the site.

Stone sculpture is rare at El Mirador in contrast to Classic Period centers, which is a general pattern for Formative Period sites. One eroded stone **stela** is decorated with iconography, possibly representing a floating long-snouted deity, and a battered **hieroglyphic** text that bears affinities to examples of written texts from **Abak Takalik** and **Kaminaljuyu** in the highlands of Guatemala. A Late Formative Period sherd from a broken **ceramic** vessel also has a hieroglyph that may read *ahaw,* or "lord." However, it is not certain if there were individual kings at El Mirador as with Classic polities, or if there was a more corporate political structure, which is reflected in the organization of large labor pools for construction and the lack of ruler portrait art.

El Mirador was abandoned by the Early Classic Period, and it was only sparsely reoccupied during Classic times. The fact that the largest ceremonial architecture and the site residences mainly date to the Late Formative Period indicates that excavations at El Mirador are essential for examining the rise of Maya states in the lowlands. Economic and social ties with other areas are evident in the art at El Mirador and also in the ceramic assemblage—for example, contact with peoples of El Salvador is apparent due to the presence of **Usulutan** wares—which needs to be further explored. Also little is known about El Mirador settlement, elite residences, **tombs,** agriculture, and **religion**.

MIRAMAR (LAKE). Lake Miramar, which has **Maya** ruins on its shores and small islands, is in the lowland jungle of northern Chiapas, Mexico. Many of the archaeological sites on this lake date to the Postclassic Period, particularly the town Lakam tun (Maya toponym, from which the Spanish name of **Lacandon** for this area and its inhabitants derives), whose ruins are found on the largest island of the lake. The ruined buildings are fashioned from thin slabs of cut limestone like other ancient Maya cities of this region. However, no large stone **stelae** or carved stone sculptures are known from this particular area. Some **caves** were explored near the lake by archaeologists who found stone cutting tools, **ceramics,** and several burials.

In the middle of the 17th century, Spanish **conquistadores** once again entered the jungle lowlands to make their final attempts at subduing the last free indigenous people and their territories around Lake Miramar. The Spanish captured and killed many of the Chol-Lacandon inhabitants of the lake settlements, but a large number of them were driven farther into the bush. These people eventually founded the center of **Sac Bahlan** near a savanna just to the east of Lake Miramar, which was discovered and colonized by the Spanish at the beginning of the 18th century.

MIRRORS. These objects appear to have been connected to the supernatural world and important for elite power and divination in the **Mesoamerican** past. The **Olmec** and coeval cultures in the highlands of Oaxaca, Mexico, like at **San Jose Mogote,** and on the south Chiapas coast (**Ocos** people), used magnetite mirrors. These mirrors functioned as pendants and were perhaps used to light fires, to reflect light, or as portals to the supernatural during religious ritual. Mirrors may thus have been crucial religious items for shaman-leaders and **priests.** Mirrors are often depicted in the art of **Teotihuacan** and the Classic **Maya.** In Mesoamerican iconography, people wear mirrors around their waists, and frequently the faces of **deities** and ancestors peer out from them.

Sometimes serpents and human figures come forth from mirrors, as seen in paintings and stone sculpture in different Mesoamerican cultures. On Maya polychrome **ceramics,** elites are shown gazing into mirrors in bowls that contain a dark substance, which is probably either an **obsidian** backing, an iron pyrite mosaic, or water. At archaeological sites, especially those of the Classic Maya (**Copan, Dos Pilas, Kaminaljuyu,** and **Tikal,** to name a few), round mirror backings of fired clay and oxidized pieces of mosaic pyrite mirrors are recovered in **tombs,** residences, and **temples.** In the art of the **Aztecs,** an important deity called **Tezcatlipoca** is depicted with a smoking obsidian or pyrite mirror for a foot. God K, or *K'awil,* of the Maya carried what appears to be a smoking mirror in the forehead.

MITLA. An often-visited highland site in Tlacolula near the Valley of Oaxaca that was more than likely initially built and occupied by the **Zapotec** people. Most of the construction at this center was during Postclassic times and after the Classic florescence of **Monte Alban.** At Mitla several clusters (five main ones: three of the North Group and two of the Group of the Columns) of long palace-like structures are arranged around central patios, or **plazas.** These buildings were made with compartments of long narrow rooms. Although the ruins await more extensive archaeological exploration, some of these buildings have been excavated and restored. Some structures have painted murals on their walls that show people and animals on a dark background. A row of eyes that may represent stars on one mural indicates darkness or night.

The building facades may demonstrate **Mixtec** influence from centuries of marriage alliances with the Zapotecs in the Postclassic Period, since the structures are covered with carved stone geometric and linear scrolling, or "greca," designs (called step frets and *greca* motifs) found at Mixtec sites. Walls were painted red, and the designs were left white for a striking contrast. These building facades may have mimicked aboriginal **textile** designs from the area. Few buildings of ceremonial nature are found at Mitla, including only a small number of **temple** pyramids. Hence, it is believed that the site functioned principally as a secular and civic center and not as a religious one.

However, a number of **tombs** have been found at the site, which shows that it had some ritual significance and that it may have been important for ancestor worship. These burials contained **gold** beads, copper bells, and polychrome **ceramics,** which once again suggest interaction with the Mixtec people. Burials in the Palace Group of the Columns appear to have contained mummy bundles of the Zapotec **Zaachilan** nobility, as described at the time of the conquest. Additional research is needed at Mitla to examine indigenous lifeways and the functions of the center's buildings and to explore the nature and significance of Mixtec influence.

MIXE-ZOQUE (**Me**-hey **Soh**-kay). This is an indigenous linguistic family found today in parts of Veracruz and Chiapas, Mexico. It is believed by many archaeologists and linguists that the **Olmec** of Formative Period Veracruz and Tabasco spoke a Mixe-Zoquen language. This language family is distinctly different from its **Aztec, Maya, Mixtec,** and **Zapotec** neighbors. It is also felt that "Isthmian" **hieroglyphic** texts found in this area, like those on the La **Mojarra stela** from Veracruz, may record sounds and meanings from the Mixe-Zoque languages.

MIXTEC (Mish-**tehk**). The name of a language and people of Oaxaca in southeastern Mexico. The Mixtec culture area of the past and present is divided into the Mixteca Alta of the highlands in central Oaxaca, the Mixteca Baja in the hills and lowlands to the northwest toward Puebla, and the Mixteca de la Costa on the Pacific Coast of Oaxaca. Mixtec archaeological sites are found mainly in valleys and on hilltops, indicating these people were in need of additional land and defense. The **Zapotec** people lived in adjoining areas of Oaxaca, and they interacted heavily and fought with the Mixtec kingdoms.

Many Mixtec centers had a large Postclassic Period occupation, such as Tilantongo, Tlaxiaco, and Yanhuitlan in the highlands, and Tututepec on the coast. The Mixtec centers and ruling families were never unified under one polity or ruler. The Mixtec governments can be better classified as small-scale regional states, or kingdoms, centered on a town that controlled settlements in a limited surrounding territory. These polities also collected **tribute** from the local populace.

The Mixtec were renowned craftspersons in Postclassic **Mesoamerica.** Some Mixtec communities in Oaxaca today still specialize in the production of certain items, such as pottery vessels and woven mats. The Pre-Columbian Mixtec crafts and industries in **metallurgy, gold, ceramics, textiles,** and stone carving were among the finest, and Mixtec goods and craft specialists were much sought after, especially by the **Aztecs** of central Mexico. Because of their artistic skill and high-quality manufactured goods, the Mixtec were conquered by the Aztecs and forced to pay **tribute** to **Tenochtitlan**.

Examples of Mixtec artistry include fine gold ear, finger, and lip ornaments in the shape of animals, beautiful polychrome ceramics with designs depicting animals and people, and metal axes, pins, and awls, necklaces of shell, **jade,** turquoise, and coral, and elaborately carved animal bones. High-quality artifacts of this type were found in a **tomb** burial of a Mixtec noble at the Zapotec site of **Monte Alban.** Richly stocked Mixtec tombs that contained many of these same items were also found at **Mitla,** a Postclassic site in the Zapotec area.

Many of the finest painted **codices,** or pictographic books, such as the **Codex Nuttall,** are from the Mixtec area. The codices depict historical events and persons (like the well-known ruler **Eight Deer**), Mixtec **deities** and rituals, and buildings, including **ball courts** for the ball game. The Mixtec people also made thousands of small human figures crudely carved in green or white stone for general distribution and some unknown use, or they were intended for rituals and ancestor worship.

Ancient Mixtec society was organized in rigid socioeconomic segments that included the ruling elite, the supporting commoner population, and slaves. These social groups were separated by marriage taboos, clothing styles, status at birth, and occupations and roles. The Mixtec elites even used a language and vocabulary that differed from that of the masses. The nobles also practiced royal incest to produce heirs in order to perpetuate ruling bloodlines, preserve kingdoms, and consolidate economic holdings. The nobles from different centers and kingdoms also practiced marriage alliances between themselves to create wider political and economic cohesion, and to lessen **warfare** and competition. *See also* NUINE

MOJARRA (LA). The name of some ruins and a now famous carved stone **stela** from the banks of the Acula River in Veracruz, Mexico. The ornate La Mojarra stela was recently stumbled upon while it was still submerged in the Acula River. The carved stela is made of basalt, and it shows a richly dressed noble or ruler with several columns of **hieroglyphs** above and in front of him. The text contains approximately 400 hieroglyphs, making it one of the longest stela inscriptions in ancient **Mesoamerica**.

This monument has **calendar** dates (A.D. 143 and A.D. 156) that place it at the end of the Formative Period. Stylistically, the artwork on the stela is comparable to contemporaneous sculptures and iconography at **Abak Takalik, Chalchuapa, Izapa, Kaminaljuyu,** and El **Mirador,** among other Late Formative sites. The elite personage depicted wears an impressive zoomorphic headdress, **jade** jewelry, and a cape, while he carries unidentifiable objects in his hands. Attempts have been made to decipher the hieroglyphic text, which may represent an ancient **Mixe-Zoquen** language that is found written on only a few objects, such as a sculpture called the Tuxtla Statuette.

MONTE ALBAN. This remarkable city is perched on a hilltop overlooking the highland Valley of Oaxaca. It was founded in this location around 500 B.C. by people living in earlier villages in other parts of the valley; no previous settlement is known in this location. Many of the stone masonry buildings and **temples** were restored at Monte Alban, and archaeologists have encountered defensive walls, stone sculpture, **tombs** rich with fine **jade** and **gold** artifacts, **hieroglyphic** texts, and elaborately carved and modeled **ceramics**.

The early occupations and Classic era of Monte Alban (until A.D. 900) are traditionally associated with the **Zapotec** people, whereas **Mixtec** influence is recognized at the site during the later Postclassic era (A.D. 1000–1400) when the site was eclipsed by neighboring centers such as **Mitla.** Contact with the **Olmec** and **Teotihuacan** cultures is also seen in examples of art at Monte Alban. Population at the site and adjacent slopes may have risen to 15,000–20,000 people at its peak.

The site is well known for its many "**danzante,**" or "dancer," sculptures depicting contorted humans on carved stone slabs. More than likely, these images and their accompanying short hieroglyphic texts record captives taken in **warfare** by the Monte Alban elites and then **sacrificed.** Besides the representations of captives and the building of many stone structures, the power and prestige of the Monte Alban elite is witnessed by several rich tombs and the wide distribution of their ceramics.

These tombs contain painted murals, hieroglyphic texts and images in stone, and finely made exotic items, which provide clues to the history, influence, and socioeconomic ties of the Monte Alban rulers. By forging external ties with other powerful peoples, controlling labor for construction and crafts, enticing population concentration at the center, and gathering food and supplies throughout the valley, the ruling elite were able to create and manage a successful polity and cultural tradition for hundreds of years. The Classic Monte Alban rulers created a large realm and extensive networks of interaction that reached the Pacific Coast of Oaxaca.

MONTE ALTO. An archaeological site that is located near the town of La Democracia in Escuintla (where stone monuments decorate the town **plaza** close to a small museum with many artifacts from the site) on the Pacific Coast of Guatemala. This site is known for its large sculptures of volcanic rock, consisting of **"pot-bellies"** and disembodied heads that resemble other Late Formative monuments in Guatemala and El Salvador (see photo). These monuments may depict rulers or perhaps **deities.** Little archaeology has been done at Monte Alto, but the known **ceramic** chronology points to a Late Formative to Early Classic (approximately 300 B.C. to A.D. 500) occupation.

The south coast of Guatemala was one of the richest areas geographically and culturally in ancient times, and more excavations are needed in this zone. It has been hypothesized that the art of Monte Alto was contemporaneous with or even predated the **Olmec** culture because of its aesthetic style. However, the evidence suggests that although there may have been some Olmec influence from the Gulf Coast region, this sculptural art developed much later and from local antecedents. Nonetheless, a local **jade** mask and some ceramic vessels bear close affinities with Olmec art and attest to interaction with these people.

MOTAGUA RIVER. A major river valley that extends to the Caribbean after stretching through the mountainous region of eastern-central Guatemala near the border with Honduras. The Motagua River flows through the northern portion of a great tectonic depression that connects with the valley of Chiapas to the southwest. The largest single source of **jade** is located in the lower Motagua Valley, and this precious stone has been exploited since Early Formative times. This jade resource area was tapped by the ancient **Olmec** civilization and the later **Maya** people, probably through **trade,** who prized this greenstone for making portable sculptures and jewelry.

What is particularly interesting about the Motagua River Valley is that despite the existence of jade and prime agricultural land on alluvial soils (banana plantations and extensive farms and ranches are found there today) ancient populations were relatively low in this region. There are no large urban centers, such as **Monte Alban, Teotihuacan,** or **Tikal,** found in this region of rich land, active trade routes, water, and abundant natural resources, and most archaeological sites consist of villages and small towns that mainly date from the Formative to the Classic Periods.

However, **Quirigua,** the Classic Maya site that has the tallest stone **stelae** and was home to a ruler who captured a king from the nearby center of **Copan** around A.D. 738, is found here. But even this site is comparatively small compared with other major Maya and **Mesoamerican** sites. Like areas around **obsidian** mines, it is possible that the jade-rich Motagua basin was used by several peoples and sites and no large centers were created to control the land or the jade resource that was available to all.

MOTECUHZOMA (Moh-tey-kuh-**soh**-mah). One of the last **Aztec** leaders, or *tlatoani,* whose kingdom was finally conquered by the Spanish in A.D. 1521. Motecuhzoma (II) Xocoyotzin ("The Younger"), who began his rulership around A.D. 1502, was an important ruler of the Mexica dynasty, because he achieved distant conquests and he attempted to consolidate and extend the Mexica (Aztec) empire in **Mesoamerica** through **warfare** and political and economic reforms. He also attempted to transform Aztec Imperial strategies toward the end of his reign in order to gain power and avert internal strife with the empire.

This ruler's fame, however, stems from his apparent ambivalence toward the newly arrived Spanish **conquistadores** (he alternately treated them as beings with supernatural connections, enemies, and allies) and his tenacious efforts to accommodate the Spanish colonizers while retaining rulership over his empire. Motecuhzoma II was killed in **Tenochtitlan,** during an initial skirmish in 1520 between the Aztecs and Spanish, before the final siege and capture of the Aztec capital.

One of the earliest autonomous rulers of the Aztec state was also known by this name, Motecuhzoma (I) Ihuilcamina ("Heaven Shooter" who ruled from A.D. 1440–1469). Motecuhzoma I helped to engineer the building of the Mexica-Aztec empire in central Mexico and the expansion of this state into other parts of Mesoamerica, particularly into the **Huastec** area in Veracruz and the **Mixtec** region of Oaxaca, Mexico. This ruler also participated in the transformation of Aztec history, **religion,** politics, and economy that would help create and maintain the empire. Motecuhzoma I began large construction programs in the capital that eventually made Tenochtitlan one of the largest and most impressive cities of the aboriginal New World.

MOTUL DE SAN JOSE. *See* IK SITE

MOUNTAIN. Mountains were important sacred places to many ancient **Mesoamerican** societies. Being prominent natural features in the landscape, mountains were named and incorporated into mythology, religious beliefs, and ancestor worship. Mountains also contained **caves,** which were significant ritual and burial places. Many settlements and cities were located near important mountains, volcanoes, and hills, which were conceived of as places of the gods. Some **Maya** sites were constructed into or on hills or mountains, and their buildings were aligned with them. Maya **temples** were viewed as *witz,* or human-made mountains, where rituals took place and ancestors and gods were worshiped. A tall conical earthen mound at the **Olmec** site of La **Venta** appears to be an effigy volcano or mountain, making it a monumental symbol of these geographical features.

At **Teotihuacan** in central Mexico, the Pyramids of the Sun and the Moon are directly in front of, or in lines of sight with, surrounding mountains. The **Aztecs** believed that their ancestors emerged from **caves** in a sacred mountain and a major female **deity, Coatlique,** resided on a mountain. Thus at their capital of **Tenochtitlan, temples,** such as the **Templo Mayor,** represented these sacred landscapes. **Mount Tlaloc** was also an important Aztec shrine to **Tlaloc,** the rain deity. Clouds formed around mountain peaks, which signaled the coming of rain and the beginning of life in the Aztec agricultural cycle. The mountains also yielded important materials, including **obsidian** and **jade,** and were sources of sought-after plants and animals like the **quetzal** bird for headdress feathers and pinewood for torches. *See also* MOUNT TLALOC and TUXTLA MOUNTAINS

MOUNT TLALOC. Sacred **mountain** of the **Aztecs** (Mexica) of central Mexico. Mount Tlaloc is located just to the east of Lake Tetzcoco and the capital center of the Aztecs, **Tenochtitlan.** The mountain is surrounded by ancient paths, aqueducts, residences, gardens and fields, and shrines. On the summit of Mount Tlaloc rests a **temple** to the god **Tlaloc,** the Aztec rain **deity.** The low stone and earthen walls of the temple form a long entrance hall and a rectangular superstructure. This temple probably housed images of Tlaloc and the offerings, including **sacrifices** of children, presented to the deity.

Aztec pilgrims in Postclassic central Mexico would visit the shrines and temple to Tlaloc at certain times of the year, especially on the onset of the rainy season, to leave offerings and perform rituals and sacrifices. These rites would help ensure rain and abundance for the **maize** fields, and the continuation of the cosmos and human existence. The ceremonies were seen as successful when clouds formed around the summits of this and other mountains at the beginning of the rainy season. Rituals and beliefs related to Mount Tlaloc and the rain deity are described in ethnohistoric documents, depicted in **codices,** and studied through archaeological excavations and surveys.

N

NAHUA. Name for a large number of **Mesoamerican** peoples and language groups that are indigenous to central Mexico. Nahua and related languages are spoken by the **Aztecs, Tlaxcalans,** Tepanecs, possibly the **Toltec** and **Teotihuacan** populations, and other peoples in ancient Mexico. Nahua peoples are still found today in Veracruz, Tabasco, and other parts of Mexico and have been since the expansion of the Aztec empire and relocation of Nahua peoples during Spanish colonial times. The Nahuatl-speaking **Pipil** Nahuas have been found in Guatemala, Honduras, El Salvador, and in lower Central America ever since their migrations into these areas from central Mexico in antiquity. *See also* NAHUATL

NAHUATL (Nah-wahtl). Language specifically spoken by the **Aztec** people of **Tenochtitlan** in central Mexico. Nahuatl is described as a melodious tongue that, in addition to its use for everyday speech, was used for poetry, elaborate public oration, and hymns to **deities** in ancient Mexico. Nahuatl words are typically long and rich semantically; many meanings, modifiers, and qualities are embedded in the words that cause much debate on their translations among scholars and linguists working to understand the language. For example, the deity name **Huitzilopochtli** means "Hummingbird on the left" or "Hummingbird to the south," which illustrates the **Mesoamerican** conceptual connection of "south" to "left." Also, **Aztlan,** the homeland of the Aztecs, may be glossed as "Place of Whiteness" or "Place of Herons."

NAJ TUNICH (Nah Tune-eech). A large **cave** system located in the **Maya mountains** in northeastern Guatemala near the border with Belize. This cave is famous for its Maya **hieroglyphic** texts and figures painted in black on the walls, its many offerings of **ceramics,** some of which are entire vessels, interior features of masonry, and signs of ritual and burning. The entrance to the cave is on a hill, and it opens into a large antechamber. Several passageways branch out from a central natural tunnel, and a new corridor, complete with ceramic vessels and hieroglyphic texts, was recently discovered and mapped.

The hieroglyphic texts in Naj Tunich ("House of/in Stone") describe the "seeing" of the cave (named the "black hole in the earth") and the rituals performed there by Maya pilgrims from different areas and sites in the vicinity. The name or the title "Mopan" is repeated in the painted texts, which is interestingly enough the name of the Maya people and area today where this cave is located. The name of a Maya king of **Caracol** also appears to be listed here. The ceramics at Naj Tunich indicate that the cave saw its greatest ritual use from Late Formative to Classic times.

NAKBE. A **Maya** site in northern Guatemala that is located near and is contemporaneous with the large Late Formative Maya site of El **Mirador** in the Department of **Peten.** An ancient raised road, or **sacbe,** through a swampy **bajo** area connects the two sites. Like El Mirador, Nakbe exhibits large stone built **temples** (between 20 and 45 meters tall) that are adorned with huge carved and painted stucco masks representing Maya **deities.** Nakbe contains some of the earliest temple constructions and **ceramics** in the Maya lowlands, which begin around the Middle Formative Period. Much like El Mirador, Nakbe contains clustered groups of monumental constructions with temples placed in the common triadic pattern of three temples facing a central **plaza** area. This site also has a **ball court** for playing the bouncing **rubber** ball game.

A stone **stela** at the site shows two persons, presumably Maya nobles, facing one another. This monument, which was originally placed in an upright position, shares iconographic similarities with sculptures at **Abak Takalik, Izapa,** and **Kaminaljuyu.** Excavations in bajos and ancient areas of cultivation near the site have demonstrated that the Maya removed rich organic soils from the low swampy areas and placed them on their nearby agricultural fields to enrich them.

A less dense Classic Period occupation existed at Nakbe. At this time, craftspersons living in a residential group manufactured Classic **codex**-style vessels, which are brightly painted with human, deity, and animal figures with adjacent **hieroglyphic** texts. Many of these vessels have been looted from this ruin and other adjacent sites and sold on the international art market.

NARANJOS (LOS). The archaeological site of Los Naranjos is situated on the north shores of Lake Yojoa in west-central Honduras, and it is located in the **Ulua River** drainage. This site is significant for its early occupation and formidable defensive ditches. According to the initial **ceramic**

assemblage (the Jaral Phase wares), Los Naranjos was first occupied during the Middle Formative Period and had ties with other contemporaneous sites, such as **Playa de los Muertos.** The early material culture at the site closely resembles that of the **Olmec,** including fired clay figurines, pottery types, and finely worked **jade,** which was found in burials of people of high rank and status. Large constructions were present at this time, and an impressive ditch that runs to the lake was initially made. This ditch measures about 20 meters in width and seven meters in depth.

The subsequent Late Formative habitation of Los Naranjos was even greater, and several monumental buildings were constructed. One building, Str. IV, had a stepped substructure that was arranged according to the cardinal directions, and it supported four buildings on its summit. This building was made of a rubble and earthen core that was finished with roughly faced limestone blocks but with no plaster covering. At this time an even larger defensive ditch was constructed around the main group of buildings and a large patch of cultivable land.

NETZAHUALCOYOTL (Net-sah-uh-**ahl**-koh-yotl). A great ruler of the important Postclassic center of Tetzcoco in central Mexico. This king was instrumental in creating and maintaining the Triple Alliance around A.D. 1423 to the 1460s that was the backbone of the **Aztec** empire. He was crowned king of Tetzcoco after he assisted in the overthrowing of the Tepanecs (who were involved in the murder of his father, which he witnessed as a young prince) and other previous ruling peoples in central Mexico and helped bring the Aztecs to supreme power in the **Basin of Mexico**.

Netzahualcoyotl was remembered as a wise man, an artist, and an educated thinker who lived in a sumptuous palace. He was also crucial in making major decisions involving the alliance and the Aztec empire. He assisted in the engineering of the imperial political, military, and economic organization of the Late Postclassic. To reform a centralization of elite power, Netzahualcoyotl implemented strict standardized laws and rules, or a legalist system, overseen by elites and judges, which were designed to punish people for crimes and define proper behaviors and social positions in society.

NUINE. A relatively little-studied area, art style, and culture found in the Mixteca Baja region between the site of **Cholula** in Puebla and the **Mixtec** peoples of highland Oaxaca in Mexico. The people of this region are known for their external contacts with **Teotihuacan** and **Xochicalco** in central Mexico, the Mixtec highlands, and the Gulf lowlands to the northeast. Small "**colossal heads**" of clay are known from this area, which points to contact with the Formative Period **Olmec** peoples. The Nuine culture developed a **hieroglyphic** writing system that differs from other **Mesoamerican** writing systems, including that of the Mixtec and **Aztec codices,** and it has not been completely deciphered to date.

O

OBSIDIAN. This volcanic glass was mined and gathered in nodules from the mountainous regions of highland Guatemala, **west Mexico,** and central Mexico during pre-Hispanic times. The obsidian nodules were prepared as cores for the removal of flakes and blades, which were used as cutting tools. Obsidian is more brittle than **chert** for use as stone tools, but it is more easily worked and extremely sharp. Not only was it used for knives and **weapons** in ancient **Mesoamerica,** but it is currently used for making fine surgical instruments. Obsidian was also used in the manufacture of **mirrors,** jewelry, masks, and clothing and for pigment grinders. Some major obsidian workshops have been identified at the sites of **Kaminaljuyu** and **Teotihuacan**.

Early hunters and gatherers fashioned their spearheads and knives from this volcanic glass. Ever since Formative times, obsidian nodules, cores, blades, and flakes made their way around Mesoamerica from various natural sources. Grey obsidian from the major sources of Ixtepeque, San Martin Jilotepeque, and El Chayal in the highlands of Guatemala are found throughout the **Maya** area. Green obsidian from the Pachuca source in central Mexico is also found here, but is more common to the west of the Maya region. The presence of green obsidian can be taken as evidence for **trade** and interaction with central Mexican polities (especially Teotihuacan and **Tula**), and the obsidian's dark shade of green, a sacred color in Mesoamerica, made it a prized and sacred item. Obsidian from the Ucareo source in central Mexico has a distinctive blue-grey color, and it also rarely turns up in the Maya area.

Besides the simple visual identification, obsidian is subjected to neutron activation, which is more costly and destructive, to determine its source and area of origin. Experiments with inexpensive obsidian hydration for use as a dating method are increasing in Mesoamerican archaeology. The amount of water absorbed by the obsidian incrementally over time can be measured. By measuring this "hydration rim" on the edge of the obsidian with a microscope, the time since the obsidian artifact was made and deposited in the ground can be calculated. Obsidian hydration dating is currently being developed for absolute chronologies in several regions in Mesoamerica, but it is currently a more reliable source to relatively date archaeological deposits within single sites or small regions.

OCOS. Name of a coastal region in southern Guatemala that is applied to an Early Formative culture and **ceramic** vessel types on the Pacific Coast of Chiapas, Mexico, Guatemala, and El Salvador (**Soconusco**). The Ocos culture dates to approximately 1500–1300 B.C., making it one of the earliest sedentary societies in ancient **Mesoamerica.** Ocos life is a continuation of even earlier cultures in the same region, **Barra** and Locona, and Ocos ceramics are found in earlier levels at some **Olmec** sites on the Pacific and Gulf Coast areas. Archaeological sites of Ocos peoples that are scattered over this vast region are characterized by groups of large earthen mounds near streams and estuaries.

This culture can be recognized by the presence of globular, gourd-like ceramic pots with long tripod supports with linear, cross-hatched and cord marked designs on them. This society and the previous Locona culture were among the first peoples to exhibit social ranking, with some individuals owning larger and more elaborate houses and exotic **trade** goods, such as hematite **mirrors** and painted pottery. People of higher rank and status may have managed the exchange and distribution of **obsidian** tools, or they may have obtained their higher position in society as religious specialists. *See also* COLIMA

OLMEC. A premier civilization (ca. 1750 B.C. to 400 B.C.) in Formative Period **Mesoamerica** that had a cluster of sites containing monumental architecture and stone art on the Gulf Coast of Veracruz and Tabasco, Mexico. Scattered archaeological sites bearing Olmec or "Olmec-influenced" art and artifacts of this early "horizon culture" are also found in central Mexico (**Chalcatzingo, Tlatilco**), **west Mexico** (Teopantecuanitlan), and southeast Mexico (**San Jose Mogote**) and in scattered sites in **Yucatan,** southern Guatemala (La Blanca), western Honduras (**Copan**), and western El Salvador (**Chalchuapa**). Olmec culture is mainly identified by a distinctive iconographic style found on white kaolin clay **ceramics, jade** figures, and stone sculpture, which includes **deities** (often called "were-**jaguars**") with cleft heads, opened and down-turned mouths, fangs, almond shaped eyes, thickened lips and noses, and crossed band motifs.

Large centers in the Gulf Coast region, including Laguna de los Cerros, **San Lorenzo, Tres Zapotes,** and La **Venta,** have impressive buildings constructed mostly of piled earth. They also contain the greatest number of stone sculptures, such as **colossal heads** depicting helmeted men, large stone **altars,** and carved representations of a variety of deities, and a high concentration of imported and worked jade. Stone for monumental sculpture was transported from the **Tuxtla Mountains** in Veracruz, possibly by river rafts part of the way. Many other sites are only identified by smaller buildings and sculpture, diagnostic artifacts, and burials with Olmec materials. A newly discovered deposit in a bog at El **Manati,** found inland from the Gulf Coast, contains **rubber** balls and wooden statues fashioned in the typical Olmec style.

Olmec sites typically have some large pyramids at their cores and a dispersed resident population that varied from a few hundred to a few thousand people, depending on the site and period. Subsistence was based on **maize** agriculture and the collecting of abundant wild forest and water resources. The Olmec obtained **trade** goods from distant regions throughout Mesoamerica and worked them into utilitarian and religious artifacts and some of the most exquisite artworks of any early culture.

Many anthropologists believe that the Olmec were organized principally into chiefdoms or perhaps even early states. Recent debate on the origins of the Olmec divides archaeologists who believe that Olmec civilization either grew and expanded from the Gulf Coast heartland, or that the Olmec evolved through interaction between the various Formative sites throughout Mesoamerica, or finally that the culture has its roots in the South Coast of Guatemala and Chiapas.

A few diffusionist theories state that Olmec civilization was founded by migrating African peoples, because of similar facial characteristics on sculptures and figurines. But hard supporting material evidence for Old World contact, like diagnostic ceramics, **metallurgy,** and writing, is lacking. Current research focuses on Olmec settlement patterns, interregional trade and interaction, the functions of large public buildings, and the origins and spread of Olmec iconography.

P

PALENQUE. Palenque is one of the most beautiful and architecturally spectacular of the Classic **Maya** sites in the southern lowlands. Palenque is located near the foothills of the Chiapas highlands and near the **Usumacinta River,** and is one of the furthermost western Maya sites. This site is well known for its elegant architecture, sculpted wall panels in its **temples,** long and beautifully executed **hieroglyphic** texts, and royal **tombs.** The name *Palenque* denotes "fenced-in (place)" in Spanish and was probably given to this area or site during late colonial times, because of the presence of palisaded Maya villages in this region. An ancient place name for this area and for the site is *Lakam ha,* which may refer to the pools of water at the site or one of the large rivers nearby. Palenque was one of the first sites discovered and frequently visited by outsiders and explorers in the mid-19th century.

Much archaeological research has been conducted at Palenque, and many of the site's stone masonry buildings have been excavated and restored. The palace area that is set upon an artificial platform contains long range-type structures with **vaulted roofs,** roof combs (vertical ornamentation placed over the top center of the roof), eroded mural paintings, interior courtyards, aqueducts, exterior stucco facades depicting nobles, and stone sculpture. A unique four-story tower with windows facing the cardinal directions on each floor is part of this architectural complex. Stone thrones with hieroglyphic texts and stone carvings depicting war captives are found in the palace group.

One of the most impressive constructions at Palenque, the Temple of the Inscriptions, is located near the center of the site and main **plaza** and is built into a natural hill. This structure is a nine-terraced funerary monument that exhibits a central stairway and a large temple superstructure with multiple entrances between columns and monolithic wall panels with finely carved hieroglyphic writing. These texts, among others, have the Palenque emblem glyph, which is a depiction of a bone (*Bak'*).

While the Temple of Inscriptions was being excavated in the early 1950s, a descending staircase from the temple superstructure into the core of the building was cleared and a fabulously rich royal tomb was discovered. This large tomb has a vaulted roof, walls adorned with stucco figures of Maya elite personages, and a stone sarcophagus that has an elaborately carved limestone slab for a lid. The sarcophagus contains the skeleton of an elderly male who wore a mosaic **jade,** shell, and **obsidian** mask and a large quantity of worked jade jewelry. The inscriptions on the sarcophagus lid and in the temple superstructure identify the tomb as that of "K'inich Hanab" Pacal, who was one of the greatest of the Palenque kings. Pacal was responsible for the creation of much of the architecture and artwork at the site, which were made during his reign.

The Temples of the Sun, the Cross, and the Foliated Cross are monumental buildings found to the north of the Temple of Inscriptions. This series of temples was built and dedicated by King Pacal's son, "Chan

Bahlum." These impressive and beautiful buildings are currently being excavated by Mexican archaeologists who are uncovering the buildings' terrace substructures, hieroglyphs, sculpture, and elite tombs. Wall panel inscriptions in these temples describe the events in the lives of the Palenque nobility, their parentage, their connections with certain Maya **deities,** and their participation in important ceremonies. **Calendar** dates projected into the distant past relate to the birth of the Palenque triad of deities. These gods were believed to have been born in these structures, which are symbolic **sweat baths,** according to new decipherments and architectural studies.

Palenque had ties with many local and distant Maya sites. The nobles interacted with other sites of the western Maya area, such as Comalcalco, Pomona, Tonina, and Tortugero. In fact, a later Palenque ruler, "Kan Xul" (or "Kan Chitam"), was captured by the Tonina king and presumably **sacrificed.** Palenque was one of the westernmost Maya sites that collapsed early on during the Classic Period. Much more excavation in the main group of ruins and in the settlement area are needed to examine this crucial problem in Maya prehistory and to learn more about the site and culture history as a whole.

PETEN. In Yucatec **Maya** *peten* means "island," and the term appears to signify the round shape of these geographical features. Peten was a toponym used in the Central Lake District of the northern lowlands of Guatemala by the Yucatec-speaking **Itza,** who lived on islands in these lakes. The "Great Peten" was the name given to the large island capital of the Itza, **Tayasal** on Lake Peten Itza, which was conquered by the Spanish in A.D. 1697 and named Nuestra Señora de los Remedios (later "Flores"). Peten may also appear as a toponym in Classic Maya **hieroglyphic** texts of northern Guatemala.

Today Peten is the name of the northernmost state or department of Guatemala that consists of the lowland rainforests, the central lake region, and the northern foothills of the Guatemalan highlands. In ancient times, Peten was rich in forest products that were widely **traded,** such as honey, **cacao,** incense, or **copal, rubber, jaguar** pelts, parrot feathers, and **chert** stone, and had a dense concentration of Classic Maya sites with hieroglyphic texts in stone, multicolored **ceramics** and masterfully carved stone **stelae** and **altars.** Currently Peten is being massively developed for settlement, vehicle transportation, logging, ranching, oil extraction, and farming. Subsequently, much of the natural jungle and archaeological sites are under attack.

PIEDRAS NEGRAS. Piedras Negras is an important Classic **Maya** center in the **Usumacinta River** region that has some of the most beautifully carved limestone **stelae, altars,** and panels in the Maya area. Piedras Negras rests on the east bank of the Usumacinta River in northwestern Guatemala, which made it accessible by canoe travel much like the Maya site of **Yaxchilan** farther upriver in Chiapas, Mexico.

Piedras Negras has many **temples** and **plazas** that are placed on natural hills like at nearby **Palenque,** and the site has an extensive residential zone and rich soils for agricultural production. Recently, a **cenote,** or large sinkhole in the limestone, that may explain an ancient **hieroglyphic** place name for the site, was discovered nearby. **Ball courts** for the ball game, palaces, a finely sculpted throne that was smashed in antiquity, and **sweat bath** structures for ceremonial cleansing and health are also found at the ruins. Piedras Negras probably controlled several smaller settlements in the area that have similar sculpture and architecture.

Piedras Negras was made famous by early and recent excavations at the site and their discoveries. From local carved stone monuments the recognition of **calendar** dates associated with births, accessions to the throne, and deaths of Maya rulers led to initial decipherments of Maya hieroglyphic writing. Early rulers of Piedras Negras are mentioned in carved texts at Yaxchilan, and inscriptions at Piedras Negras suggest alternating alliances and **warfare** with this neighboring site. Some of the Piedras Negras stone stelae depict young Maya heirs seated in niches upon wooden scaffolding, while others show rulers dressed as warriors, some of which wear costumes with imagery related to **Teotihuacan** or other central Mexican cultures. The sculpted panels contain gatherings of Maya nobles wearing their ceremonial finery. One excavated burial at the site contained worked **jade** ornaments with hieroglyphic texts that name the female owner of the jewelry and quite possibly the occupant of the grave.

PIPIL (Pee-**peel**). When the Spanish arrived in Central America, they encountered **Nahua**-Pipil peoples (a linguistic and cultural group related to the **Aztecs** that may have split off from them some 500 years or more before the conquest) settled in scattered towns and villages in Guatemala, Honduras, Nicaragua, and El Salvador. These people had migrated from north-central and central Mexico to these areas in Central America probably during the Early to Middle Postclassic times (ca. A.D. 1000–1200) and after the collapse of **Mesoamerica**'s Classic Period civilizations.

The Pipil influx into Central America at this time may have been related to the large-scale migrations of Mexican peoples after the Classic

Period collapse around Mesoamerica, the movements of Nahua peoples into areas being abandoned by other cultures at this time, or perhaps the political and economic expansion of Nahua speakers throughout Mesoamerica. The Late Classic Period **Cotzumalhuapa** culture and art style of this area, which appears to have had strong ties to Mexican societies, is probably too early to be attributed to the Pipil according to the linguistic and archaeological data. However, earlier Pipil and Nahua migrations into this area cannot be ruled out.

The name *Pipil* comes from the Nahua word *pipiltin,* which means "children" or "nobles." Some major Pipil sites are Itzcuintepeque (which led to the naming of the state of "Escuintla" in Guatemala), Iztapa, Mita, and Mixtan in Guatemala, which had a very large Pipil population, Chapagua and Papayeca in Honduras, Cuscatlan, Cuxutepeque, Izalco, and Nonualco in densely Pipil-settled El Salvador, and Chinandega, Quauhcapolca, and Tezoatega in Nicaragua (the name of this country is from a Pipil-Nicarao chief contacted by Spanish travelers in 1523). Material culture found at Pipil sites includes green **obsidian** from the Pachuca source in central Mexico, **Chacmool** sculptures, **plumbate pottery,** Nicoya Polychrome **ceramics,** Silho Orange **fine paste ceramics,** and large ceramic figures of the central Mexican deities **Tlaloc** and **Xipe Totec.**

The individual, small-scale Pipil states were interacting and involved in war and **trade** (particularly in **cacao**) with other Central American cultures. This interaction, plus the organization of **warfare** and **tribute** payments from subject polities, helped to create Pipil territorial states during the Late Postclassic Period. However, Pipil polities were losing ground and commerce to the Late Postclassic **Maya** states in Guatemala and Honduras. Later, the Spanish **conquistadores** met large armies of fierce Pipil warriors, and only after bloody campaigns, like those fought against other Nahua peoples in Mexico, were they able to conquer and colonize the Pipil regions.

PLANCHON DE PIEDRA. An unusual site on the Lacantun River (a tributary of the **Usumacinta River**) in Chiapas, Mexico, where drawings and figures are etched into a limestone bedrock shelf that juts out into the water. The site is also called "Planchon ('wide flat area' in Spanish) de las Figuras." This geographic feature may also have figured in the Classic **Maya** place name *Lacam Tun,* or "wide stone," from this area, and from which the present terms *Lacantun* and *Lacandon* were derived.

Some of the carved figures on the rock include **temples,** humans in ritual dress, animals, Maya iconography, and geometric figures. No large archaeological sites have been reported in the immediate vicinity, but the limestone shelf was probably visited and carved by the Classic Maya peoples who inhabited this area. Perhaps this site was the destination for pilgrimages or canoeing expeditions from neighboring **Bonampak** and **Yaxchilan.** It is also conceivable that these carved figures either predate or postdate the Classic Maya, since it is difficult to date the carving style on the rock. No archaeological work or reconnaissance has been carried out in this area, which further complicates interpretations of the history and dating of this site.

PLAYA DE LOS MUERTOS. Unique archaeological site known for its burials that is located near the banks of the **Ulua River** just north of the site of Los **Naranjos.** Much of what is known of Playa de los Muertos comes from earlier excavations of multiple interments and their rich and interesting offerings. The material culture found here dates to the Middle and Late Formative Periods, and it closely resembles items found in other parts of **Mesoamerica,** such as **Copan,** Los Naranjos, **Tlatilco, Yarumela,** and **Colima** sites. **Ceramic** types include long-necked bottles, handmade figurines, **Olmec** influenced shallow bowls, and a stirrup spout effigy pot that resembles examples from Colima, **Cuyamel,** and Tlatilco. Finely worked **jade** jewelry, mainly beads, were also recovered at Playa de los Muertos.

PLAZA. A plaza is a flat, open area surrounded by **temples** and residences in ancient **Mesoamerican** settlements. In the **Maya** area, plazas are rectangular, whereas in the **Teuchitlan** tradition of Classic Jalisco in **west Mexico,** plazas are round, and they often contain round temples in the middle. Plaza areas were used for rituals, public gatherings, **markets, dance** spaces, and festivals. These areas were often leveled and paved with stones or lime plaster. Maya sites typically contain several plazas where carved stone **stelae, altars,** and **ball courts** for the ball game are present. Maya **hieroglyphic** texts even have a sign for "plaza" in descriptions of where rituals and stela erections took place.

PLUMBATE POTTERY. A very distinctive shiny dark brown **ceramic** ware that dates from Terminal Classic to Early Postclassic times (ca. A.D. 900–1100) in the **Maya** area and in central and eastern Mexico. Plumbate is the only true glazed indigenous pottery in the New World resulting from special clays and high firing temperatures. This ceramic type has a semi-glossy and waxy surface that is brown to copper in color. A production area on the Pacific Coast of Guatemala has been identified with the discovery of large quantities of broken plumbate pots and the enclosed kilns needed to achieve the high temperatures for the firing of this special ceramic type. These ceramics were decorated not by painting but by carving, molding, or modeling on the surface of the vessels. Plumbate wares were **traded** by their manufacturers throughout the southeastern region of **Mesoamerica**.

POCHTECA. Elite merchant class of the **Aztecs** of ancient central Mexico. Pochteca is derived from the **Nahuatl** term *Pochotl,* which also names the giant ceiba tree (the sacred "tree of life") and may be glossed as "father, mother, leader, progenitor, protector." The Aztec Pochteca traveled long distances throughout **Mesoamerica** on trading expeditions often accompanied by a large caravan and warrior escorts. The Pochteca were important to the Aztec empire for they brought back exotic materials, such as **jade, jaguar** skins, **textiles,** and **quetzal** feathers, many necessary **trade** items, including honey, **cacao,** and other flavorings, to Mexican **markets** and palaces. They also supplied important news from afar upon their return to the capital center of **Tenochtitlan**.

These travelers also served as spies for the Aztec leaders and military who were constantly watching enemies and subject provinces on the brink of revolt. The Pochteca were often granted safe passage in foreign lands because of their high rank and purpose as traders, and their deaths would bring retribution by the Aztecs. They also provided **tribute** and tax payments of materials and exotics to elites and rulers. For their political and economic importance, the Pochteca were granted special status, housing, clothing, and privileges by the Aztec rulers. Soon after the Spanish conquest and the subjugation of the Aztec nobility, long-distance trade and espionage was halted with the elimination of the Pochteca traders.

POPOL VUH (Poh-pohl Vooh). The name of the "council book" of the **Quiche Maya** of the central highlands of Guatemala. This sacred book contains information on Quiche history, religious beliefs, myth, social organization, and other insights on the lives and culture of this important Maya group. The copy of the Popul Vuh that comes down to us was written in the mid-16th century by the Friar Francisco Ximenez, a Spanish **priest** who spoke Quiche fluently. This padre learned of a manuscript called the Popul Vuh written in Quiche in the town of Chichicastenango, and it was Ximinez who rewrote the Quiche text with a Spanish commentary. The original was probably written in Spanish orthography by

Quiche priests, nobles, or diviners who spoke from **hieroglyphic** and pictographic **codices.** This manuscript is now housed at the Newberry Library in Chicago.

In the initial part of the Popul Vuh the creation of the Quiche people and the world is described. The Earth is created by the Maya **deities** who then brought into existence the sun, heavens, and the animals. Since the animals could not praise the deities or provide offerings to them, people had to be made to perform these tasks. The first people were created unsuccessfully from mud, and then in a second, but also failed attempt, they were fashioned from wood. Only the last section of the book, which provides a discussion of Quiche lineage history and events, gives the final success of the creation of humans from **maize**.

The middle section of the Popol Vuh relates stories of the demigod hero twins, Hunahpu and Xbalanque, who are initially born, subsequently survive successive trials, and eventually defeat and kill the **underworld** deities. The hero twins are miraculously born of an underworld maiden and a demigod father, himself a twin, and the twins and their mother eventually go to live with their brothers and grandmother. Here the twins trick their evil-minded brothers, magically provide food for the household from an unproductive maize field, and learn how to be prodigious ball game players. Because of their skills and their constant disturbing presence on the **ball court,** the twins are invited to play ball with the gods in the underworld. Here they intelligently survive several trials in underworld houses ("bat house" and "house of knives," for instance) and on the ball court. After they trick the underworld lords to self-**sacrifice** as traveling **dancers** and magicians, the hero twins rise into the sky as the sun and moon.

POT-BELLY. Sculptural style or iconographic complex that is witnessed to the greatest extent on the Pacific Coast and nearby highlands of Guatemala and El Salvador. Another example is known from **Copan,** Honduras. This accurately descriptive term of these sculptures was coined following studies of the anthropomorphic stone carvings that have a disproportionately large and distended belly with arms and legs wrapped around it (see photo). These monuments are typically surmounted by a round head with closed eyes and lips. It is believed that these works of art represent either dead human ancestors, sacrificial victims, babies, or possibly a **Mesoamerican deity,** such as the little-understood "Fat God."

It has also been hypothesized that the pot-bellied sculptures predate the **Olmec** stone carvings on the Gulf Coast. However, archaeological investigations at **Monte Alto** in Guatemala and especially Santa Leticia, El Salvador, demonstrate that the sculptures are of local origin and date to the Late Preclassic Period. The Pot-bellied sculptures then are tied to belief systems and art styles of Late Formative societies in southern Mesoamerica.

POTTERY. *See* CERAMICS

PRIESTS. In state-level societies in ancient **Mesoamerica,** like the **Aztec, Maya,** and **Mixtec,** the priesthood was an important religious and political office. Priests were often born into their societal roles, or many were elites who achieved the priestly office or status. The priests were responsible for the organization of rituals and for mediating between humans and the supernatural. They also kept the count of the **calendar,** carried out astronomical observations, performed **sacrifices** to **deities,** maintained the **temples** and images, and advised the ruling elites.

Frequently, the heads of state were also priests, or their priestly advisors were members of the royal family. Mesoamerican priests lived in the temples, and they could be recognized by their special clothing and physical appearance. For example, in Aztec society people in the priesthood did not wash themselves and they made blood offerings from cuts in their ears. Thus they were recognized by their scarred faces and blood-caked hair, skin, and clothing. In Classic Maya society, some priests may have used the title *its'at,* which means "sage" or "wise man," **ahaw,** "ruler," or *ahkin,* "he of the sun," referring to counts of days and heavenly connections.

PULQUE (**Puhl**-kay). The fermented drink made from the sap of the **maguey** plant that had widespread use in **Mesoamerican** societies. It was with ancient societies in central and eastern Mexico where pulque had special importance and abundant use, since maguey grows well in the drier highland ecozones. Pulque is a thick, milky liquid that is often compared to mother's milk or semen in some ancient Mesoamerican cultures. Pulque was used as a sacred drink in ceremonies, and intoxication from it helped people attain an altered state of being, which in turn assisted them in their communication with the supernatural. Today it is also left as an offering in bowls to be drunk by **deities,** or it is thrown on the ground as an offering or **sacrifice** to be similarly consumed.

The **Huastec Maya** of northern Veracruz were famed pulque drinkers, and a relief sculpture from El **Tajin,** Veracruz, depicts maguey leaves and blood from a figure's penis added to a vat of pulque during auto-sacrifice. The Bilimek Pulque Vessel is a Late **Aztec** drinking vessel that depicts the pulque goddess with the beverage streaming from her breasts. The pulque goddess and deities drinking pulque from cups are also shown in **Mixtec** painted books. *See also* CACAO

PUTUN. The term used to designate the **Maya** groups, particularly the Chontal ("foreigner") Maya, of the area of extensive swamps and rivers of the plains of Tabasco and Campeche. It has been hypothesized that the so-called Putun Maya flourished during Terminal Classic and Postclassic times (about A.D. 900–1300), and that they may have been involved in the downfall of Classic Maya states in the lowlands. They may have been merchant specialists that also disrupted **trade,** interaction, politics, and society during the Classic Maya collapse (ca. A.D. 800).

The Putun Maya are said to have focused on regional canoe trade in southern **Mesoamerica** by making their way through the rivers of the Maya area and navigating around the **Yucatan** Peninsula. These merchant and war-like Maya peoples are felt to have interacted heavily and intermarried with people from rising states in central Mexico after the Classic Period. The Putun Maya are presumed to have extensively traded with settlements along the coasts of Yucatan throughout the Postclassic Period.

Terminal Classic stone **stelae** at the southern lowland Maya site of **Seibal** differ from Classic Period monuments and are often cited as being portraits of Putun Maya nobles who intruded into the central Maya area during the collapse. Putun Maya merchant-warriors may also be depicted as being defeated in **warfare** by central Mexican warriors in murals at the Terminal Classic to Early Postclassic site of **Cacaxtla** in Mexico. However, it is also possible that the **Huastec** Maya, and not Putun Maya, are shown as the defeated in these mural paintings. *See also* POCHTECA

PUUC. A fairly dry region in southwestern **Yucatan,** where a range of low hills is found. Puuc is also a name that refers to a type of **Maya** architecture and archaeological sites that are found in this ecological zone. Puuc sites are medium to large, and they contain rectangular, terraced buildings whose exterior facades are filled with ornate sculpture mosaics. These structures also have false columns around or near their doorways. Some well-known archaeological sites in the Puuc region include Kabah, Labna, **Sayil,** and **Uxmal,** which, contrary to what is seen elsewhere, had sizeable Terminal Classic populations.

The Puuc region has some of the richest agricultural soils of northern Yucatan for growing **maize.** However, the area has much less rainfall and surface water compared with other geographical zones in the northern Maya lowlands. Streams and **cenotes** are practically nonexistent, therefore, the ancient Maya inhabitants constructed **chultunes,** or underground cisterns, for capturing and storing runoff from the seasonal rains. Ancient ruins are situated near the most agriculturally productive soils in the region and chultunes can be seen all over the sites.

PYRAMID. *See* TEMPLE

Q

QUELEPA. An intriguing archaeological site in eastern El Salvador that appears to have had separate occupations of different cultures. In the Formative Period, Quelapa had ties with much of El Salvador and Honduras, as seen in the comparable **ceramic** assemblages from this region, including the diagnostic **Usulutan** pottery. Yet by the advent of Early Classic times the architecture at Quelepa did not resemble buildings at most **Mesoamerican** sites, except for Los **Naranjos,** which is located to the north in Honduras. These two sites contain huge artificial terraces that support residential structures with paved entrance ramps. Perhaps the early inhabitants of this site were associated with populations farther south in lower Central America and not with the **Maya** to the northwest.

Quelepa architecture became "more Mesoamerican" in the Late Classic when rectangular buildings were built around **plazas.** Ceramics, plus ball game equipment made of stone and an I-shaped **ball court** show affinities with the Gulf Coast region of Veracruz. Perhaps this site contains valuable information related to early migrations in southern Mesoamerica, and perhaps further research will help reveal the mystery of the **Cotzumalhuapa** and **Pipil** incursions into the area. *See also* CHALCHUAPA

QUEMADA (LA). "The burned place/one" is situated atop a steep hill in central Zacatecas near the northern frontier zone of **Mesoamerica.** This site may be the place described in west Mexican indigenous lore that involved past **warfare,** the burning of structures, human **sacrifice,** and the abandonment of an important center in Pre-Columbian times. Current archaeological data show that La Quemada dates from Middle Classic to Terminal Classic times (A.D. 500–900) and not to the later Postclassic or **Toltec** period as initially postulated. This site has several large **temples, plazas,** courtyards, terraces, extensive road and wall systems, **altars,** and **ball courts,** which attest to its great political and economic power in the region. Like **Casas Grandes** and the centers in the **Chalchihuites** region of northern Mesoamerica, La Quemada was probably an important node in the **trade** networks with peoples located in what is now the southwest United States.

QUETZAL. The bird most prized in past Mesoamerican societies for the extremely long iridescent green tail feathers of the male that were used exclusively in the costumes, fans, parasols, and headdresses of elites and high status warriors. For these peoples, quetzal feathers were as precious as **jade, gold,** silver, and **jaguar** pelts. A magnificent headdress of approximately 500 quetzal feathers (called **Motecuhzoma**'s headdress), currently located in Vienna, was given to the Spanish **conquistadores** by the **Aztecs.** The quetzal bird (*Pharomachrus mocinno*), or *quetzalli* in **Nahuatl** and *k'uk'* in Mayan languages, is found today mainly in the cloud rainforests of the mountainous regions of Chiapas, Mexico, Guatemala, and Honduras. It can be recognized by its scarlet colored chest feathers, small round head with green feathers and short yellowish-white beak, and long green tail feathers, which can grow to about one meter.

Quetzal feathers were **traded** throughout **Mesoamerica,** were paid in **tribute** by subject towns to the Aztec capital of **Tenochtitlan,** and they were acquired by traveling merchants (**pochteca**) from people living near the bird's habitat, particularly the **Maya.** The quetzal is extremely shy, and its feathers can only be taken from hunted birds or from ones that have been stunned by blow gun pellets and bird bolt arrows shot from a bow. Because of the importance of its resplendent plumage, the quetzal and its feathers are often depicted in Mesoamerican art, are important in Mesoamerican folklore, and even appear in Maya **hieroglyphic** writing in names of persons and places. Many Classic to Postclassic Maya rulers and other elites even carried the name or title "quetzal" in their epithets. One of the earliest kings of **Copan,** Honduras, was named Yax K'uk Mo' ("Great Quetzal Macaw"), and the **Quiche** war captain **Tecum Uman** was said to have transformed into a quetzal upon his death in the battlefield while fighting the Spanish intruders.

QUETZALCOATL (Ket-sahl-**coh**-atl). "**Quetzal**-feathered serpent" in **Nahuatl,** this **deity** is called *K'uk'ulkan* in Yucatec **Maya.** This is perhaps one of the oldest and most important of the ancient **Mesoamerican**

gods. It is found in the belief systems and iconography through time across the Mesoamerican cultural area. Quetzalcoatl is described as a feathered serpent (usually a rattlesnake) that connects the earth and sky (the sky was often believed to be the underside of a snake's belly in many Mesoamerican cultures), and it was associated with the wind and rain. In contemporary **Mixtec religion,** a similarly described serpent lives among the clouds in the sky and brings rain. In past Mesoamerican societies, this deity was also associated with the elite. Additionally, the ancient **priests** claimed to communicate with or actually be descendants from Quetzalcoatl, whom they often provided with **sacrifices** and food offerings.

Depictions of the feathered serpent may appear as early as the Early Formative Period (about 1000 B.C.). An **Olmec stela** at the site of La **Venta** in Tabasco (Monument 19) shows a large rattlesnake with a feather-like crest and bird-like mouth floating around an elite personage. The feathered serpent is a common motif in the polychrome mural art of **Teotihuacan** from A.D. 300–700. Here the body of Quetzalcoatl frequently frames scenes of the afterlife, people performing rituals, and depictions of the watery worlds.

In other later central Mexican societies dating to the Postclassic Period (A.D. 1000–1500), including the **Toltecs** and **Aztecs,** Quetzalcoatl was prominent in their art forms, religion, and culture history. The deity was usually worshiped in **temples** with round sides at Mesoamerican sites dating after the Classic Period. Even in Pueblo cultures of the Southwest United States, a feathered serpent is associated with water and fertility. A winged serpent is even found in the carvings of Mississippian peoples (ca. A.D. 1000) of the Southeast United States, suggesting a pan-Amerindian belief system or, more than likely, cross-cultural interaction.

The myths of Postclassic Mesoamerican peoples demonstrate the multifaceted nature of their deities, of which Quetzalcoatl (wind, rain, priestly elites) was a prime example. For instance, Quetzalcoatl is associated with, or is an aspect of, the wind god **Ehecatl** of the Aztecs. Quetzalcoatl was also connected with **Tlaloc** the rain deity.

At the time of the conquest in central Mexico, Mesoamerican myths spoke of Topiltzin Quetzalcoatl, who was a wise, more peaceful, and powerful ancestral ruler of the ancient great city of **Tollan** (possibly **Tula,** Hidalgo in Mexico and/or Teotihuacan). This divine ruler was banished from Tollan by a rival, **Tezcatlipoca,** and he then floated across the sea to the east on a raft. But he vowed to return to his realm one day. Spanish **conquistadores** arrived in Mexico during the same year name (1 Reed) that Quetzalcoatl was expelled from Tula. Hence, the Aztecs believed that Hernan Cortes was the deity who was finally returning to claim rightful rulership over their domain.

QUICHE (Key-**cheh**). The Quiche **Maya** were one of the most powerful state societies encountered by the Spanish **conquistadores** during the conquest of Central America. The Postclassic Quiche kingdom was located in the highlands of central Guatemala where they politically subjugated and controlled a large region by A.D. 1520. This Quiche-dominated region even included territory that stretched to the hot **cacao**-growing country of the **Soconusco** area on the Pacific Coast. The Quiche controlled this territory and their subject towns, which paid **tribute** through a confederacy centered at their capital called **Utatlan,** or *Kumarcaaj* ("Old Reeds" or another Mesoamerican **Tollan**) in the Quiche language. A large number of Quiche archaeological sites with stone architecture are located on highly defensible hilltops, which attests to the fact that **warfare** was commonplace here during the Postclassic. The Quiche were also farmers and hunters, and they **traded** with other Mesoamerican peoples.

Additionally, these people were the bitter enemies of the nearby **Cakchiquel** Maya (who spoke a related language) of the capital center of **Iximche,** and the **Nahua**-speaking **Pipil** of eastern Guatemala and western El Salvador. The Quiche claimed to have blood ties with the ancient **Toltecs** of central Mexico and are said to have come from **Tula** or Tollan. However, they may have originated as part of the "Mexicanized **Putun** Maya" in Postclassic Tabasco to the north.

The Quiche polity has been viewed as being segmentary in nature, or governed by different lineages at several centers. The Quiche Maya and their fabled war captain, **Tecum Uman,** were finally conquered by the Spanish conquistadores under Pedro de Alvarado in A.D. 1524 after several fierce battles. The Quiche fought with **atlatls,** bows and arrows, **obsidian**-edged swords, and lances, which were commonly used in conquest-era **Mesoamerica.** The **Popol Vuh,** a colonial document that recounts Maya history and mythology, is written in Quiche and perhaps was originally created in Utatlan during the 16th century.

QUIRIGUA. This relatively small Classic **Maya** site located near the banks of the **Motagua River** in southeastern Guatemala is famous for having several of the largest carved stone **stelae,** or portraits of Maya rulers with written texts, made of fine limestone or sandstone. The tallest monument, Stela D of the Late Classic (A.D. 766) king of Quirigua colloquially known as "Cauac Sky," stands approximately 6 meters (or about 20 feet) tall. This ruin is also well known for its massive and unique sculptures carved from river boulders called "zoomorphs" that depict humans, **deities,** and animal-like supernatural beings. Some examples of the stone monuments, sculpture, and buildings resemble those of **Copan,** which is located near Quirigua just across the border into Honduras. Copan probably played an important role in the history and development of Quirigua.

Quirigua is situated near fertile alluvial agricultural soils (extensive banana plantations are there today) and was found along important terrestrial and canoe-borne **trade** routes on the eastern frontier of the Maya area. The Maya at Quirigua more than likely controlled the course and prevented flooding of the Motagua River to protect the city. The river passed near the site in antiquity, thus archaeologists believe that there may have been a canoe landing in the area. The site is also found near major sources of **obsidian,** a volcanic glass used for cutting tools, and **jade,** which was traded and carved all over **Mesoamerica** to be used for ceremonial items and jewelry. Much of the architecture, residential structures, and even sculpture at Quirigua has been covered by recent and past episodes of flooding. Hence, it is difficult to locate archaeological remains at the site and many buried deposits and buildings have been discovered through deep excavation and trenching. It is difficult to comment on the exact chronology or population size at Quirigua, because much of the site is buried, but the site was probably largely inhabited during the Classic Period and it may have held only a few thousand people.

Nonetheless, we know considerable detail of the history and past lifeways at Quirigua through excavation and study of the **hieroglyphs** on the stone monuments. Even though there was an earlier occupation in the area, Quirigua appears to have been settled by ethnic Maya peoples during the Early Classic Period (ca. A.D. 400–500). The colonization could have been initiated by Copan, or according to local inscriptions the Copan rulers may have installed the first Maya rulers at the site. Early monuments indicate that Copan rulers visited the site and that they may have overseen enthroning rituals of Quirigua kings. Additionally, it is possible that portions of the supporting population of Quirigua and the inhabitants of the nearby hills were not ethnically Maya in this frontier zone.

Quirigua was at its height during the Classic Period, and some of the largest constructions, tallest stelae, a **ball court,** the great **plaza** (one of the largest in the Maya area), and the site's own "emblem glyph," or royal title, were created after a crucial historical event: the sacrifice of the Copan king "18 Rabbit" (*Uaxaclahun u bah k'awil*) by the Quirigua ruler

"Cauac Sky" in A.D. 738. "Cauac Sky" then claims to be the succeeding ruler of Copan and the fortunes of the Quirigua elites increased even though it is uncertain if they held power over Copan after possible victories in **warfare.** Also according to the hieroglyphs, the Quirigua kings were continuously successful in a number of later military campaigns against unknown enemies.

Evidence from hieroglyphic texts suggests that Quirigua and Copan once again became allies at the end of the Late Classic Period. However, they both experienced collapse at about the same time during Late Classic to Terminal Classic times instead of one site becoming prominent when the other fell. The downfall at Quirigua may have been triggered by war, changing trade routes, environmental destruction, or migration to other sites. One of the last sculptures reported at the site is a reclined **chacmool** figure, which is rare in the southern Maya lowlands, but more common at the later Terminal to Early Postclassic sites of **Chichen Itza** in **Yucatan** and **Tula** in central Mexico. Therefore, there may have been a late occupation of Quirigua, the local inhabitants may have been in contact with other peoples to the north and west, or this type of sculpture may have had its beginnings in this region.

R

RAMON (BREADNUT). The ramon or breadnut tree (*Brosimum alicastrum*) was believed by some archaeologists to be a staple crop of the ancient lowland **Maya.** Found in and around Maya sites in the rainforest, this tree was probably cultivated by the Maya, who collected the fallen food. Monkeys and birds flock to ramon trees, thus the Maya also may have used the groves of trees for hunting.

The ramon tree yields a tasty fruit and a nut that can be soaked and ground with a **mano and metate** to make tortillas or gruel. The nuts are plentiful and store well (experiments show that they can be kept in underground **chultun** pits for a long period). However, contemporary populations in the lowlands typically relish the fruit as a snack and consider the nut a not-so-savory starvation food only to be used when the **maize** crop fails. Therefore, it may have been similarly "underutilized" by the ancient Maya as well. *See also* DIET

RELIGION. Religion was extremely important in all **Mesoamerican** societies. It permeated all aspects of their lives, including even agriculture, so-

The ancient city of Teotihuacan in central Mexico with the monumental Pyramid of the Sun and the Street of the Dead in the background. (Copyright © Jean Pierre Courau. Used by permission.)

The Great Plaza of the Classic Maya site of Tikal, Guatemala, with Temple I (foreground), Temple V (background), and palaces of the South Acropolis (center). Note the two uncarved stone stelae and altars placed on the plaza floor before the steps of Temple I. (Copyright © Jean Pierre Courau. Used by permission.)

The main ball court in the central plaza at the Classic Maya ruin of Copan, Honduras. Carved stone stelae depicting Maya rulers are found on the north and west steps of the court structures. (Copyright © Jean Pierre Courau. Used by permission.)

Classic Maya carved stone stela depicting a male ruler of the site of Machaquila, Guatemala, flanked by hieroglyphic texts. The ruler wears jade jewelry as earplugs, a necklace, and wristlets. (Copyright © Jean Pierre Courau. Used by permission.)

Carved stone danzante, *or captive figure, of the ancient Zapotec culture from the center of Monte Alban, Oaxaca, Mexico. Hieroglyphic inscriptions above the left elbow of the figure name the captive or the date of his capture. (Copyright © Jean Pierre Courau. Used by permission.)*

Monumental stone altar or throne from the Formative Period site of La Venta, Tabasco, Mexico, showing an Olmec person, possibly a male ruler or religious specialist, in a cave. (Copyright © Jean Pierre Courau. Used by permission.)

Olmec colossal head sculpture, which may be a portrait of a male ruler, from La Venta, Tabasco, Mexico. (Copyright © Jean Pierre Courau. Used by permission.)

Formative Period Pot-Belly stone sculpture from La Democracia (Monte Alto) near the Pacific coast of Guatemala. (Copyright © Jean Pierre Courau. Used by permission.)

Aztec Coatlique statue from the capital Tenochtitlan, discovered in excavations in Mexico City. A necklace of hearts and hands covers the breast and streams of blood represented by serpents issue from the dismembered deity. (Copyright © Jean Pierre Courau. Used by permission.)

Aztec Calendar Stone or throne fragment from Tenochtitlan with the fifth and current sun in the center. (Copyright © Jean Pierre Courau. Used by permission.)

A meeting of Maya nobles from a replica of the brilliantly painted murals of the Classic Period site of Bonampak, Chiapas, Mexico. The nobles wear textiles, jade beads from their ears, and Spondylus shells around their necks. (Courtesy Gainesville Museum. Copyright © Jean Pierre Courau. Used by permission.)

Mask of worked jade from the ancient Olmec culture. (Copyright © Jean Pierre Courau. Used by permission.)

Painted and carved ceramic vessel of the Postclassic Mixteca-Puebla style. (Copyright © Jean Pierre Courau. Used by permission.)

Painted ceramic vessels from the Classic Maya culture of the highlands of Guatemala. (Copyright © Jean Pierre Courau. Used by permission.)

Postclassic Mixtec gold jewelry from Tomb 7 at Monte Alban, Oaxaca, Mexico. (Copyright © Jean Pierre Courau. Used by permission.)

Mam Maya woman wearing huipil textile, San Ildefonso Ixtahuacan, Guatemala. (Copyright © Jean Pierre Courau. Used by permission.)

cial organization, **warfare,** architecture, and dress. Ancient Mesoamericans believed in forces or powers in nature and the cosmos. Everything and everyone was infused with this cosmic power and essence. There were **deities,** supernatural beings, and forces associated with the earth, sky, heavens, **underworld,** plants, animals, wind, rain, and even diseases.

Ancestor veneration was also central to Mesoamerican religions. People were frequently buried in house platforms or **tombs** in **temple** pyramids, where they remained close to and communicated with the living. **Sacrifices** were essential for the perpetuation of the universe, ancestors, and human existence, and human, animal, and food offerings were commonly given to the deities and supernatural forces to request something or to placate them. Many Mesoamericans also believed that they had various kinds of souls and personal energies, one of which was a companion spirit, or co-essence, in the form of an animal or some otherworldly creature. *See also* PRIESTS

REMOJADAS. In Central Veracruz, Mexico, and around the archaeological site of El **Tajin,** a large quantity of Classic Period pottery figurines of the Remojadas tradition are found. This largely mold-made **ceramic** tradition is named after the site where these figurines are most common and possibly were manufactured. The large hollow figurines are very naturalistic representations of humans and animals, and **deities** are often depicted as well. What is especially unique about this distinct **Mesoamerican** ceramic style is that many figurines are lifelike and show emotion.

In this figurine art, males and females hold hands or embrace, and most of the human figurines are gesturing and smiling. Some of the figures are life size. Incredible detail regarding ancient Veracruz clothing, regalia, headgear, and dental modification is witnessed in this tradition. Extraordinary animal figurines even have wheels and axles. This finding demonstrates that human porters were more important and practical in Mesoamerican societies than the use of the wheel for most transportation and construction purposes.

RUBBER. Rubber comes from a tree (*Castilla elastica*) native to **Mesoamerica;** ancient Mesoamericans were the first to play games with a bouncing rubber ball, which was later taken to Europe after the conquest. Large quantities of rubber were taken from the Gulf Coast region of the **Olmec** (meaning "rubber people/people of land of rubber"), and peoples from this area paid **tribute** in rubber to the **Aztec** empire. The rubber tree also is common in **Peten,** Guatemala, where it was extracted in the 19th and early 20th centuries. The Spanish word for rubber, *hule* was taken from the **Nahuatl** term *olli* for this substance.

Black rubber balls and scenes from the ball game are frequently depicted on Classic **Maya** painted **ceramic** vases, but the earliest rubber balls were found at the Early Formative site of El **Manati** in Veracruz. These rubber balls were recovered along with wooden Olmec statues in a bog near a natural spring, which were probably left as offerings at a sacred site. Rubber balls were formed in wooden molds and then often left in them when not in use, so they would not lose their round shape. Rubber was also used as offerings to be burned in balls or as shaped figures (humans or animals in the case of the **Lacandon** Maya) because of the strong smell and black smoke that was received by the gods.

S

SAC BAHLAN. After fleeing their center Lakam tun in Lake **Miramar,** Chiapas, during the Spanish conquest in the 16th century the Chol-**Lacandon** created this small capital near the Lacantun River. The site of Sac Bahlan was later encountered by Spanish **conquistadores** marching to subdue the **Itza Maya** of the northern Guatemala rainforests in A.D. 1695. According to some Spanish written sources, Sac Bahlan was reported to have three large communal structures and about 100 houses all made of pole and thatch, which were located near a savanna, hills, and a stream.

After they subjugated the population of Sac Bahlan, the Spanish built a fort here and used the site as a mission and garrison for up to 50 years until the people were forced to move to the cooler Guatemalan highlands. In the **mountain** pueblo of Huehuetenango many of the relocated Chol-Lacandon died. Recent surveys near the savannas of the southeastern Chiapas lowlands may have encountered Sac Bahlan, but the veracity of the identification of this site has to be proven archaeologically. A study of the ethnohistoric and archaeological records at Sac Bahlan could yield interesting results regarding culture contact, conquest, and indigenous cultural transformations.

SACBE. Term meaning "white road" in many Mayan languages. These white roads were first described by the Spanish who visited **Yucatan.** **Maya** *sacbeob* (plural) are raised causeways that are constructed of stone and earth fill, which are paved with a thick layer of stones and white lime plaster. Hence, this gave the physical appearance of the Maya "white roads."

Sacbeob are more common in the lowland Maya centers in Guatemala, Belize, and especially Yucatan. These roads connected ceremonial precincts within sites, like at **Caracol, Copan,** and **Tikal,** and often connected one major center with another, such as between El **Mirador** and **Nakbe** in northern Guatemala. One of the longest of the known sacbeob, which stretches 100 kilometers by connecting several centers, is found between Yaxuna and Coba in eastern Yucatan. These roadways were used collectively for transportation, walking paths, and avenues for ritual processions. Impressively long and wide stone and plaster causeways were also marveled at by the Spanish **conquistadores** at the **Aztec** capital of **Tenochtitlan**.

SACRIFICE. Sacrifice of humans and animals was crucial for the successful outcome of Mesoamerican ceremonies and held a central position in ancient belief systems. People and animals were decapitated, dismembered, and their hearts, blood, and other parts were given as food or burned offerings to the gods and ancestors. Even the burning of objects such as plants and **jade,** plus the spilling of **pulque** and **maize** gruel on the ground, was seen as ritual sacrifice and necessary for the continuation of life and the cosmos.

Additionally, self-sacrifice, or auto-sacrifice, which includes bloodletting and self-mutilation, was widely practiced. **Priests** extracted blood from their ears and loose skin, men let blood from their penises, and women drew blood from ropes and thorns through cuts in their tongues. During rituals this blood was thrown on the ground, smeared on idols, offered with food to **deities,** or burned on paper in bowls and incense burners. Sacrifice was not viewed as a punishment, but as the ultimate sacred offering to deities in order to sanctify a ritual and enter a pact with the supernatural.

Human sacrifice is widely described by the Spanish **conquistadores** and colonists who obviously detested the practice. The Spanish were shocked by what they viewed as cruel and unholy practices, and were astounded by the number of victims killed in sacrificial rituals on the **Templo Mayor** (main temple) in the **Aztec** capital city of **Tenochtitlan.** They describe how the victims were held by their feet and hands on an **altar** and how the native priests removed hearts by cutting through rib cages with sharp **obsidian** and **chert** knives. The victims and their blood were believed to help the sun and its warrior protector, **Huitzilopochtli,** through the **underworld** and sky each day.

The Spanish also mention that predestined sacrificial victims were purposely drowned, burned, buried alive, decapitated, or shot with arrows during ceremonies for different occasions or at certain times in the ritual **calendar.** The human blood was often smeared on idols and the walls of the **temples.** Sometimes the victims were cannibalized by the victors who wished to partake in and retain the essence, power, or energy of the noble sacrificed person. Since there was plenty of food in ancient **Mesoamerica** and only certain people participated in a ritual cannibalistic act, human sacrifice probably had little nutritional importance.

There is abundant evidence for human sacrifice in the archaeological record throughout Mesoamerica. Human bone fragments, whole limb bones, and heads that are worked or have cut marks are often found in special deposits or burials. Phalanges placed in small **ceramic** vessels are associated with some burials, particularly in the **Maya** area, and they may have been removed by **women** and kin of the deceased in funerary rites. In the Temple of **Quetzalcoatl** at the central Mexican site of **Teotihuacan,** burials were discovered where adult males, presumably sacrificial captives, had their hands bound behind their backs. Large stone knives, sacrificial altars, and pointed obsidian blades for bloodletting also are commonly found in archaeological sites. Additionally, skull racks, or **tzompantli,** displaying the heads of the victims are found in several Postclassic Mesoamerican sites.

Maya art and Mexican **codices** depict human sacrifice; often the victims are captives from **warfare** or people predestined by their birth date, social position, and ritual status for this purpose. Maya art also shows scaffold sacrifice where victims are bound to the poles and killed with arrows and heart extraction. Stone monuments also depict women pulling cords through their tongues. Additionally, Maya **hieroglyphs** contain references to sacrifice with the decapitation or "the axe event" verb (*chakah*) and the verb *nawah,* which appears to refer to the ceremonial stripping of the original clothing and then the adornment of human captives for sacrifice. Many times Maya sacrificial victims were powerful kings taken in combat whose lives were the ultimate ritual offering to the deities.

SALT. The production and distribution of comestible salt was an important economic pursuit in ancient **Mesoamerica.** Salt works, or *salinas,* are found throughout the region since the beginning of sedentary villages. Formative Period salt manufacturing sites have been encountered on the south coast of Guatemala and Chiapas (**Soconusco**), central Guatemala, and on the coasts of **Yucatan**. From the archaeological evidence and descriptions by the Spanish, we know that large-scale salt making in Yucatan, especially in the Chikinchel Province of the northeast, and on the south coast of Guatemala and Chiapas, took place in Postclassic and early Colonial times.

Salt was extracted from seawater, coastal estuaries, and salt-laden soils. Water was boiled and evaporated in large **ceramic** vats or pottery vessels to collect the salt. Enormous round ceramic vats for this purpose were found in situ at the Formative to Classic Period (ca. A.D. 100–600) site of Salinas de los Nueve Cerros, probably a Formative to Classic Period **Maya** site near salt mineral deposits in the foothills of central-northern Guatemala. Seawater was also evaporated in large, shallow pans of compacted earth near the coasts of Yucatan and Guatemala. The process of evaporating and refining salt was also carried out by adding water and brine in wooden troughs, which were slowly drained, leaving the salt behind.

The salt was then traded from the production areas to the interior and was transported as small blocks or cakes, or in sacks and ceramic vessels. Where salt was scarce, or when **trade** ties were severed, salt was obtained from the ashes of burned palm leaves as done today by some contemporary Mesoamerican peoples like the **Lacandon** Maya.

SAN JOSE MOGOTE. Located in the Valley of Oaxaca, Mexico, San Jose Mogote was one of the largest initial settlements in the area around 1600–1300 B.C. (Early Formative Period), and was inhabited until about 400 B.C. (Middle Formative). This site was occupied by approximately 20 to 30 families, or about 150 people in total, during the Early Formative, and it grew to over 500 persons during the last phase. The people of San Jose Mogote cultivated **maize,** avocado, chile, and squash, among other plants. For supplementing their **diets** they also hunted deer, rabbits, peccaries, and turkeys. This site is well known for its early dates for village life, **temple**-like buildings, and a **danzante,** or sculpture, depicting a naked captive who had his heart extracted. This monument was discovered in a masonry temple that dates to about 800–600 B.C. It is one of the earliest examples of Mesoamerican writing since the captive's name (possibly "One Earthquake" or the word for "heart") is shown in the space between his legs.

One of the earliest public structures in ancient **Mesoamerica,** a large building with lime plastered walls and floors, was built during the Early

Formative phase of the site. Domestic structures through time consisted of walls of sticks plastered with mud and a lime covering, that were topped with a thatched roof. There were also four main residential wards corresponding with the cardinal directions. Inside the buildings were signs of possible working areas for **women,** where spindle whorls for making thread and bone needles for weaving **textiles** were found. Bell-shaped pits near residences were made to store food and then were eventually used as trash and burial sites.

At this site we also have early signs of craft specialization and **trade:** the residents manufactured magnetite (an iron ore) **mirrors** and artifacts of shell and mica that may have been traded to the **Olmec** to the northeast. They may have exchanged these items for shark's teeth, shells, turtle carapaces, and stingray spines used for ritual purposes. Burials at San Jose Mogote showed status differentiation, with people of higher rank being buried with **jade** and shell artifacts, polished iron ore mirrors, and **ceramics** bearing Olmec designs that varied possibly according to rank and lineage. Perhaps the builders of San Jose Mogote were **Zapotecs** who later constructed nearby **Monte Alban**.

SAN LORENZO. This site was first excavated in the 1940s when a report of a "large stone eye and face looking up from the ground" surfaced and the **Olmec** were discovered. This is one of the earliest Gulf Coast Olmec sites in Veracruz; it dates to about 1700–700 B.C. (Early to Middle Formative Period) and is contemporaneous with **San Jose Mogote.** When San Lorenzo was abandoned it is possible that people moved to the later Olmec site of La **Venta** to the east. The people who founded and lived at this site may have been **Mixe-Zoque** speakers according to several linguists and archaeologists.

The early **ceramics** at San Lorenzo also demonstrate ties with the **Ocos** peoples on the south coast of Chiapas and Guatemala. Olmec culture is fully recognizable at San Lorenzo after 1200 B.C. when culturally diagnostic white kaolin clay ceramics and figurines, stone sculpture, and monumental architecture made of packed clay prevail at the site. Worked **jade** artifacts, a hallmark of Olmec culture, however, are conspicuously absent here. Settlement is scattered throughout the hinterland of the site, and these people, who probably farmed **maize** and hunted in the area, helped build and maintain San Lorenzo. What appears to be a simple earthen **ball court** and figurines depicting ballplayers that were found here suggest that the ball game was played early on at the site.

San Lorenzo is located on a raised platform, much of it artificial or modified by humans into a distinct form (possibly a large effigy mound?), surrounded by level savanna and floodplain near the Coatzacoalcos River. To the south is found the important ritual site of El **Manati,** which contains a spring and bog that has preserved **rubber** balls, wooden busts, and worked jade artifacts. On the large platform of San Lorenzo three-dimensional stone sculptures and mounded earthen buildings are arranged. The stone for the sculpture was procured in the **Tuxtla Mountains** about 70 kilometers to the northwest. Some of the most impressive and beautiful Olmec sculpture is seen at San Lorenzo: **colossal heads, altars** (which were probably large stone thrones), and anthropomorphic figures carved in the full round.

The colossal heads may depict rulers, ancestors, or ballplayers. The "table-top" **altars** usually depict people emerging from **caves** carrying babies in their arms, and in one case dwarf figures hold up the tabletop. Many of the stone sculptures were defaced and buried in a line on top of the site platform presumably when the elites who commissioned them died. Also, an extensive water drain system made of stone was found deeply buried at San Lorenzo. These drainage lines may have been used by **priest**-leaders for rituals or to show that they controlled the existence of this precious resource. Also found in the excavations were **obsidian** artifacts from sources in Guatemala and highland Mexico, and bones of dogs, snook fish, and psychoactive toads, which may have been used to make hallucinogens for ritual use.

SAYIL. One of the largest archaeological sites of the **Maya** of the **Puuc** region in **Yucatan,** where there are rich soils in a comparatively dry area. Sayil is famous for its unique large palace structure, which is made up of three different levels and an elaborate sculpture facade of stone mosaic patterns and **deity** masks (probably of **Chac,** the rain god) and stone columns at the central doorways. This palace is connected to other palace-like structures, **temples,** and a **ball court** for the ball game by a long causeway or **sacbe.** Recently, a large portion of the site was mapped (about four square kilometers) and it is estimated that approximately 10,000 people lived here, which makes Sayil one of the more densely populated sites in the Puuc region. The site was probably occupied by Yucatec Maya.

Occupation zones, **ceramic** densities, and activity areas were identified through intensive surface collection near the site core. **Chultunes,** or subsurface storage pits for water, were found to be common around residential structures. The larger, more complexly built domestic buildings are believed to have belonged to high status families, who had a longer history of occupation and land tenure at the site. The artifacts collected at the site show that Sayil had its greatest population during the Terminal Classic Period (around A.D. 800–900). Some carved stone **stelae** are found at the site, but they are too eroded for their **hieroglyphs** to be read. *See also* UXMAL

SCHOOLS. Education and training of young people is a priority in human cultures and schooling is usually organized into formal institutions with teachers in societies that have large populations and social inequality. In some ancient Mesoamerican societies like the **Aztecs** and the **Maya,** youths attended schools to learn about their history, **religion,** combat, ceremonial practices, and occupations. Most schools in ancient **Mesoamerica** were probably much like the ones in the Maya area where young men were educated in men's houses; here young men lived apart from their families while learning special skills, and they practiced for their eventual roles in society.

The imperial Aztecs of central Mexico had two main types of highly structured schools for their youth: the *calmecac* and *telpochcalli.* The calmecac was a special kind of school found in major centers of the Aztec empire where the more promising children of the nobility and some commoners were groomed for religious, political, social, and military service. Usually there was one school for boys and one for girls in each city. At the school the students' lives were highly regimented and they had to perform specific duties, tasks, lessons, purifications, and ceremonies. The children of the nobles were instructed to become **priests,** administrators, war leaders, and judges.

The telpochcalli, or "youth houses," were responsible for the education and training of commoner children. Each Aztec **calpulli,** or a clan-like ward in the cities, had this type of school where the young people were exposed to religious and moral life, the arts and rhetoric, and history and science. Boys were given military instruction and the girls were trained in religious matters. As in other Mesoamerican schools, these Aztec youths were taught humility, cleanliness, proper behaviors, discipline, social roles, and information about their culture in order to educate and indoctrinate them. Punishments for students were severe, and as the Aztec **Codex Mendoza** shows, youths were pricked with cactus needles or held over a fire stoked with chile peppers when they did not obey their elders or if they failed to complete their assignments.

SEIBAL. A popular **Maya** site for visitors because it is accessed by traveling on the picturesque Pasion River through the southern **Peten** rainforest and because it has large **temple** structures and beautifully carved stone **stelae.** Seibal is a large site that is crucial for understanding the Classic Maya collapse and culture change in the southern lowlands around A.D. 825. This important center had a large Terminal Classic population when most other sites in the region were being abandoned. Many **Fine Paste ceramics** dating to the Terminal Classic, which point to ties to regions to the north and west, were recovered from excavations.

Many of the Terminal Classic stone stelae at Seibal are rendered in a style different than other carved Maya monuments in the lowlands. These monuments may have been commissioned by only one or two rulers. The Seibal stelae may exhibit influence from contemporary cultures in central Mexico, **Yucatan,** or Tabasco (**Putun** Maya?) since the figures have more angular faces, thick moustaches, nose plugs, and unique hair styles. These figures are similar to ones seen on painted murals at **Cacaxtla,** central Mexico. Some of the stelae have "speech scrolls" in front of the figures' mouths and square cartouche **hieroglyphs,** both of which are common further west in Mexico. A building in the center of the main **plaza** at the site that has distinctive architectural elements, plus a round structure at the end of a **sacbe,** or causeway, are unique to the southern lowlands and also are similar to Terminal Classic constructions to the west and north.

Seibal has several large groupings of monumental public buildings that are connected to one another by sacbe paths. For the ball game, this site has two **ball courts** that are built on an east-west axis instead of the usual north-south one; a large ball court is found in the acropolis in the main group of structures (Group A), and a smaller playing court is found in the middle of the site along a sacbe leading to the above-mentioned round structure. Another large cluster of buildings (Group D) is found on a steep hill near the west bank of the Pasion River. This group is very defensible with easy access gained only by a sacbe from the central group of structures (Group A). Seibal also has a large settlement zone with structures of every size and shape (many of which were occupied during the Terminal Classic Period) that stretch for several kilometers beyond the site core.

Through archaeological investigations and decipherments of hieroglyphic texts in the Pasion River region, much is known about the history of Seibal and its rulers. Most of what we know about the site is associated with events in the Late Classic Period. Many of Seibal's monumental temples and residential structures were built in the Late Classic and before the numerous Terminal Classic stelae were carved. Although the site may have been autonomous early on, it eventually came under the aegis of the Late Classic rulers of **Dos Pilas,** since Dos Pilas Ruler 3 captured "**Jaguar** Paw" of Seibal in A.D. 735 and Dos Pilas Ruler 4 was involved in rituals and the commemoration of a carved hieroglyphic text at Seibal. Seibal kings are identified in the texts through their association of the emblem glyph for Seibal, which contains three hearthstones.

According to later monuments and population growth in the Terminal Classic, Seibal probably became independent again at this time. Many of the latest carved stelae at the site were dedicated by a Terminal Classic ruler named Wat'ul-Chatel. Stela 10 at the site mentions an important **calendar** period ending ritual by the Seibal ruler in A.D. 849 that was attended by the rulers of Dos Pilas (or perhaps **Tikal,** which uses the same place hieroglyph), **Calakmul,** and Motul de San Jose. However, like other sites in the region during the Late Classic, Seibal became abandoned by Early Postclassic times. It is possible that regional political, economic, and social systems were breaking down because of **warfare** and abandonment, and maybe people were heading to the north to the **Puuc** area in **Yucatan,** or to Tabasco.

SOCONUSCO. This is the name of an extensive area in southern **Mesoamerica** that figured prominently in the history of many Pre-Columbian societies. The name *Soconusco* was used by the Spanish **conquistadores** when referring to the native land of *Xoconochco,* or "On the Sour Cactus Fruit." This is the **Nahuatl** place name of a town and a southeastern province that was subjugated by and paid **tribute** to the **Aztec** empire. Soconusco refers to the narrow strip of coastline and piedmont area that borders the Pacific Ocean in Chiapas, Mexico, and western Guatemala.

Diverse ecozones are found here, such as rivers, mangroves, flat plains, jungles, and hills. This territory was rich in products both from the ocean and from the land that were desired by many ancient Mesoamericans. The area is hot and humid with fertile lands that are enriched by volcanic ash and alluvium. Some of the lushest tropical rainforest and **cacao**-growing plantations in ancient times thrived here, and today it is one of the largest sugarcane-producing, farming, and cattle ranching areas in Latin America.

Because of its rich environment and myriad resources, Soconusco was a focal point for human occupation throughout the Mesoamerican cultural sequence. Archaic hunters, gatherers, and fishers moved about this region while living in seasonal camps and living off both the land and the rivers, mangroves, and sea. Some of the earliest permanent Mesoamerican settlements are found in Soconusco in the Early Formative Period, like the **Barra** and **Ocos** people and sites with contact with the **Olmec** civilization to the north. These early societies began experimenting with the cultivation of **maize** and other plants, but they still relied on the collecting of local resources for their survival. These Formative Soconusco cultures remained remarkably homogeneous with regard to architecture, material culture, subsistence, and settlement patterns, which attests to strong interaction and frequent migrations and contact.

Later in the Classic Period, Soconusco supported a large population; ruins dot the landscape and are found in many of different ecozones. This area more than likely was occupied by **Maya, Mixe-Zoque, Nahua,** and **Zapotec** peoples, beginning in the Formative Period and leading up to the Spanish conquest. The central Mexican metropolis of **Teotihuacan** was in contact with or perhaps dominated the peoples of Soconusco. Artifacts from Teotihuacan, such as green **obsidian, ceramics,** and incense burners, and local material culture showing the influence of this great center are found in large quantities in this coastal area. Teotihuacan may have been interested in exchanging with the inhabitants of Soconusco or controlling **trade** in cacao, seashells, animal skins, feathers, and forest products.

Just before the Spanish conquest, portions of this region and its products were controlled by the **Quiche** and **Cakchiquel** Maya and the Aztec empire. A main reason for targeting Soconusco for subjugation and tribute payments was its wealth in cacao, bird feathers, **jaguar** pelts, and sea resources. A further incentive for Aztec conquest of the area was for support for the military harassment of adjacent territories and to appease traveling **pochteca** merchants seeking wealth here.

SPONDYLUS. One of the more common types of seashell used by elites in ancient **Mesoamerica;** these shells were found throughout the lands and at different times. *Spondylus* shells, or "spiny oysters," are found in deep waters of both the Atlantic and Pacific Oceans. Thus these precious shells had to be acquired from afar and traded. As jewelry, they were prized for their orangish-red color when the interiors were scraped and polished. Often bits of worked spondylus shell are used in mosaic masks or headdresses. These shells were also prized by many cultures near the west coast of South America.

Whole polished Spondylus shells were used on necklaces and cape clasps of **Maya** nobles, as seen in the **Bonampak** murals. Maya **women** often are depicted on stone monuments and **stelae** with Spondylus shells below their waists, which may symbolize their female anatomy, femininity, or fertility. Also, Spondylus shells were often placed near the waists of noble men or women in their **tombs.** In Maya art water is symbolized with stylized Spondylus shells, and the rain god **Chac** is frequently depicted by what appears to be a Spondylus shell for an ear.

STELA. Term from Old World archaeology that is applied to freestanding carved stone monuments of ancient **Mesoamerica.** Stelae (plural) are mostly found in the **Maya** area, especially in the southern lowlands of **Peten** and Chiapas, but there are also many seen in Tabasco and Veracruz, Mexico. Many stelae were set up in the Classic Period (A.D. 400–800), particularly in the Maya region. It is quite possible that a large number of similar standing carvings were made of wood and found throughout Mesoamerica, but they have been destroyed by time and the elements.

A large number of stone stelae have carved human figures in low relief, and mainly the Maya stelae have **hieroglyphic** inscriptions, as do some from Oaxaca and Veracruz (see photo). The Formative Period sculpted stela at La **Mojarra** has one of the longest written texts in ancient Mesoamerica and is written in a non-Mayan language. At the Classic Maya sites of **Copan,** Honduras, and Tonina, Chiapas, and in the **Huastec**a area in Veracruz, human portrait stelae were carved in the full round, or three-dimensional form. The Maya mainly used limestone for these monumental artworks, but at Copan and in **Olmec** Veracruz, volcanic rock was used.

The Maya are said to have a "stela cult," but they merely took the carving and placing of these monuments dedicated to rulers to a much greater extent than other cultures of Mesoamerica. The Maya often commemorated these monuments at "period endings" in their **calendar,** which were at 5-, 10-, or 20-year intervals. The Maya also erected stelae following war events, life crisis rites of the elite, or after important rituals and gatherings. Many Maya sites have carved or "plain" stelae (shaped as a stone slab, but no carved figures or texts were added) that are set up behind round stone "**altars,**" which in some cases may be "seats" or "thrones" according to hieroglyphic and iconographic clues. The most numerous and largest stelae are located in the Maya area. The Classic Period site of **Quirigua,** Guatemala, has the tallest stelae, such as Stela D, that rise some six meters high.

Much social, religious, and political information relating to ancient Maya society is taken from the iconography and hieroglyphic writing on Maya stelae. We now know when and where important battles, marriages, ball games, sacrificial rites, visitations, and funerals took place. Elite personages and events in their lives are frequently depicted on the carved surface of the stone and discussed in the written texts. Even important information on the Maya stelae themselves can be found in the texts: a stone stela was called *lakam tun* or "wide banner stone," they had sacred personal names, and were "planted" (*ts'apah*) or set up on certain days and for specific occasions. Many times offerings of **jade** and **ceramic** vessels were placed in front of or beneath the planted stone monument. Occasionally, Maya carvers and artists, especially near the **Usumacinta River** in Chiapas and Peten, put their names in smaller secondary texts on the stelae, or "signed" their works, which is quite unusual in the creation of art in the ancient world as a whole.

SWEAT BATH. Important for cleansing and ritual purification of the body and for healing and medicinal purposes, sweat baths were ubiquitous in ancient **Mesoamerica** and are still found in many indigenous communities today. Ancient sweat baths were small circular or rectangular structures with stone or mud-plastered wood walls and roofs. Sweat baths were tightly sealed and had narrow entrances that could be closed so that the hot vapors made from pouring water over heated stones in an attached chamber could not escape. Flues and dampers were installed to control the amount of heat and vapor, and low benches and seats were provided for the occupants taking a steam bath. Sweat baths have been identified at the archaeological sites of **Ceren,** and **Chichen Itza, Piedras Negras,** and **Tikal,** while sweat baths are painted in the **Codex Mendoza, Codex Nuttall,** and Codex Borgia from Postclassic Mexico.

Sweat baths, called *temascalli* in **Nahuatl** of the **Aztecs** ("temazcal" in Spanish) and *pibna* ("hot bath house") in Classic **Maya hieroglyphs,** were not only used for cleansing and invigorating the skin and body. They were important buildings for ritual gatherings, religious ceremonies, sexual encounters, and for healing sick persons who needed the curative "heat" put back into or maintained in their bodies. Human **sacrifice** was also carried out in these buildings. The sexual and procreative aspects of sweat baths were central in pre-Hispanic times where pregnant **women** and recent mothers with their infants were frequently bathed. Additionally, Maya hieroglyphic texts indicate that some **temples,** particularly at the Classic Period site of **Palenque,** were symbolic sweat baths where **deities** were said to have been born from ancestral goddesses and then subsequently worshiped in these structures.

SWIDDEN. *See* MILPA

T

TAJIN (EL). The ruins of El Tajin are found in the lush tropical hills near the Gulf Coast in Veracruz, Mexico. The majority of the monumental structures made of stone blocks at this beautiful site pertain to the Classic Veracruz culture (ca. A.D. 600–900), but the ethnic affinities of the population, like at ancient **Teotihuacan,** are unknown. Archaeologists continue to be divided as to whether the ruins were built by ancient **Huastec Maya** or the **Totonacs,** which were both ancestors of contemporary populations that live near El Tajin. At the ruins today these people sell crafts and perform *volador* or flying **dances** while swinging down from ropes attached to the tops of tall poles.

Contacts between the Maya, **Zapotecs,** Teotihuacan, and other Central Mexican peoples and the ancient population of El Tajin likely occurred at many times in the past. This is evident in the art style and material culture found at the site. **Trade** between these cultures is seen with the presence of exotic **ceramics,** ornaments, and **obsidians.** Ceramic figurines at the site show affinities with the **Remojadas** style. El Tajin is remarkable for its in-the-round and relief sculptures. Many of these three-dimensional freestanding stone **stelae** depict rulers, elites, or possibly **dieties.**

Additionally, a large number of **ball courts,** some of which have very long playing alleys, are also found at El Tajin. At least nine ball courts are present, but there could be more unidentified ones (most **Mesoamerican** cities had only one or two of these). It is not surprising then that much of the art and artifacts at this site relate to the ball game and rituals associated with it, including human **sacrifice.** Ceremonial carved stone ball game paraphernalia, such as waist yokes, hand stones, and ornaments, are common here. Also, stone sculpture depicts elites in game regalia and human sacrifice. One ball court relief shows ballplayers removing hearts from other players and a deity performing genital bloodletting for rain. The perpetuation of the cosmos and fertility were also important results of the game and the ensuing sacrifice and rituals.

Many structures continue to be excavated and restored by Mexican archaeologists at El Tajin. One of these, the 18 meter-high Pyramid of the Niches, contains a high staircase and what appear to be 365 niches that may be associated with ceremonies of the tropical year. However, the exact number of the niches and their use may never be known because of destruction and wall fall at this **temple** in antiquity. In palace-like structures at El Tajin, architects used columns and a one-of-a-kind cement made of sand, shell, and wood fragments in their construction. Many of the structures and ball courts at this site have been recently excavated, restored, and opened for tourists to visit.

TARASCANS. The Late Postclassic Tarascan kingdom (ca. A.D. 1350–1450) was centered in Michoacan (**Aztec** "place of the masters of fish" or "place of the fishers") near Lake Patzcuaro in **west Mexico** just west of the Aztec capital **Tenochtitlan.** The Aztecs never conquered these militaristic people and fine craftspersons who spoke a language unique to the area. Because of their distinct language, dress, social organization, and material culture, it has been hypothesized that the Tarascans were from western South America, or at least had been in extensive contact with South American cultures since Formative times.

Differing from other **Mesoamerican** civilizations, it appears that Tarascan society (who called themselves the "Purepecha") did not have formal **ball court** constructions, the 260-day ritual **calendar,** or a principal rain **deity.** Their style of architecture and building construction also differed from other Mesoamerican societies. With other Mesoamerican societies they shared a similar solar year calendar, human and self-**sacrifice,** stone **temples, tombs** of kings and elites, and religious specialists and **priests.** Among the principal deities of the Tarascan state were the creator earth goddess, the sun deity, and the moon goddess. Tarascan **metallurgy** was also one of the more advanced of this technology in ancient Mesoamerica since they produced many artifacts made from copper, in addition to **gold** and silver.

The Tarascan empire consisted of an urban capital (**Tzintzuntzan** at the time of the Spanish conquest) and many smaller dependent centers that were dispersed throughout a large territory. Although the Tarascans were often at war with the Aztecs, Tarascan goods and crafts, such as turquoise, smoking pipes, gold and silver ornaments, and worked **obsidian** (local volcanic glass), crossed the fortified frontier and were traded in Aztec **markets.** Tarascans even visited Aztec cities while participating in **trade** and ritual. But the Tarascans protected their lands and people from **warfare** with the Aztecs with fortified posts on hilltops along the eastern frontier with the Aztec empire.

Comparatively little archaeology has been conducted in the Tarascan zone despite the fact that the last capital of Tzintzuntzan and many other large ruins still stand. But much is known about this pre-Hispanic society because of the lengthly and highly descriptive colonial document called *Relación de Michoacán,* which was written by a Spanish priest who may have put down in writing portions of an indigenous document or oral histories. Information on Tarascan political organization, religious beliefs and gods, economic systems and trade, plus burial rites of the rulers (*kasonsi*) is contained within this important ethnohistoric source.

TAYASAL. When the Spanish arrived at the central lakes of **Peten, Guatemala,** in A.D. 1697 to conquer and subjugate the **Itza Maya** kingdom they encountered dense populations concentrated on a peninsula and on a nearby large island *Noh Peten* (now named "Flores") in Lake Peten Itza. The Spanish called the island fortress and adjacent populated peninsula shores "Tayasal" from the words *Tah Itza* ("of the Itza" or "place of the Itza") in Mayan. Excavations on the peninsula itself and the shoreline have shown that habitation of the area dates from the Formative to the Postclassic Periods, with a uniquely large occupation in Terminal Classic times. However, the island site of *Noh Peten* had a particularly dense population from the Postclassic Period to after the conquest.

Hernan Cortes and Spanish **conquistadores** happened upon the Tayasal island and nearby peninsula settlements in A.D. 1524, while marching south toward Honduras to punish a rebellious governor. They had a peaceful encounter with the Itza Maya, and Cortes described the numerous **temples** and residences at Tayasal in subsequent letters to the Spanish Crown. He also left the Itza his injured horse, which later died in their care, and this prompted them to keep the horse's bones and many carved stone horse effigies in their oratories. Contemporary inhabitants of Tayasal still recall legends of stone horses at the bottom of Lake Peten Itza.

Later, Spanish priests visited Tayasal and their ruler **Canek** to persuade them to submit to the Crown. When the Spanish returned to conquer them, the Itza built defensive works around the island and on their buildings to repel the foreign attackers who built ships to attack the city from the lake. Many Itza fled the confrontation and entered the forest to live with the **Cehach, Lacandon,** and other remote Maya groups. Today many Itza Maya settlements are found around Lake Peten Itza, but few of these indigenous people live near the island and peninsula of Tayasal.

Excavations on the island and adjacent peninsula at Tayasal have uncovered ceremonial structures, houses, human burials, stone **stelae** and painted **ceramics** with **hieroglyphic** writing, worked **jade** and shell, and worked stone artifacts made of **chert** and **obsidian.** Recent investigations and reconnaissance may have identified lakeside settlements that have defensive works that may have been used by the Spanish as bases while carrying out the conquest of the Itza at Tayasal. Work still continues in the area of Tayasal to learn more about the Itza Maya and how their settlements and culture changed both before and after the Spanish conquest.

TAZUMAL. *See* CHALCHUAPA

TECUM UMAN. An important personage in local histories and storytelling in the highlands of Guatemala. Tecum Uman was a valiant **Quiche Maya** war captain and grandson of a Quiche king. Tecum Uman is mostly known through stories of his defeat on the battlefield by Spanish **conquistadores** while defending his homeland. Tecum wore long green feathers on his arms and **mirrors** on his body, and it was said that he could fly to "see all around him."

This historical person has become a central culture hero figure for the people of Guatemala, especially the military, who invoke his courage, skill, and cunning as a warrior and leader. In A.D. 1524, Tecum and his army met the conquistador Pedro de Alvarado and his forces in the Quetzaltenango Valley (**Nahuatl** name given to the area of highland Guatemala by Alvarado's **Aztec** allied troops). The Quiche forces lost the battle and Tecum was slain by Alvarado. Native sources recount that when Tecum fell, a **quetzal** bird with long beautiful green plumage flew from the spot into the sky.

TEHUACAN. Some of the first evidence for wild and early cultivated **maize** in **Mesoamerica** was recovered from **cave** and rockshelter sites in the Tehuacan Valley in southeastern Puebla, Mexico. This region is more arid than central Mexico and the Gulf Coast found just to the east because of the surrounding **mountains** that trap clouds and humidity. Thus this valley presents a prime opportunity to study well-preserved sites and plant and animal remains to better understand the ancient Mesoamerican **diet.** Excavations over the last few decades have provided critical information on early plant cultivation, plant and animal collection, settled life, **ceramic-** and vessel-making technology, and social organization in Archaic and Formative Period Mesoamerica.

Small bands of hunters and gatherers lived in seasonal camps at Tehuacan from about 10,000 to 7000 B.C. This valley was cooler and drier in this period, and the people hunted antelope, wild horse, and rabbits in the grasslands on the valley floor. The climate became warmer from 7000 to 5000 B.C., and the inhabitants of Tehuacan turned to experimenting with plant cultivation (squash, amaranth, avocado, cotton, and chile peppers, among others) partially because of game die-offs. Grinding stones, including **manos and metates,** plus projectile points made of **chert** for hunting deer and small game, appear during this cultural phase. People remained living in seasonal camps, but they coalesced into larger bands at particular times, probably during hunts, rituals, or after the rainy season to exploit certain plants and their products.

Settlement patterns and culture remained essentially the same through the early periods of the chronological sequence up to 5000 to 3400 B.C. but with a significant difference in plant cultivation: for the first time we see the full domestication of maize with small cobs, gourds, beans, and squashes in the Tehuacan Valley. However, it appears as if these plants were domesticated elsewhere and earlier (7000–5000 B.C.?), perhaps in another zone in Puebla or Oaxaca, and then brought as fully developed cultigens into the valley. From 3400 to 1500 B.C., more permanent settlements appear for the first time in the valley. At this point in the cultural sequence, the first stone vessels appear, and then somewhat later the earliest ceramics are found in the archaeological record. Fired clay vessels probably were not invented here; the idea most likely originated with peoples who manufactured earlier ceramics in the Pacific Coast of Mesoamerica (**Barra** people in **Soconusco**) or from northern South America.

Occupation in the Tehuacan Valley continued into the Classic and Postclassic Periods, with populations contemporaneous with, in chronological order, **Teotihuacan, Toltec Tula,** and the **Aztec** empire. In fact, the Aztecs of central Mexico subjugated the area and exacted **tribute** from the local rulers of several settlements here. Recent excavations at the site of Tehuacan Viejo in a long, range-type palace structure revealed that the building may have housed decorated shields and **weapons** used in **warfare.** Murals depicting shields and central Mexican iconography were found on the plastered walls of this structure along with holes above each individual shield symbol, where presumably the weapons illustrated were hung on pegs. The shields contain war iconography and insignia of Aztec **deities.** The decorated shields on the murals may correspond to different deities, distinct warrior societies, or conquered towns, which paid tribute to the site's leaders.

TEMAZCAL. *See* SWEAT BATH

TEMPLE. A common structure in many ancient Mesoamerican societies from Formative to Postclassic times that was used for rituals and the storage of ceremonial items and religious images. Temples are typically placed on top of tall pyramidal substructures near large, central public **plazas,** noble's palaces, **market** places, and **ball courts. Altars** were often placed at the foot of the stairs to a temple, or at its summit, where offerings were received or **sacrifices** performed. Public rituals were frequently carried out in full view of the masses by the **priests,** who may also have lived in the temples. Temple constructions are often square or rectangular, but circular temples are seen at **Seibal,** Guatemala, **Cuicuilco,** and **Tula** in central Mexico, **Uxmal** in **Yucatan,** and in the sites of the **Teuchitlan** tradition in **west Mexico.**

In the **Maya** area, stone **stelae** and altars were placed on the ground in front of a temple. Additionally, **hieroglyphic** benches and carved stone tablets were set within temple superstructures. Oftentimes temples contained **tombs** of elites and caches of **ceramics** and exotic items, such as shell and **jade.** Some of the tallest Maya temples can be visited at **Calakmul, Caracol, Copan, Nakbe, Piedras Negras, Tikal,** and **Yaxchilan,** among others, and symbolic **sweat bath** temples are found at **Palenque.** Temples attained their height through successive constructions one on top of the other, but some temples were built in one massive building episode.

Some of the largest temples in all of **Mesoamerica,** and of the New World, are present at El **Mirador** in northern Guatemala and **Teotihuacan** and **Cholula** in central Mexico. As they are in most Mesoamerican archaeological sites, temples are also found at **Chalchuapa, Monte Alban, Quelepa,** La **Quemada,** El **Tajin, Tzintzuntzan,** and La **Venta,** and others. Excavations at the **Templo Mayor** in the **Aztec** capital of **Tenochtitlan** have uncovered the many phases of temple construction that was common in Mesoamerica and have recovered thousands of artifacts and sculptures associated with this monumental construction.

TEMPLO MAYOR. The main **temple** (*hueteocalli,* or "old god/sacred house" in **Nahuatl,** a language in ancient Mexico) at the **Aztec** capital city of **Tenochtitlan** on an island in Lake **Texcoco** in central Mexico. This temple was one of the largest ritual structures in use in **Mesoamerica** at the time of the Spanish conquest. The Templo Mayor was found near the heart of the Aztec imperial city, and it was the location for rituals and mass human **sacrifice** to the deities **Huitzilopochtli,** the war god, and **Tlaloc,** the rain **deity.**

The Aztecs used this pyramid as a lookout and redoubt during the conquest of Tenochtitlan by the Spanish **conquistadores,** and the city was taken by the Spanish when they captured and burned the Templo Mayor (also a sign of conquest and submission in ancient Mesoamerican **war-**

fare). Soon after the capture of Tenochtitlan, the Spanish dismantled the main temple to use the building materials, particularly the stone blocks, in the construction of the large cathedral in the center of the city. Recent subway expansion, road and housing projects, and archaeological excavations have uncovered the long construction sequence and the several different building phases of the Templo Mayor that date to the Postclassic Period. Some of the architectural features have been restored, and artifacts from the temple have been housed in a local museum for preservation and viewing.

The Aztec Templo Mayor was a symbolic representation of the center of the Aztec empire and cosmos. The tall structure was the place of ritual communication between the Aztecs and supernatural beings and ancestors in the **underworld** and heavens. This imposing building also demonstrated to all the power and prestige of the Aztecs. Not only did it take years to build and could it be seen from kilometers around, but it was the setting for mass human sacrifices and ceremonies for the public. Human blood coated the stairs and terraces of the structure and the walls and floors of the temples on its summit.

The Templo Mayor was topped with twin temples: one on the left dedicated to Tlaloc (rain) and the one on the right to Huitzilopochtli (war). The structure for the rain deity was painted in blue, and it contained statues and imagery depicting the deity and the watery underworld. Excavations at the base of the temple revealed cache boxes, some of which contained offerings to Tlaloc; these offerings reflect their connections with water and the underworld: **jade,** sea shells (including the **spondylus** variety), coral, crocodile skeletons, Tlaloc effigy **ceramics,** and fish carvings. The temple of the Aztec patron god of war, Huitzilopochtli, was decorated in red paint, and it held images of this deity, the sun, and human skeletons with skulls adorning the roof.

The construction of the Templo Mayor also mirrored Aztec mythology and religious beliefs. Like other monumental architecture in ancient Mesoamerica, this temple was a metaphorical **mountain** where ancestors and deities lived or came from. In this case the mountain was that of Coatepec (Coatepetl), or Hill of the Serpent. According to Aztec **religion, Coatlique,** the mother of Huitzilopochtli (the Aztec patron deity), resided and kept her temples here. When her daughter and older sister of Huitzilopochtli, **Coyolxauhqui,** threatened to kill her and then wounded her, Huitzilopochtli was miraculously born with **weapons** and the fire serpent to protect his mother. Huitzilopochtli slayed and dismembered his malevolent sister and sent her tumbling down the mountain.

This story is symbolized in the construction of the Templo Mayor: the height of the structure symbolizes the Coatepetl mountain, Huitzilopochtli's temple and his images rested at the top of the mountain, serpent or *coatl* balustrades flanked the central stairway, and a large round carved stone **altar** depicting the dismembered sister (the Coyolxauhqui Stone) was placed at the foot of the pyramid. A giant statue of the mother Coatlique, a figure with claws as feet and serpents for her head, arms, and skirt, was also found near the Spanish colonial cathedral after it was probably toppled and dragged away from this pyramid. The doorways of this temple, plus the large stone cache boxes inside the building fill, may also have been thought of as symbolic **caves**.

TENOCHTITLAN (Tay-noch-tee-**tlan**). The majestic capital of the **Aztec** empire at the time of the Spanish conquest in the early 16th century was Tenochtitlan, which was located on a large island in Lake **Texcoco** (Tetzcoco) in the **Basin of Mexico.** This is one of the largest cities in Pre-Columbian **Mesoamerica** and even in the world at the time; the city was home to nearly half a million people at its height (see photo). The Spanish **conquistadores** were astounded upon first viewing Tenochtitlan from afar while standing on surrounding **mountains,** and they felt that the sight in front of them was a vision from a dream or like a mythical, romantic place from contemporary explorers' accounts. The Spaniards described how they were impressed by the gleaming white buildings, towering **temples,** beautiful palaces, road systems, dense populations, numerous canoes, and the bustle of the city.

Tenochtitlan was founded in the early 14th century (around A.D. 1325–50) by the wandering Aztecs, or Mexica, who were trying to establish themselves politically and economically in central Mexico. After being expelled from their initial settlements by local rivals, the Aztecs came upon the large island in Lake Texcoco where they witnessed the sign foretold by **priests** indicating the place of their future city. This prophecy spoke of an eagle standing on a nopal cactus, which would mark the destined location of the Aztec capital. In fact the emblem for Tenochtitlan, which appears in Postclassic Mexican **codices,** or books, and for the modern Mexican flag is a shield and darts symbol under an eagle perched on a cactus growing out of a rock. The shield and darts are symbols of **warfare,** and they refer to the military prowess and conquests of the Aztecs. The inclusion of the rock sign in the place name probably refers to the island. In fact, the word *Tenochtitlan* in **Nahuatl** can be glossed as "the place of (or at) the rock and cactus." The Aztecs subsequently leveled off parts of the island and reclaimed lands from its shores and swamps to build the seat of their eventual empire, which would later extend to many parts of ancient Mesoamerica.

During its florescence, the city of Tenochtitlan incorporated its sister settlement, Tlatelolco, located on the north end of the island. Tlatelolco had a major **market** compound, many residences and palaces, and a minor ceremonial precinct for the Aztecs. The very center of the island and city of Tenochtitlan was the locus of the major ritual center, the palaces and buildings of the ruling elite, and a smaller market. In the core of Tenochtitlan rested the grand **Templo Mayor,** with its steep staircase and surmounting temples dedicated to the Aztec patron **deity Huitzilopochtli** and **Tlaloc** the rain god, a **ball court,** a **tzompantli** ("skull rack" for heads of **sacrificed** people), large **plazas,** a zoo, a round temple to **Quetzalcoatl,** and other minor temples and shrines. Streets ran through the city, canals for water and canoe traffic crisscrossed the island, residences and gardens were placed on all available ground, and three large elevated causeways connected Tenochtitlan with the mainland to the north, south, and west. To the east of the island was a canoe landing and off the eastern shore was a dike system designed by the great Tetzcoco king **Netzahualcoyotl** to control flooding and to retain more fresh water.

The Spanish conquistadores under Hernan Cortes and their indigenous allies occupied Tenochtitlan in 1521 after months of siege warfare and with help from the effects of disease and starvation. This location was to remain a major political and economic center for the Spanish in the New World. The temples of Tenochtitlan were razed, and the rubble was used to bury Aztec constructions and to build an impressive cathedral, which still stands at the heart of Mexico City. During recent urban construction projects, parts of the ancient Aztec city have been exposed in the rubble and fill along with Aztec stone sculptures, such as the **Coatlique** and **Coyolxauhqui** stones. Much of the remains of Tenochtitlan are still covered by the concrete and buildings of Mexico City, but some sections of exposed buildings and a museum of Aztec artifacts can be viewed today.

TEOTIHUACAN (Tay-oh-tee-uh-wah-**kahn**). This ancient metropolis, located near Mexico City in the **Basin of Mexico,** is one of the largest Pre-Columbian cities in **Mesoamerica** and has some of the most massive **temples** in the New World. Although the cultural florescence at this site dates to the Early Classic Period (A.D. 400–600), monumental construction and artworks began during the Late Formative Period (ca. 150 B.C. to A.D. 100). Teotihuacan (**Nahuatl** for "City of the Gods" in **Aztec** myth) is the center of another early archaeological "horizon" (**Olmec** is another and an earlier horizon) in Mesoamerica; similar artifacts and architectural styles are found throughout Mesoamerica in the Classic Period. This attests to the political and economic power of this huge city and its importance in regional social and **trade** networks.

Information from ancient Maya **hieroglyphic** texts suggests that Teotihuacan (or the Maya *Puh*) was an ancient **Tollan,** or "place of the reeds," which was a city and ancient people central to the royal histories of later **Toltec, Maya,** Aztec, and other Mesoamerican peoples. Clearly, Teotihuacan was involved in direct rule of and/or extensive influence on local and distant peoples alike. Recent interpretations of Maya written texts and the presence of Teotihuacan material culture suggest that people from Teotihuacan took power at important Maya centers during the Early Classic Period. However, although we now know more about the history of this city, the ethnic identity and language of its inhabitants are unknown. But its location in central Mexico and some iconographic clues on murals suggest that they may have been **Nahuas.** Despite its political might and regional significance, the city fell to possibly attackers, class conflict, and/or environmental degradation in Late Classic times.

The diagnostic architectural style of this culture is known as *talud-tablero*, which consists of outer building terraces with lower sloping walls and vertical upper faces on top of them. Large residences at Teotihuacan have carved stone pillars and brilliant polychrome wall murals that portray **deities** and supernatural places. One structure, the Temple of **Quetzalcoatl** (feathered serpent), has a sculptural facade of saurian creatures issuing forth from **mirrors.** This temple also contained many skeletons of sacrificial victims who archaeologists found buried in their finery and with their arms bound behind their backs. This temple is found in the "Citadel Compound," which is a separate, enclosed rectangular structural complex that may have been an elite palace compound and not a **market** place or fortress as initially hypothesized.

This site is also known for its stone burial masks, Thin Orange pottery, cylindrical tripod **ceramic** vessels with carved designs and painted stucco, elaborate ceramic incense burners of human figures and headdresses, and a large-scale **obsidian** manufacturing industry. Major themes in the iconography include the goggle-eyed **Tlaloc** deity, the feathered serpent, and the creator and fertility goddess called the "Spider Woman," who may have been a central figure in the pantheon. Also shown are supernatural **jaguars** and birds, and **priests** and warriors adorned with feather headdresses, **textiles,** and **jade** ornaments. Evidence from the art is used to argue for a more corporate and priestly elite rather than charismatic individual rulers as leaders of the Teotihuacan state.

This urban center covered at least eight square kilometers and held approximately 150,000–200,000 people at its height. The impressive Pyramids of the Sun and Moon, which have been restored, are framed by **mountains** surrounding the Valley of Mexico. In fact, these immense buildings were probably viewed by Teotihuacan's inhabitants as being symbolic mountains themselves. The Pyramid of the Sun is one of the largest structures in the New World and was probably built in the talud-tablero style, but it may have been incorrectly restored. It measures about 215 meters long and 60 meters high. A **cave** was discovered under the center of this pyramid and this feature may be symbolic of the cave of creation from the mythology of later Nahua peoples. The Pyramid of the Moon is the second largest temple at the site, but it is still one of the largest constructions in the New World. A **tomb** containing the bones of possibly a sacrificial victim and artifacts of shell, greenstone figures, and obsidian blades was recently discovered.

City constructions were also planned around a grid system, neighborhoods, caves, and astronomical alignments. The Street of the Dead acts as a central north-south axis of the grid systems and was a major thoroughfare of the city; it is flanked by small temples and the Pyramid of the Sun, and it meets the Pyramid of the Moon to the North. The Street, or Way, of the Dead may have received its name from the large number of mummy bundles of dead ancestors that may have been placed in the structures along this central avenue. Recent interpretations of Teotihuacan sculpture and mural art indicate that pole ceremonies—rituals, **dance, sacrifice,** and the displaying of ancestors on wooden poles—may have taken place at this city.

Residential wards at the site are large apartment compounds that have vertical exterior facades at streets and alleyways and open interior patios. Burials, food preparation areas, and living quarters are found within the residential structures. Evidence for Maya and **Zapotec** wards, plus areas of craft specialization, has been recovered by archaeologists. Conversely, the presence of Teotihuacan people is also detected at several distant Mesoamerican sites with the presence of green obsidian, thin orange ceramics, talud-tablero architecture, and artworks. The roles of Teotihuacan people abroad may have been that of merchants and members of ruling dynasties. **West Mexico,** Oaxaca, Veracruz, and the Maya area particularly have higher percentages of Teotihuacan-derived architecture, sculpture, and artifacts. Exciting research on the archaeology and iconography of this great culture continues today, which promises important discoveries and contributions to Mesoamerican prehistory.

TEPANECS. *See* AZTECS and NAHUA

TETZCOCO. *See* TEXCOCO

TEUCHITLAN. This is a regional architectural tradition of **west Mexico** that is very unique in **Mesoamerica.** The Teuchitlan tradition dates from the late Formative to the Classic Periods (A.D. 200–700). This culture area has received close attention by archaeologists in recent years. Monumental architecture of the Teuchitlan tradition and culture is seen at many centers in the highlands of Jalisco and Nayarit, while smaller structure complexes are also located in neighboring Colima, Michoacan, Guanajuato, and Zacatecas. This region is famous for its **ceramic** figurine art, which celebrates ancestors, rulers, warriors, plants and animals of the natural world, human **sacrifice** and burial, and ancient ceremonies.

Fortifications and outlying settlements along the edges of the Teuchitlan Valley in central Jalisco allude to more complex central administrative and territorial polities with demarcated boundaries rather than a loosely organized, hegemonic sociopolitical structure. The larger centers supported many thousands of people, and intensive **chinampa,** or raised field, agriculture near lakeshores was employed to help sustain this population. Only further settlement surveys and excavations at these little-known centers will provide insights on ancient population densities and sociopolitical organization.

Large Teuchitlan sites have the very distinctive circular groupings of structures that are indigenous to this region. In the center rests an impressive terraced conical building or **temple** that is encircled by smaller square structures arranged around a circular **plaza.** Often there are concentric zones of these structure groupings around a principal circular complex, which suggests that there were cultural grammars of space and its use, plus notions of ritual and social importance at the "center." These circular compounds may be patterned according to west Mexican cosmologies, views of the cosmos, or they may be large symbolic representations of sectioned **maize** cobs. Many of these complexes may even overlap, and they often contain **ball courts** wedged between them.

The larger complexes were ceremonial in function, while the smaller ones were for domestic use. Moreover, these circular complexes were recreated in ceramic figurine, diorama-like models where people were shown gathered around the central round structure and in the surrounding buildings participating in ritual, music and **dance,** the ball game, **warfare,** or domestic activities. The architectural complexes often contain shaft entrance **tombs** that were stocked with many of these pottery figurines, ceramic vessels, marine conch shells, artifacts made from **spondylus** shells, **obsidian** points and blades, plus other artifacts. Only a few shaft tombs have been scientifically excavated by archaeologists. The vast majority have been despoiled by looters seeking treasures for the illegal art market.

The circular patios of the Teuchitlan tradition additionally may have been used by *voladores,* or "flying men," swinging down from a pole in a circular motion. This ritual may also be depicted on West Mexican ceramic figurines. This pole ceremony may have symbolized the ancestors' rise to the sky and heavens, whereas the tombs below the plazas and residences were located in the **underworld.** Obsidian artifact workshops are also located near these ceremonial and domestic complexes, which may have been distribution centers for these products. It is intriguing that the abandonment of the Teuchitlan centers coincides with the downfall of other polities throughout Mesoamerica during Late to Terminal Classic times.

TEXCOCO. The Spanish corruption of the central Mexican indigenous place name Tetzcoco that was adopted in colonial times. This is the **Nahuatl** name for the capital of the Acolhua people and the large lake in the central **Basin of Mexico** where **Tenochtitlan,** the **Aztec** island capital, was located. The capital city of Tetzcoco was found on the western shore of Lake Tetzcoco. Here the Acolhua, a group of **Nahua**-speaking people, were settled when the Mexica-Aztecs entered the Valley of Mexico in early Postclassic times.

Tetzcoco eventually became one of the main centers in the Triple Alliance that gave the Aztec empire its political and military strength (along with the city of Tlacopan/Tacuba). Tetzcoco joined Tenochtitlan in overthrowing the Tepanecs to become the primary power in Postclassic Mexico. These centers expanded out of the Basin of Mexico and divided up the **tribute** gained in military conquests. A famous ruler of Tetzcoco who was instrumental in the taking of power in Mexico and expanding into other lands was **Netzahualcoyotl,** the man who also implemented a "legalist system" with state laws and punishments and helped design aquatic control systems near Tenochtitlan. When the Spanish and their **Tlaxcalan** allies returned to sack Tenochtitlan during the conquest, Tetzcoco sensed the impending doom for the Aztec capital and joined the **conquistadores** against their old allies and overlords.

TEXTILES. Textiles were, and continuously are today, widely produced throughout **Mesoamerica.** Textiles were made from native cotton, agave or **maguey** fibers, and certain tree barks, and they were colored with natural dyes and pigments (see photo). Ancient textiles made of cotton thread were often brocaded where the designs and geometric shapes were woven directly into the fabric. Textiles were made usually by **women** on backstrap looms, and this activity is shown in **ceramic** figurines and painted **codices,** or indigenous books. Archaeological evidence for textile production is witnessed by ceramic or stone spindle whorls, which were used to make spun thread. Textile patterns are also seen on ceramic vessels, carved stone sculptures, painted murals, and in ornamental building facades, like at **Mitla** in Oaxaca or **Uxmal** in **Yucatan.**

Textiles were important **tribute** items paid to Mesoamerican rulers, as seen in historic records and the **Codex Mendoza.** Textiles and clothing styles were also important symbols of cultural identity, social status, and personal roles in society. For instance, in **Aztec** society, elites wore finely embroidered capes, high status warriors wore suits of **jaguar** skin and brightly colored textiles, **priests** wore long white or light-colored robes, and commoners wore white loincloths. In Classic **Maya** art, women wore long and elaborately woven blouses and skirts, and men wore plain or embroidered loincloths and capes. The different Maya groups and the pueblos that they are from today can even be distinguished by the colors and patterns in their textiles and clothing. Textiles are still central to Mesoamerican economies and cultural survival.

TEZCATLIPOCA. An ancient **deity** of central Mexico whose name means "smoking **mirror**" in **Nahuatl,** the language of the **Aztecs.** This deity is depicted with a mirror as a foot (or on the head) in central Mexican **codices,** and mirrors were powerful tools of shamans, **priests,** and rulers. Tezcatlipoca was a patron deity of religious specialists and rulers. In this respect, this entity is similar to *K'awil,* the ancient **Maya** deity of rulership who has a smoking mirror placed in his forehead. The deity is also often characterized as an "all powerful" entity that was connected to one's destiny and fate.

In Aztec myth Tezcatlipoca is in eternal conflict with **Quetzalcoatl,** the feathered serpent deity. They battle each other over the dominion of the earth and heavens, and it was Tezcatlipoca that tricked Quetzalcoatl into incest with his sister and then forced him to leave **Tula,** according to ancient **Mesoamerican** myth. Tezcatlipoca is also associated with **jaguars,** and, according to legends, he was transformed into a jaguar by Quetzalcoatl.

TIKAL. Tikal is one of the largest and most important of all the Classic **Maya** sites (see photo). This ancient city is located in the jungles of the Department of **Peten** in the lowlands of northern Guatemala. The site is over six square kilometers in size with thousands of structures mapped, but the settlement actually continues into the unexplored hinterlands. Tikal probably had 50,000 to 120,000 occupants at its peak, and its rulers controlled an extensive territory around the site core.

Tikal also has some of the tallest structures in the Maya area, and many of these towering **temples,** plus long palace-like buildings and residences, are well preserved, considering their antiquity and the somewhat harsh and destructive environment. Much is known about this ancient Maya site because of extensive archaeological investigations since the 1960s and following decipherments of local **hieroglyphic** texts from stone monuments, standing **stelae,** buildings, carved bones, and painted **ceramics.** Tikal and its ruling elites are also mentioned in inscriptions from other Maya sites, which attests to its political importance and influence. Archaeology continues at Tikal today, and the reconstructed buildings and the natural surroundings attract thousands of tourists each year.

Tikal is found on low ridges in an area of elevated terrain, which keeps the city raised from nearby swampy areas and **bajos.** These low areas could have been used for collecting water, for agriculture, as **chinampas,** or raised fields, and for hunting and collecting certain plant products. There are no permanent water sources such as rivers or lakes near the site, even though it is only found about 40 kilometers north of the Central Lakes District and **Tayasal,** the capital of the **Itza** Maya that was conquered in colonial times. However, several large artificial water catchments are scattered throughout the site, which attest to the abilities of the Maya elite in organizing corvee labor, the control of a valuable resource, and their monopoly of water for politics and ritual.

Tikal is situated near prime agricultural land in this region, and its central position in the lowlands would have been important for **trade** and interaction with other Maya sites in Classic times. This site was occupied since Middle Formative (Preclassic) times (ca. 800 B.C.) with a small population up until the Postclassic era (ca. A.D. 1200) that had scattered remnant occupants in only a few structures. The archaeological, hieroglyphic, and iconographic data show that Tikal was at its height during Early Classic to Late Classic times (ca. A.D. 400–800), to which most of the monumental art and architecture dates.

Extensive mapping and excavations at Tikal have unveiled this Maya metropolis and its long intriguing history. Some of the largest temple structures have been cleared of vegetation and substructure terraces, central stairways, and their superstructure temple rooms and stone roof ornaments have been dug and restored. All that is missing are the plaster masks and iconography, the stucco finish, and the red paint covering on the buildings.

One of the most spectacular buildings at Tikal is Temple I (the so-called Temple of the **Jaguar**), which is located at the main ceremonial **plaza** at the site. Temple II, which is similar in construction to Temple I, is found on the west end of the plaza in front of Temple I, and these buildings are flanked by large constructions that delimit the main plaza. The main plaza also contains rows of carved stelae, or standing carved monuments, that record the local dynasty's history and important events. A small **ball court** lies just to the south of the grand Temple I.

Temple I rises some 50 meters above the plaza floor, and it is built of stone masonry and carved wooden lintels of dense chicozapote wood, which are still preserved. This building also has a tall central staircase leading up to the temple superstructure, but what is actually best preserved is the stairway used for the building's construction and not the more gently sloped, wider steps used by the Maya to reach the temple. The carved lintels depict and contain the glyphic name of an important ruler, "Hasaw" (Ruler A), who may be the person shown sitting on a throne on the roof comb over the temple door.

Temple I was designed to be a funerary monument: it is basically a single phase construction, it contains nine terraces representing the levels of the Maya **underworld,** and a rich **tomb** (Burial #116) was discovered within the temple at its base. The large burial chamber contained the skeleton of an adult male, large quantities of carved **jade** beads, finely painted ceramic vessels, **spondylus** shells, and intricately carved animal bones. The texts on these bones mention that they are owned by Hasaw, the occupant of the tomb.

The North and South Acropolises, which flank Temples I and II on the main plaza, were largely excavated and restored in the 1960s-70s. Here are many palace structures and elite residences and temples where layers of construction were discovered to date back to Late Formative times (ca. 200 B.C. to A.D. 300). In these structures, like most in the Maya area, building upon building was placed one over the other as the structures grew taller and more massive. Additionally, many human burials were uncovered, some of them being rich graves with jade bead necklaces and painted polychrome pottery.

Some of these burials are believed to be of the ruling elite class, and of some Maya kings and queens. However, the positive identification of these burials with known historical personages from the carved monuments is hampered because of the absence of corroborating hieroglyphic texts in the burials that name the occupants. Also found in earlier constructions were hieroglyphic stone monuments and caches of ceramics, jade, shell, and **obsidian** that were ritually interred.

Other tall temple constructions at the site core include Temples II, III, IV, V, and the "Lost World" (*Mundo Perdido*) pyramids, which are found near Temple I. These buildings are also constructed of stone masonry, and the majority are topped with temple superstructures and high roof combs with sculptured ornamentation. Recent studies indicate that there are some significant alignments among the monumental buildings at Tikal. For instance, viewing the high roof comb of Temple III from Temple I marks the position of the sunset on the spring and fall equinoxes, and the sighting of the roof of Temple III from Temple IV coincides with the winter solstice sunrise. Alignments with heavenly bodies, such as the sun and **Venus,** and geographic features, such as **caves** and hills, seem prevalent at Maya cities, and this demonstrates that the builders and elites strove to make their constructions part of nature and the cosmos.

The monumental temples of Tikal have ornately carved wooden lintels that are well preserved and some of the most unusual and exquisite examples of Maya art. The lintels contain portraits of Tikal kings and accompanying hieroglyphic texts that speak of their exploits. In this select iconography, the rulers sit on thrones decorated with ornaments, woven mats, and jaguar skins, while they are depicted in their richest finery of jade beads, **textiles,** jewels, staffs of office, and mosaic jade and shell headdresses capped with **quetzal** feathers. Most of these impressive temple constructions have not been completely excavated, but it is likely that they too contain richly stocked tombs of the ruling nobles.

Some of the most recent archaeological investigations have taken place in the Mundo Perdido, or "Lost World," complex near the main plaza at Tikal. The monumental constructions in this area are earlier than those on the main plaza since the Mundo Perdido buildings date from the Late Preclassic to the Early Classic (ca. 200 B.C. to A.D. 500). One of the largest pyramids at Tikal is found here, which dates to Late

Preclassic times and exhibits large stucco masks on its sides, but no masonry temple superstructure. Other large buildings here have talud-tablero architecture reminiscent of structures at Early Classic **Teotihuacan** in Central Mexico. The excavations in the area of Mundo Perdido have uncovered a vertical stone marker carved in Teotihuacan style and with early Maya hieroglyphs, a headless seated statue of stone carved in the full round (the "Man of Tikal") with early hieroglyphs on its back, buried mural paintings, and several rich burials and earlier monumental constructions.

The extensive layout of the ancient city of Tikal has many interesting architectural compounds and features and residential groups that will provide archaeologists with important research and findings for years to come. For example, a possible **market,** storage area, or palace complex is found just to the east of the main plaza. Several architectural complexes with impressive buildings and hieroglyphic monuments are scattered throughout the site, and some are connected by wide raised roads, or **sacbeob,** to the main plaza and other monumental constructions. These complexes have palaces, temples, and burials of the Tikal Maya elites. There are also Twin Pyramid groups that may have been used in special elite rituals or for marking the passage of the sun and stars. High-quality artifacts, including carved jade and shell, painted, stucco-covered wooden statuettes, hieroglyphic pottery, and stone sculpture have been recovered from these noble compounds.

The vast settlement area at Tikal remains relatively unexplored. The residential compounds have been mapped, and only a few have been excavated. These small structures of the Maya farmers, craftspersons, and laborers were typically built of stone and earth platforms that were topped with a pole and thatch superstructure. Burials of the occupants are found within these earthen domestic platforms, and these interments typically contain ceramic vessels and not the rich artifacts of the elite. Also, evidence of craft and artifact making, such as **chert** tools and shell ornaments, were found in the artifactual assemblages of the Tikal residences. In the periphery of Tikal, a long shallow moat and wall system about three kilometers to the north and south of the site that was built during the Early Classic Period was discovered during mapping operations. This extensive, peripheral construction that connects to the adjacent low, swampy areas may not have been a defensive wall but a boundary marker because of its large size. However, it could have been manned and maintained by the large residential population, and used to control foot traffic or as an early protection and warning system from outside invaders.

Perhaps some of the most interesting information on the history and ruling dynasty at Tikal comes from the hieroglyphic texts at this site and other contemporary Maya sites. Tikal's emblem glyph and place name show tied hair (*Mutul*). From the dates on monuments, a local king list and historical events have been worked out. One Early Classic ruler named "Jaguar Paw Skull" by epigraphers is mentioned on many early stone monuments at Tikal. In a stone lintel text at **Yaxchilan** in Chiapas, Mexico, this Tikal ruler is said to have sent a subordinate to visit the king of this distant site. Another early ruler, "Stormy Sky," commemorated inscriptions that documented his parentage, events in his life, and rituals that he performed. The iconography of his monuments and his dress and that of his father ("Curl Nose") point to a close interaction with Teotihuacan people. A noble associate of "Stormy Sky" named "Smoking Frog" may have been a subordinate and an eventual ruler of the nearby site of Uaxactun. However, Curl Nose and Smoking Frog may have been Teotihuacan elites who became foreign lords at Tikal, according to more recent epigraphic interpretations.

Going by the hieroglyphic texts, **warfare** may have taken place between Tikal and Uaxactun in the Early Classic, and a "hiatus" in monument- and temple-making at Tikal during the Middle Classic Period appears to be the result of the defeat of Tikal in battle by the elite of **Caracol** in Belize. A Late Classic Tikal ruler, "Shield Skull," was also defeated in combat by Ruler 1 of **Dos Pilas** and a **Calakmul** ally. We also know that the Late Classic Ruler A ("Hasaw") waged successful military campaigns against the sites of Calakmul and Yaxha and subsequently implemented a major building campaign at Tikal. Additionally, the inscriptions state that Ruler A was the father of Ruler B, who probably was responsible for the construction of the largest temple at Tikal, Temple IV, which may be his tomb. Some of the latest stone **stelae** in the Maya lowlands with a cycle 10 baktun **calendar** date of the Terminal Classic are found at Tikal and at other nearby sites. Tikal was eventually abandoned in Terminal Classic times possibly because of military conflict and the fragmentation of the Tikal polity and the dispersal of its population.

TIPU. A Late Postclassic to early Colonial Period site in Western Belize near the border with Guatemala. Tipu was a small settlement of Yucatec **Maya** who had constructed a few small platforms and houses. Later, it was transformed into a colonial town and mission by the Spanish living in **Yucatan.** Colonial Tipu was located on the frontier of the Spanish colonial world, and the independent Maya kingdoms of the **Itza, Cehach,** and **Lacandon** were dispersed in the vast rainforest wilderness to the west.

A small church was built by the Spanish at Tipu, and they used the site to house and convert subjugated Maya. This town was also in a strategic location for contacting, converting, or trading with the distant unconquered Maya groups. A large quantity of burials was excavated in the floor of the church, and these provide interesting evidence for the examination of religious syncretism, changing burial practices, **diet,** and disease. Traditional stone tool technology was still important to the Tipu Maya during colonial times; **chert** tools and projectile points are commonly found. Also, Maya **ceramic** vessels were still commonly used, and some modeled effigy ceramics were associated with the construction and use of the church. This is convincing evidence of the continuation of non-Christian beliefs and ancient Maya religious practices and **deity** worship.

Tipu was eventually abandoned after a series of raids by unconquered Mayas, epidemic diseases, relocation of the inhabitants, and through flight into the wilderness by some of the occupants. Some of these refugees may have joined Lacandon populations found to the west in **Peten,** Guatemala, and Chiapas, Mexico. A similar settlement and Spanish mission center was located at nearby Lamani in Belize and is currently being excavated.

TLALOC. Nahuatl term for the rain **deity** of the **Aztecs** and other central Mexican Pre-Columbian cultures from the Classic to the Postclassic Periods. This god is recognized by his round goggle-like eyes, fangs, pointed teeth, and blue paint or clothing. Many times the deity pours water from the hands or **ceramic** vases that are held, and Tlaloc often carries bolts of lightning. Tlaloc lived in the sky, clouds, on tops of **mountains,** in **caves** with water, and in a water paradise where drowning victims and sacrificed people were destined to arrive. The deity arose from mountain peaks in the midst of cloud cover and storms and poured water from the sky to replenish the supply on earth for plant and human use.

The Aztecs and other Mesoamerican peoples provided many offerings to Tlaloc during rituals, especially human **sacrifices** and children drowned during the rites, on the onset of the rainy season and during droughts. Tlaloc may also be associated with the coming of meteor showers after the beginning of the rainy season in June/July in Mesoamerican societies. Tlaloc iconography is found all over **Mesoamerica** with early examples found in the Early Classic **Teotihuacan** culture of central Mexico and the Classic **Maya**.

At Teotihuacan, Tlaloc imagery appears abundantly in polychrome murals and also on ceramic incense burners, **ceramic** vessels and figurines, sculpture, and on marine shells. In the Maya area, the deity Tlaloc generally is depicted on carved stone monuments and on painted pottery, and there appears to be a **hieroglyph** naming this deity. Additional examples from contemporaneous cultures can be found in sculpture and ceramics at **Matacapan,** painted ceramics at **Kaminaljuyu,** and on incense burners and ceramics in the **Soconusco** region of southern Chiapas and Guatemala. Classic to Terminal Classic Period Tlaloc art is represented in the Maya area, at **Xochicalco, El Tajin** in Veracruz, and the **Cotzumalhuapa**-related cultures of southern Guatemala and western El Salvador.

Besides rain and storms, Tlaloc was also associated with **warfare.** Classic Maya rulers are often depicted wearing Tlaloc masks or headdresses during times of war. The usage of Tlaloc paraphernalia among the Maya may be related to the concept of "butterfly warriors" among the Aztecs. The face of Tlaloc resembles a butterfly or the head of an insect. The souls of dead Aztec warriors were thought to be butterflies fluttering to the overworld, since butterflies covered bloody bodies on the battlefield. The hieroglyph for this deity appears in Classic Maya texts following the verb for "to possess" or "hold/possess in a basket or bowl," which probably refers to the presentation of a Tlaloc mask or other ritual objects that are held. In the Maya texts this object is post-fixed with the syllable *ta,* suggesting that this deity or object ended in a *t* or *ta* in a Mayan language.

The Aztecs performed ceremonies and sacrifices to Tlaloc on **Mount Tlaloc** in the **Basin of Mexico** and in the temple of Tlaloc on the summit of the **Templo Mayor** at the capital of **Tenochtitlan.** With the Aztecs, Tlaloc is commonly depicted on blue painted ceramic vessels and stone sculpture. Depictions of Tlaloc on stone sculpture of other Postclassic societies can be seen with the **Toltecs** of **Tula,** other central Mexican cultures, the **Pipil** states of eastern Guatemala and western El Salvador, and with the **Mixtec** of Oaxaca. *See also* CHAC

TLATILCO. This is an interesting Formative-era archaeological site that was stumbled upon by workers making bricks near Mexico City. Most of the cultural features recovered by excavators at Tlatilco were human burials with rich grave goods. However, a few storage pits, trash deposits, and fragments of mud and pole houses were also encountered in the relatively limited excavations at the site. The materials from Tlatilco date to the

Early and Middle Formative Periods, and the **ceramic** types found demonstrate ties with the Gulf Coast **Olmec,** Formative Period **Copan,** and the early **Colima** culture in **west Mexico.** Unfortunately, Tlatilco was excavated over 50 years ago, and we can no longer excavate the site, because it was destroyed and covered by the expanding Mexican capital.

Approximately 350 interments have been dug at this site, and many earlier Olmec-period burials were mixed with somewhat later deposits. Nonetheless, most of the material culture and burials date to the early part of the Formative Period (ca. 1500–1200 B.C.), when sedentary life was becoming the norm and **Mesoamerican** civilization was blooming. Diagnostic artifacts of the Early Formative at Tlatilco include Olmec-style ceramics and figurines, flat-bottomed dishes, long-necked bottles, and stirrup-spout jars, which demonstrate contacts with early west Mexican societies.

Also, a great variety of effigy jars and other ceramics in the form of ducks, fish, peccaries, turtles, and other zoomorphs date to this time. The large and small ceramic figurines at Tlatilco are a fascinating mix of human forms: **women** holding children or animals, elite persons, possible players of the ball game, **dancers,** and religious specialists. These figurines depict rich adornments and clothing. Some figurines show ugly and deformed people. Still others illustrate dualism with figures with two heads and bodies, plus faces that are halved with two different expressions (possibly good and evil, for example).

Judging by the sheer number of recovered human burials in a small portion of the site, Tlatilco was probably a rather large Early Formative town. Conversely, this site may have been a cemetery or sacred burial site, such as seen at Copan, **San Jose Mogote,** and the **Cuyamel cave** Formative burial sites, where people from the surrounding area were brought for interment. The Tlatilco site and ceramics resemble early remains in South America, and these may be a legacy of earlier but indirect contact bridging cultures between the two continents and culture areas.

TLATOANI. The title of "tlatoani" was reserved for **Aztec** rulers or kings before the conquest of Mexico. The **Nahuatl** word *tlatoani* is glossed as "he who speaks." Tlatoani was a prestigious political title for the Aztec rulers since public speaking and eloquent oration were important skills and gifted talents of the noble person. Also, this title shows that the ruler "spoke" and the people and his followers "listened."

The Aztec tlatoani was the chief political officer of the state and in many cases the religious one as well. Upon the death of an Aztec ruler, the succeeding tlatoani was chosen by a council of nobles from a pool of legitimate candidates who consisted of close male relatives of the deceased king. The ruler was considered a divine being, and his subjects and nobles had to treat him in a specified manner and observe many taboos and customs when dealing with the tlatoani. For example, the foods and drink of the ruler had to be prepared and served in a certain manner, and many people could not touch him or gaze upon him. *See also* AHAW

TLAXCALA (Tlash-cah-**lah**). The name of the people and area that was never subdued by the **Aztecs** and that became one of the first indigenous allies of the Spanish **conquistadores.** Although many archaeological sites remain and much was written about the Tlaxcalans by the Spanish, comparatively little research has been done on this region and its Postclassic culture. Many large settlements and fortified centers are found in Tlaxcala, which is situated between the Aztec capital of **Tenochtitlan** and the **Totonac** area on the Gulf Coast of Veracruz.

The Tlaxcalans successfully repelled repeated attempts at conquest by their bitter enemies, the Aztecs. However, they had been surrounded by Aztec enclaves and were surrounded and cut off of critical supplies, such as cotton cloth **textiles** and **salt** for example, upon the arrival of the Spanish. For these reasons and for the opportunity to become a regional power, the Tlaxcalans joined the European newcomers marching to conquer the Aztec capital. The Tlaxcalans also had "flower wars" with the Aztecs in which ceremonial **warfare** was undertaken to test army strengths and weaknesses and in order to take captives for human **sacrifice.**

TOLLAN. This is the name of a sacred place, or city, from ancient **Mesoamerican** myth and history. *Tollan* signifies "place of the rushes or reeds," and the term signifies the locale of the beginnings of civilization, the glory of great achievements in the past, and the home of the **deities** and ancestors of ruling elites. It is believed that this is a place where some of the most grandiose structures and palaces were built, and where some of the most exquisite artworks and sumptuary goods were to be found.

Tollan is revered by many Mesoamerican peoples, such as the **Quiche Maya** of **Utatlan,** Guatemala, and central Mexican societies. The **Aztecs** held that their capital city of **Tenochtitlan** was a "Tollan." There is much archaeological and ethnohistoric information that suggests that **Teotihuacan** in the Classic Period and that the ruins of **Tula** of the **Toltecs** in Postclassic central Mexico were also considered cities called "Tollan." The Classic **Maya** referred to a place called *Puh,* or "place of the cattail reeds" (or "Tollan"), which most likely was the metropolis of Teotihuacan in the **Basin of Mexico**.

TOLTECS. The name of these people means "great artificers," and they founded a large Early Postclassic Period state at **Tula** in central Mexico from A.D. 900–1200. The Toltecs were honored by subsequent **Mesoamerican** peoples from the **Aztecs** to the **Maya** for being great warriors, kings, architects, and craftsmen. Legitimate rulers in later Mesoamerican states had to reckon their kinship and bloodlines back to a Toltec ancestor. The Toltecs were more than likely **Nahua** peoples who wandered into central Mexico from the north and initially settled in the **Basin of Mexico** at Culhuacan. According to legend, the Toltec people were led to central Mexico by a mythical hero ancestor and ruler named *Mixcoatl*, or "cloud serpent," who was also associated with **Quetzalcoatl** and **Ehecatl**. Together these deities founded a sacred ancient site called **Tollan**.

The son of Mixcoatl was Topiltzin Quetzalcoatl, who founded Tula and set up a theocratic state during the year 1 Reed in the Mexican **calendar.** This peaceful and pious ruler was eventually banished from Tula by way of a raft on the eastern sea by the aggressive **Tezcatlipoca,** who created an expansionist **warfare** and conquest state. This myth of the Toltecs has been used in an attempt to explain the similarities between the cities of Tula and **Chichen Itza** in **Yucatan** to the east of central Mexico. Postconquest accounts also mention that **Motecuhzoma,** the ruler of the Aztec empire, may have believed Hernan Cortes to be Topiltzin Quetzalcoatl returning from the east once again to retake the throne of this powerful Mesoamerican state that had its roots in Toltec society.

TOMB. Mesoamerican kings and elites were frequently interred in tombs placed in **temples** and palaces. The tombs are chambers constructed of limestone blocks that contain the human skeletons and offerings and possessions of **jade** jewelry, fine **ceramic** vessels, **jaguar** pelts, shell artifacts, and food items. Burials in the **Tarascan** region of **west Mexico** typically contain metal items as well, and **Mixtec** tombs were stocked with **gold.** Oftentimes, important persons and rulers were buried in tombs and funerary monumental architecture designed just for this purpose. In the **Maya** area, as in **Copan, Dos Pilas, Palenque,** and **Tikal,** for instance, **hieroglyphic** data from carved stone **stelae,** stairways, and panels help pinpoint the location of royal tombs in a city's acropolis. In early west Mexican cultures, large tombs, which contained rich burials with ceramic figurines and shell artifacts, were dug at the base of deep vertical shafts.

TONANTZIN. A central aspect of the earth mother was Tonantzin in the religious beliefs of the ancient **Aztecs** of the city of **Tenochtitlan** in central Mexico. This **deity** had feminine connotations and was associated with procreation and agricultural fertility. Tonantzin means "Honored Mother" in Aztec **Nahuatl.** The sun **(Tonatiuh)**, water **(Chalchiuhtlicue** and **Tlaloc)**, and the earth gave life, but it was particularly the earth goddess who helped control soil and plant productivity on the surface of the earth. By extension this deity affected human reproduction and fertility. Additionally, this deity was associated with **maize** and insects, especially spiders, and **women.**

TONATIUH. This is the **Nahuatl** name (meaning "He Who Makes the Day") of the sun **deity** and a primary source of life of the **Aztecs** and other indigenous societies in Postclassic central Mexico. Tonatiuh appears seated in a round sun disk with triangular solar rays that emanate from the edge of the disk in iconography at the Postclassic **Maya** site of **Chichen Itza,** which had connections with central Mexico, and in Postclassic central Mexican **codices.** In Aztec religious beliefs, Tonatiuh and his protector **Huitzilopochtli,** the Aztec warrior god, needed blood from human **sacrifices** to keep the sun in the sky and to defeat the **underworld** forces, which it moved through each night. This belief helped to fuel Aztec political and economic expansion in **Mesoamerica** during Late Postclassic times. Aztec warrior impersonators of the sun wore sun disks on their backs during ceremonies and sacrifices.

Tonatiuh is also associated with the east and the direction of the rising sun. The Spanish **conquistador** Pedro de Alvarado, who was instrumental in the conquest of the Aztecs and the **Quiche** Maya, was called Tonatiuh by the inhabitants of Mexico because of his light skin and light and shiny reddish-blonde hair and since the conquistadores came from the east, from the Gulf of Mexico and Veracruz when they marched inward toward the Aztec capital of **Tenochtitlan** in central Mexico.

TOTONAC. The Totonac people were located in the rich tropical region of the Gulf Coast of Veracruz, Mexico, near the **Huastec Maya** and the ancient ruins of El **Tajin** and Cempoala. The Totonacs were **tribute**-paying subjects of the **Aztec** empire, and they were organized in small regional states and through inter-elite alliances. These people were the first defeated in major skirmishes with the conquering force of the Spanish led by the **conquistador** Hernan Cortes. After losing the initial battles with the Spaniards, the Totonacs then became their first indigenous allies. The Totonacs seized the chance to remove the Aztec threat and tribute obligation and join the powerful European intruders to become new rulers of Mexico.

The Spanish placed their first base at Cempoala, a Totonac city with monumental architecture, palaces, and large **plazas.** Several ring-shaped structures built of rounded cobbles with small pillars around their edges were excavated and restored at this site, and these buildings may have been used in recording **calendar** dates and astronomical cycles.

It is not clear if the Totonac people or others built the city of El Tajin or made stone sculptures and **Remojadas ceramic** figurines in central Veracruz or not. Today, the Totonac people still reside in the tropical rainforests of coastal Veracruz where they entertain visitors at the ruins of El Tajin as *voladores,* or men who spiral down from spinning poles with ropes tied around their ankles.

TRADE. The exchange of materials and information between settlements and across whole regions was well developed since the beginnings of civilization in ancient **Mesoamerica.** Raw materials, worked artifacts, foods, natural resources, and even people were traded within each society and across ethnic and political boundaries. Trade has been given a major role in some theories on the formation of the Mesoamerican state, the initial appearance of elites, and the rise of political leaders. Trade has also been invoked by archaeologists who speak of regional integration, **warfare,** economic organization, and collapse when reconstructing past social organization, lifeways, and interaction.

Even though trade existed in the earliest cultures of the Archaic and Formative Periods, it grew in importance with the Early and Middle Formative societies, such as the **Barra** and **Ocos** peoples of **Soconusco,** and the **Olmec** civilization, where sedentary life led to increased interaction. Some of the earliest trade items were **obsidian, jade, ceramics,** shell, and hematite **mirrors.** The evolution of complex societies in the **Basin of Mexico** is believed to have revolved around the exchange of local resources between communities and the creation of an advanced political structure in order to finance and manage it. The movement of goods in the lowland **Maya** area was through both local and interregional trade, as seen in artifact assemblages from excavations of trash deposits and **tombs.** Local **chert** stone tools and ceramics were acquired from nearby Maya sites, but jade, shell, and obsidian artifacts came from afar. The Maya "Merchant God" is shown in Postclassic Period art in **Yucatan** and in painted murals at the site of **Cacaxtla,** which also was an important trading center between the Gulf Coast and central Mexico.

The **Putun** Maya of Tabasco and the **Aztec pochteca** were special merchant groups and traders. Traders often traveled with armies for protection, and they carried great burdens filled with different goods. The Aztecs traded with distant areas, such as Yucatan and the **Tarascan** cities, and this may be an indication of pan-Mesoamerican exchange at least since Olmec times, if not before. Additionally, very long-distance trade of turquoise from the Southwest United States cultures and tropical bird feathers is witnessed at **Casas Grandes** and other sites. Items from distant sources were used as prestige goods that carried sacred and supernatural connotations. Many Mesoamerican centers, like Cacaxtla, **Chalcatzingo, Chalchuapa, Copan, El Tajin, Teotihuacan,** and **Tikal,** may have grown and flourished along major trade routes. *See also* MARKETS

TRES ZAPOTES. Often thought of as a major early **Olmec** site in Veracruz, Mexico, Tres Zapotes actually has a larger late Olmec to post-Olmec occupation (ca. 400 B.C. to A.D. 100). However, it does have an earlier, smaller-scale population, which may be contemporaneous with the Olmec ruin of La **Venta** in Tabasco. Tres Zapotes may have been a major center after the fall of La Venta; perhaps people migrated to this center during Middle to Late Formative times. Late Formative stone architecture at Tres Zapotes differs from the earthen mounds of the earlier Olmec sites, and these buildings plus the **ceramic** styles are more similar to **Izapa** and **Maya** sites in **Peten** to the south. Tres Zapotes is located near the **Tuxtla Mountains,** some 150 kilometers northwest of La Venta and about 100 kilometers north of the Olmec site of **San Lorenzo** in Veracruz. Two Olmec **colossal heads** are known at Tres Zapotes, and the presence of others has been reported.

The site of Tres Zapotes contains about 50 large mounded structures, some of which are large **temples** arranged around central **plazas.** Besides the stone colossal heads, many other sculptures are scattered about the ruin. One of these stone monuments, **Stela** C, contains an early **calendar** date in its **hieroglyphic** text. When the lower part of this monument, which contains part of the calendar date and Olmec-derived iconography, was discovered in the 1930s, it spurred controversy on the dating of the monument and Olmec civilization itself.

When the upper portion containing crucial calendrical information was found, archaeologists supporting the Formative Period date for the Olmec were vindicated. Tres Zapotes Stela C was found to date to September 3,

32 B.C. (7.16.6.16.18) when correlated with the Christian calendar. Recent research shows that this date occurs three days after a total solar eclipse at dawn in the area of Tres Zapotes. This stela provides good evidence that the Olmec or other early cultures in Veracruz had developed complex calendars, **astronomy,** and writing.

TRIBUTE. Taxes were paid all across ancient **Mesoamerica** through tribute given in labor, natural products, and manufactured goods. Rulers also exacted tribute from their subjects that was collected and in turn used to support and persuade the masses to build **temples, plazas,** and palaces. The elite also demanded labor and periodic payments of food and other items from the peasantry to sustain themselves. Mesoamerican nobles also gained tribute from victory in **warfare;** the conquered towns and peoples had to make payments of food, materials, and slaves to their new overlords. For example, the **Codex Mendoza** lists the tribute payments of various subject provinces and cities to the **Aztec** empire centered at the city of **Tenochtitlan.** These payments included **jaguar** skins, **quetzal** feathers, **jade** beads, honey, firewood, **gold, textiles,** and warrior costumes. The Classic **Maya** probably had a similar tax system; the word *icatz'*, "tribute," appears in conjunction with iconography showing people bearing bundles or on actual tribute items in several **hieroglyphic** inscriptions.

TULA. An important ruin and the center of the **Toltec** state in Hidalgo, Mexico, Tula is located some 50 miles northwest of Mexico City. Tula is one of the more sacred sites to ancient Mesoamericans; it is one of the cities called **Tollan,** or "Place of the Reeds," a name given to just a few important centers, including **Teotihuacan** in central Mexico and **Utatlan** in Guatemala.

Although there was an earlier settlement in the vicinity, the city of Tula itself was initially founded on a hill for defensive purposes during the Early Postclassic Period (ca. A.D. 900). Tula was sacked and burned at the time of its collapse at approximately A.D. 1200, probably by marauding **Chichimecs** from the north. The **Aztecs** of central Mexico venerated ancient Tula and made pilgrimages there for ritual purposes and excavated the site for sacred relics of the "great artisans and elite people" of Tollan.

The site of Tula contains a number of large **temples** and palace-like structures. It also has two large **ball courts** (one of them is similar to the ballcourt at **Xochicalco**), **plazas,** a **tzompantli,** or skull rack, and a structure with round sides that may have been a temple for the worship of

Quetzalcoatl, who was the feathered serpent **deity** of ancient Mexico. Pyramid B, the largest structure at the site, is a five-tiered, terraced building that has many columns arranged at its base in front and carved columns on its summit. The square columns on the top of the structure depict Toltec warriors in rich costume, plus ancient deities. However, Tula is well known for its immense three-dimensional columns that show helmeted warriors in battle dress carrying **atlatls.**

At its height during Early Postclassic times, Tula covered nearly 16 square kilometers and was home to an estimated 30,000 to 40,000 people. People lived and were buried in gridded apartment-like compounds like the ones seen at Teotihuacan, and they irrigated their crops with canals and dammed water. Wheeled figurines of animals, similar to those of the **Remojadas** tradition in Veracruz, were found in houses. The wheel was neglected for transportation probably because of the hilly, rocky terrain and ignored because of the importance of using and controlling human labor. Many people at Tula were also dedicated to the procurement of **obsidian** and the production of obsidian artifacts for **trade.** There is little material evidence for the "great elites" and talented artisans at Tula, since no rich **tombs** or signs of extensive and high-quality Toltec craft and art production have been found. The artwork from this site itself is not as aesthetically fine or well executed as that at other Mesoamerican ruins.

With Tula rests one of ancient **Mesoamerica**'s most intriguing mysteries: the nature of the connection between Tula and **Chichen Itza** in **Yucatan.** There are striking resemblances between the art and architecture of these two contemporaneous cities: reclining stone **chacmool** figures, feathered serpent columns, carved warrior columns, a skull rack depicted in stone, stone bas-relief friezes with eagles and **jaguars** consuming hearts, a large ball court **plumbate pottery,** and a hall of columns adjacent to the main pyramid at each city. The shared similarities are beyond coincidence and the debate continues as to whether the influence ran both ways or was imposed on one center by the other. The expansion of the Toltec state into the Maya region may explain the similarities and interaction. However, recent work on the chronology and culture history at Chichen Itza suggests that this center may have been more important in the development of distant Tula than previously felt.

TUXTLA MOUNTAINS. The Tuxtla **mountains** are located in southeastern Veracruz, Mexico, near the Gulf of Mexico. This area is one of the more picturesque regions in southeastern Mexico because the mountains, which can be seen from several kilometers away, rise up from the tropical coast and plain into the clouds. At the top of the mountains rests Lake Catemaco and the cloud forests where small contemporary farming villages are present. Among the Tuxtla Mountains are volcanoes, cinder cones, and large deposits of volcanic rock.

These volcanoes were the models for effigy volcano **temples** at **Olmec** sites, such as the conical earthen mound seen at La **Venta.** The Tuxtla Mountains also provided the source for volcanic rock for carving Olmec monuments, **altars,** and **colossal heads.** This stone was also used in making **manos and metates** for grinding **maize,** other foods, plus different pigments. Occupation in this area dates from Early Formative times to the Colonial Period. Also the famed Tuxtla Statuette, a Late Formative Period artifact, depicting a winged and duck-billed human figure with an inscribed Long Count **calendar** and Isthmian-style **hieroglyphs,** is reported to be from this region.

TZINTZUNTZAN. The capital center of the Late Postclassic **Tarascan** empire was Tzintzuntzan on the shores of Lake Patzcuaro in Michoacan, **west Mexico.** Much of this large center is still intact and undisturbed by modern settlement, which is not true for many Late Postclassic Mesoamerican cities. The remarkable preservation of this city presents a prime opportunity for archaeologists to study this ancient civilization. This important archaeological site has been mapped and only partially excavated; much more has to be done in order to understand the site chronology and history. Excavations and surveys continue to explore other Tarascan sites near Tzintzuntzan to learn more about their political organization, craft specializations, and **religion.**

A large rectangular platform was constructed into a hillside at the site, and this structure supports five *yacata* buildings, which have a rounded exterior and a T-shaped inner chamber. These buildings, some of which have been restored, were used for administrative purposes, elite visitations, and as **temples.** The architecture at Tzintzuntzan is unique in that the buildings contain finely fitted, but irregularly shaped volcanic stones instead of the standard superimposed courses of rectangular cut blocks usually found in **Mesoamerica**.

The Yacatas also contain rich **tombs,** and colonial sources speak of the cremation and burial of kings in these structures. Many human burials have been uncovered at the site, and it is assumed that they were the graves of nobles and of sacrificial victims who accompanied the nobles in their deaths to serve them afterward. Artifacts found in the burials, on the occupation surfaces, and in trash deposits include **ceramic** vessels, copper bells and axes, clay smoking pipes, **obsidian** artifacts, **gold** jewelry, and turquoise. Here the Tarascan people specialized in **metallurgy,** and they made objects of gold, silver, and copper. They also gilded other artifacts and materials such as wood with these metals.

TZOMPANTLI (Sohm-**pahn**-tlee). One of the first things that horrified the Spanish **conquistadores** when they entered the **Aztec** capital of **Tenochtitlan** was the presence of the *tzompantli,* the **Nahuatl** term for the Mesoamerican skull rack. The tzompantli is a scaffold-like construction of poles on which heads and skulls were placed after holes had been made in them. The heads displayed on the skull rack in **Mesoamerica** were usually from captives in **warfare** and victims of **sacrifice,** some of whom were killed after the ball game. Thus, these architectural features are found near **ball courts, temples,** and ceremonial/public precincts.

The skull rack at Tenochtitlan was a large construction that contained hundreds of displayed skulls. Eventually, the heads of Spaniards and of their horses would decorate this tzompantli. At other sites in ancient Mesoamercia, such as **Tula** and **Chichen Itza,** a tzompantli is depicted in stone carvings on platforms that may have supported actual skull racks. Skulls found in the sacred well, or **cenote,** at Chichen Itza bear holes from placing them on a pole rack. An early tzompantli made of wooden poles and scaffolding typical of this construction and complete with human skulls was found at the small Late Formative site of La Coyotera in Oaxaca, Mexico.

U

ULUA RIVER. The Ulua River in northwest Honduras runs through a wide valley and rich alluvial plain. This river, plus the Comayagua, Chamelecon, and other rivers, make up the Comayagua drainage of northwest Honduras. Many archaeological sites are found in this area, and some of them have been extensively surveyed and excavated. Because of the large river system and connections to the northern coast of Honduras and the sea **trade,** sites in the Ulua Valley interacted with centers in Veracruz, **Yucatan,** and in the **Maya** area immediately to the west.

The important Postclassic site of Naco, which participated in interregional exchange, is located on the Chamelecon River just to the west of the Ulua River. In the Classic and Terminal Classic Periods, large quantities of carved marble vases were produced by peoples in this region. These vessels, which exhibit designs and iconography (especially scrolls and reptilian heads) similar to those found at El **Tajin** in Veracruz, are found at many sites in eastern **Mesoamerica,** such as **Copan** and **Quirigua.**

UNDERWORLD. For ancient **Mesoamerican** peoples, the concept of the underworld was a salient part of their belief systems and lives. The realm of the underworld was called *Xilbalba* by the **Quiche Maya** and *Mictlan* by **Nahuas** in Central Mexico. In the underworld the death **deities** ruled, and they brought disease and death to those living on the earth's surface; death and illness were great concerns for ancient Mesoamericans. Human **sacrifices** and other offerings were given to these gods to appease them and promote health and life. The **Aztecs** provided human hearts and blood to nourish the sun and its protectors during its travels through the underworld each night.

The ancient Maya believed that the underworld was accessed through **caves,** where the Maya performed rituals, left offerings, and buried some of their dead. In the Quiche Maya book **Popol Vuh,** the Hero Twins underwent a series of trials in houses and in ball games with the underworld lords. These trials were repeated by dead Maya kings at the **ball court** in the afterlife, and they would eventually outsmart and defeat these malevolent deities and ascend into the heavens. Many other people who died were destined to remain in the underworld. It was believed that food and materials buried with the dead were needed in the afterlife, and dogs helped to guide them on their journeys in the underworld. Mesoamerican iconography shows the underworld gods and denizens with skeletal features, bone imagery, foul smells, screech owls, and disembodied eyes and limbs.

USULUTAN. Area of west-central El Salvador where a distinctive style of **ceramics** was developed. Archaeologists discovered this type of ware in this location and now have identified its spread into eastern El Salvador during the Middle to Late Formative Periods, and then to the central **Maya** area during Late Formative times. Usulutan pottery is easily distinguished by its rounded bowl shapes and thinly painted wavy lines. Usulutan ceramics are found at many major sites in southern **Mesoamerica,** including **Chalchuapa, Copan, Quelepa,** and **Tikal.** This special ceramic was produced in mass quantities in some archaeological sites in El Salvador and then **traded** to other areas. Other contemporaneous and more distant sites copied the Usulutan shapes and decoration instead of acquiring the originals.

Usulutan wares have a dark orange or brown background and wavy parallel lines of a cream-colored or slightly yellowish tone. The lines may have been created by painting them on separately, or by the application of a chemical or wax-like substance to create the lines during the production process. In this case, the pottery is fired to a light cream-brown color, an unknown substance is painted on in lines (beeswax, or a resin?), and then it is burned off in a second firing that turns the rest of the vessel a darker orange or brown.

USUMACINTA RIVER. One of the largest rivers in **Mesoamerica** that creates the border between Chiapas, Mexico, and **Peten,** Guatemala, is the Usumacinta. The Usumacinta River is fed by several large tributaries in Chiapas and Guatemala, and its swelled waters rush to the Gulf Coast in Tabasco, Mexico. Being wide and deep, the Usumacinta River has been used for water transport in ancient and modern times, but its rapids and whirlpools often make it hazardous for boats, especially during the rainy season. **Trade** and interaction among **Maya** centers spread out along this river was facilitated by canoe and boat travel. A **hieroglyphic** stone panel at the site of **Piedras Negras,** located on the banks of the Usumacinta in Peten, mentions the visitation of a king, "Bird **Jaguar,**" who arrived by canoe from another Usumacinta site, called **Yaxchilan.** Important for regional exchange, trade goods such as **jade, ceramics,** shell, and feathers, were shipped up and down this river.

UTATLAN. The **Nahuatl** name of the Postclassic capital of the **Quiche Maya** people in the central highlands of Guatemala. The center was locally known as *Gumarcaaj,* but Utatlan became the more widely used name after the Spanish **conquistadores** and their **Aztec** soldier allies occupied the area. This city is known for its densely packed settlement, many elaborately constructed palaces, various **temples** made from stone blocks, multicolored mural paintings, a large **ball court,** and several **altars** and shrines. Settlements, residential structures, minor temples, and agricultural lands are also found on the surrounding hills and on nearby **mountains.** Utatlan was founded by the great Quiche lord "Gucumatz" (**Quetzalcoatl** in Nahuatl or "feathered serpent") in the early 15th century on a plateau surrounded by steep cliffs and deep ravines. This site was chosen for its highly defensible location against the traditional enemies of the Quiche—the **Cakchiquel** Maya—and other warlike peoples. Also there were only two narrow roads leading in and out of the city. Some excavations have been carried out at Utatlan, and a wealth of information regarding the city and the Quiche kingdom has been gleaned from ethnohistoric sources.

Utatlan was a major highland Postclassic political, economic, and ritual center, and it was the seat of the expanding Quiche Maya polity. The Quiche name for the city, *Gumarcaaj,* is glossed as "Place of the Reeds." This place name signifies that Utatlan was perceived by the Quiche inhabitants to be **Tollan,** or a sacred center that is occupied by descendants of the **Toltecs** of **Tula** in central Mexico. The Quiche rulers are said to have originated in Tula according to their myths and histories, such as seen in the **Popol Vuh** accounts. Elite Quiche Maya lineages were associated with palaces that were called "big houses" at Utatlan. These palaces and lineages were distinguished by their specific placement in the city and identified by the individual ornate building facades and artworks of their houses. The largest residence known was probably the palace of the ruling *Cawek* lineage at the time of the conquest. Some of the temples at the center were the locations of worship and **sacrifice** to the sun **deity,** the moon god, the sky god, fertility deities, and the feathered serpent.

In A.D. 1524 the center of Utatlan was home to an estimated few thousand people when the Spaniards took the staunchly defended city, aided by their newly acquired Cakchiquel allies. Although the Quiche had destroyed one of the main entrances to their capital to better protect themselves, the Spanish tricked them into letting their guard down, and the city was attacked and razed by the powerful attacking army. The city was largely abandoned after this decisive Spanish military victory over Utatlan and following the subsequent subjugation and relocation of the Quiche. Archaeological investigations at Utatlan have uncovered burials, murals, architectural features, and **gold** jewelry, but large portions of the site, particularly large trash deposits in the adjacent ravines, still await excavation. Some of the earliest reports of ruins in Guatemala during the first half of the 19th century included descriptions of Utatlan, and they also contain drawings of the then relatively well preserved buildings. *See also* IXIMCHE

UXMAL (Ush-**mal**). An important Late Classic to Terminal Classic Period (ca. A.D. 750–950) **Maya** site located in the **Puuc** Hills region of western **Yucatan,** Mexico. This is the largest center in the Puuc area, and Uxmal was the seat of a powerful, regional Maya state in the Terminal Classic Period. The impressive size of the site (perhaps two square kilometers or more) and its monumental structures, plus information from studies of **hieroglyphic** inscriptions and the abundant stone sculpture, attest to the importance of this site and its ruling lineage.

At the time of the Spanish conquest of the Maya in Yucatan in the mid-1500s, the area of Uxmal was the seat of the royal Xiu lineage. This Maya family claimed a Mexican ancestral connection, and it is possible that they were not of the original royal lineage of Uxmal. An earlier ruler of Uxmal in the Terminal Classic era, "Lord **Chacahaw**," may have been a Yucatec Maya, since his titles include the name *Chac,* which was a central **deity** in the Yucatec pantheon. The kings of Uxmal appear to have been a significant power in Yucatan before the ascendancy and regional domination of the rulers at **Chichen Itza**.

The center of the archaeological site of Uxmal contains several large buildings, **plazas,** palaces, **temples,** and a **ball court** for the ball game enclosed within an encircling defensive wall. The ball court has vertical playing walls and stone disks for the ball to pass through that have **hieroglyphs** inscribed on them. Additionally, a raised causeway, or **sacbe,** runs from Uxmal to the neighboring smaller sites of Nohpat and Kabah, which may have been in a political and economic allegiance with Uxmal. A sinkhole with water, or **cenote,** in Yucatec Maya is not enclosed within the wall, but the inhabitants probably trapped water in **chultunes,** or human-made underground cisterns, that are common in the dry Puuc Hills region. Many stone sculptures on buildings or scattered about them, a few carved stone portrait **stelae,** and a stone **jaguar** throne—the seat of power for Maya kings—are also found at the site.

One of the tallest structures at the site is called the House or Pyramid of the Magician. This temple was a center of public ritual, possibly to Chac because of the numerous mosaic stone masks of this deity that adorn it, and perhaps the structure was a place of burial for Uxmal elites. This building can be seen from kilometers around in the low dry forest of the Puuc area, and it also may have functioned as a lookout post and redoubt during **warfare.** This building, like many others at Uxmal, has only been excavated on the exterior; more investigations are needed to explore these and the smaller residences surrounding the center. In reconnaissance operations within and near the site, a round temple, perhaps dedicated to **Quetzalcoatl** (*K'uk'ulkan* in Yucatec Maya), was discovered in the site core.

Next to this pyramid is the Nunnery Quadrangle, a large palace and courtyard complex containing four long rectangular structures that may have been the residences of important Uxmal nobles and their retainers. The iconography of the stone sculptures on these buildings suggests possible interaction with Mexico, because the central Mexican deity Quetzalcoatl, the feathered serpent, appears prominently in the facade of the North Building. Research has also pointed out the cosmological symbolism of the stone sculpture. The Nunnery Quadrangle is like a map of the Maya cosmos, because the buildings represent the heavens, sky, and celestial realms, the middle world where humans dwell, the surface of the earth where the sun was born, and the layers of the **underworld** associated with death and malevolent deities. Geometric patterns on the structure's facade also resemble ancient woven **textile** designs.

To the south of the Nunnery Quadrangle is the House of the Governor, a long range-type palace structure that has an ornate exterior sculptural facade. The House of the Governor is a large multiroomed building that rests on an artificial platform. This palace probably housed a powerful Uxmal ruler, Lord Chac, whose stone portrait statue is seen in the facade. Also, other nobles are seated on cushioned thrones, so this house may have been a council or meeting house in addition to being the residence of the Maya king. This building has nicely planned rooms with well-made corbeled arches or **vaulted roofs** in their ceilings. *See also* SAYIL

V

VAULTED ROOF. Common roof type in ancient **Maya** stone **temples,** palaces, and **tombs,** but which is not as frequent in other regions in ancient **Mesoamerica**. A vaulted roof consists of two slanted masonry walls (up to about 45 degrees) that meet and rest against one another at the top to form an upside-down V. These angled walls are created by stacking blocks with sloped faces in the vaulted roof, and they are held together by lime and mud cement. The walls and roofs themselves, plus the solid core of fill and capstones, help to sustain the vaulted roof and support its weight. Hence, these vaulted roofs are not rounded, load bearing archways with keystones as seen in ancient Europe. In actuality, vaulted roofs mimic the slanted, inverted "V" roofs of Mesoamerican houses built of pole and thatch that are designed to resist heavy rain and the sun. Intact and beautiful vaulted roofs can be viewed at the Maya sites of **Chichen Itza, Copan, Palenque, Tikal,** and **Uxmal,** to name a few.

VENTA (LA). The **Olmec** site of La Venta is located on elevated ground in a swampy area near several streams and the Tonala River on the Gulf Coast of Veracruz, Mexico. A large part of the site of La Venta dates to the later Olmec period (ca. 800–400 B.C.), and most of the monumental constructions and sculptures at the site postdate the earlier Olmec center of **San Lorenzo.** Visible today at La Venta are large earthen mounds, some of which are round and others of which are long and narrow. One of the more fascinating monumental constructions is the possible "effigy volcano" construction at La Venta, which is found near a central **plaza** at the site. This cone-shaped structure is complete with ravines on its sides and a flattened, slightly concave summit that is much like the ones seen on volcanoes in the nearby **Tuxtla Mountains.**

Many carved basalt monuments and **stelae** are found at La Venta, which is remarkable since the heavy stone had to be transported a considerable distance from the Tuxtla Mountains. One plaza at the site and a probable elite **tomb** were lined with tall basalt columns. **Colossal head** sculptures—a hallmark of Olmec civilization—are found at the site. These huge, three-dimensional portrait stones may depict rulers or men of high standing. Colossal heads are being discovered today through excavations and subsurface magnetometer surveys.

Also present are rectangular "**altars,**" or what are now believed to be thrones. One of these sculptures depicts Olmec personages holding "**jaguar babies,**" which are small anthropomorphic **deities** with cleft heads and down-turned mouths. On the other side of one tabletop monument, Altar 5, an Olmec man, or possible deity, appears to be exiting the mouth of a **cave** carved into the stone with a baby laying in his arms (see photo). Similar themes are shown on Altar 4. Standing stone stelae at La Venta have representations of Olmec rulers and elites dressed in their finery. Stela 2 shows a personage carrying a scepter and surrounded by smaller deities or ancestor figures. On a similar monument, two men greet each other while wearing elaborate headgear, as seen in most Olmec stone carvings.

Monument 19 at La Venta is a freestanding stone sculpture that is particularly interesting because it may depict one of the earliest versions of the **Mesoamerican** feathered serpent. On this monument, a large serpent encircles an Olmec noble, or possibly a **priest,** who carries a bag. Also of great significance is Monument 13, or "the Ambassador," for it contains **hieroglyphs** that surround a standing figure who holds a banner or flag. A drawing of a foot found to the left of the figure may denote "travel" or "walking," and the glyphs in front of the figure may actually be his name and titles.

Excavations are under way in and near monumental architecture at La Venta, particularly on the large cone-shaped earthen structure. A museum is also being built on site. Large scale digs here in the 1930s and 1940s also were some of the earliest archaeological investigations of the Olmec. Along the long axial line of the center many exciting finds appeared in these first excavations. Burials with carved **jade** and other offerings, a stone sarcophagus, and caches of large amounts of imported greenstone were encountered. One cached offering included small three-dimensional human figurines made of jade and serpentine that surround and face one figure made of a porous reddish-brown stone. This may depict a confrontation or a scene of **sacrifice.**

Another major find at La Venta was a large mosaic mask or geometric shape whose several hundred blocks were arranged and then buried beneath layers of soils of different colors below a plaza floor. Concave magnetite **mirrors,** some of which may have been manufactured in highland Oaxaca, were also found, and they could have been used by Olmec elites to start fires or signal over long distances, or they might have been used as ritual items connected to the supernatural world.

Settlement surveys and excavations near La Venta indicate that the supporting population lived near the edges of rivers and streams in the surrounding areas beginning around 1500 B.C. These Olmec people relied on aquatic life, terrestrial resources, and cultivated plants for their subsistence. La Venta seems to have been abandoned at the start of the Late Formative Period, since its occupation drops off at this time and only a slight scatter of **ceramics** dating to this time have been recovered. Possible competition or interaction with the developing **Maya** civilization may have something to do with the decline at La Venta and the restructuring of society in general in the Gulf Coast region at this time.

VENUS. Ancient **Mesoamerican** cultures made great advances in **astronomy** and developed **calendars** and religious beliefs based on sky watching and the tracking of the movements of heavenly bodies. Along with the sun and moon, viewing Venus was important to many of these people. The **Maya, Aztecs,** and the **Mixtecs,** plus many other indigenous peoples, had specific beliefs and **deities** associated with Venus. The movements of Venus were carefully watched; it often appears as the morning star heralding the rise of the sun, and it rises as the evening star that sets after the sun at certain times in the year.

The Maya and the people of central Mexico recorded the 584-day cycle of Venus in their **codices,** or indigenous books. For these people the periods were Venus appearing after being hidden in front of the sun (eight days), becoming the morning star (around 263 days) before hiding behind the sun (approximately 90 days), and appearing as the evening star (250 days) before it disappears in front of the sun again. Five Mesoamerican Venus cycles were completed in eight solar years so the different calendars could mesh and be correlated with one another. Maya **hieroglyphic** texts on stone **stelae** indicate that the cycle of Venus may have at times determined episodes of **warfare** and human **sacrifice**.

W

WARFARE. Warfare for **Mesoamerican** societies had many causes and outcomes. The scale of warfare ranges from raids on villages and merchants to the all-out conquest war of the **Aztecs.** Evidence for ancient Mesoamerican warfare is obtained from carved stone monuments and **stelae, codices,** or books, wall murals like at the **Maya** site of **Bonampak** and the central Mexican site of **Cacaxtla,** information from Spanish **conquistadores,** and from excavations of archaeological sites with defensive works, such as **Aguateca, Becan, Dos Pilas, Mayapan, Tenochtitlan,** and **Xochicalco,** to name a few. War was undertaken for revenge, **tribute** payments, to gain land and riches, for political favors, or for the building and maintaining of alliances. The Aztecs also had "flower wars" with the **Tlaxcalans** and other enemies to procure captives for human **sacrifice**.

In Mesoamerican states, warfare was carried out by elite specialists and armies who carried various **weapons,** such as shields, spears with **chert** tips, wooden swords lined with **obsidian** blades, **atlatl** spear throwers, and later in the Postclassic, the bow and arrow and possibly slings. People fought in open areas, or near populated centers, and the goal often was victory on the battlefield by routing and scattering the enemy army, plus the taking of captives. Also, conquest over a town and people was symbolized by the sacking and burning of local **temples,** which is seen in Mexican codices, such as the **Codex Mendoza,** and possibly in the archaeology of **Dos Pilas.** In some Classic Maya sites in **Peten,** Guatemala, polities seem to have collapsed during a period of intensified warfare over land, resources, and elite competition.

WEAPONS. Common weapons for **warfare** throughout ancient **Mesoamerica** in different periods were clubs, lances, and **atlatls,** or spear throwers. These weapons were often tipped or fixed with **obsidian** or **chert** points. The worked stone portions of the weapons, such as chert lance heads and projectile points, are recovered during archaeological excavations. At the time of Spanish contact in **Yucatan,** central Mexico, and Central America wooden swords edged with obsidian blades (**Nahuatl** *macuahuitl* used by the **Aztecs**), thrusting spears (*tepoztopilli* in Nahuatl), the bow and arrow, and stone projectiles were also frequently employed in battle. Mesoamerican weapons are depicted in native sculpture, painted ceramics, and books, or **codices.** Descriptions of weaponry are also mentioned often in Spanish ethnohistoric documents.

WEST MEXICO. This is a region of rich cultural and ecological diversity that includes the states of Jalisco, Nayarit, Michoacan, Guerrero, and **Colima.** Some of the earliest villages, **tomb** builders, and **ceramic** makers in **Mesoamerica** were found in west Mexico. These people exploited the abundant resources located in the **mountains,** lakes, rivers, and coastlines throughout this region. There is evidence of an **Olmec** and a later **Teotihuacan** presence or influences in west Mexico during the Early Formative and Classic Periods, respectively. Some of the Classic and Postclassic civilizations located in this part of Mesoamerica include the **Teuchitlan** tradition (ca. A.D. 600–800) and the later Postclassic **Tarascan** empire that was toppled by the Spanish **conquistadores.** This region has recently come under more intense focus in archaeological research and important discoveries are made each year.

WOMEN. Generally speaking, women, particularly of the commoner classes, were associated with the domestic sphere in many ancient **Mesoamerican** societies. Women were instrumental in the local economy, and they were crucial for the maintenance of the household and important for carrying out production for **trade** and exchange. Women also cooked, attended fields, gardens, and domesticated animals, wove **textiles,** manufactured ornaments and utilitarian goods, and they made **ceramics.**

Elite women are often depicted in Mesoamerican iconography in traditional and ceremonial dress, shown dancing, participating in rituals, and attending nobles in court, and they are also represented as elites of the highest rank and status, especially in ancient **Maya** culture. Works of art also connect women to important rituals and beliefs regarding fertility, the ancestors, the **calendar,** and culture history.

Mesoamerican women were believed to be linked with the moon, past warrior leaders, the earth and its fecundity, water, and the lineage founders. Some Mesoamerican **deities** with female aspects or gender characteristics were **Coatlique** and **Coyolxauhqui** of the **Aztecs** and **Ixchel** of the **Maya.** Elite women held important posts in ancient governments and councils. Their status and heritage were crucial for maintaining royal bloodlines, producing legitimate heirs to the throne, and nurturing capable rulers. Women inherited their own kingdoms and estates, and they were an integral part of forging and sustaining dynastic alliances through marriages and participation in ceremony, as witnessed in Maya and **Mixtec** society. Maya **stelae** often depict women as pivotal members of ruling families, and they are shown undertaking critical ceremonies.

X

XIPE TOTEC (She-peh **Toh-**tehk). An important **deity** of the **Aztecs** of Postclassic central Mexico. The Aztecs may have developed beliefs and ceremonies related to this god through interaction with people in Veracruz. This supernatural being was generally associated with the earth and fertility, and rituals for this god were frequently performed just before the rainy season. Xipe Totec is known as "Our Lord, the Flayed One," since Aztec **priests** would wear the skin peeled from a sacrificial victim when worshipping him. People impersonating Xipe Totec while wearing human skin appear on Aztec sculpture and in **codices.** This deity can be recognized in Aztec iconography by the mask-like skin over the face and mouth, a hole in the skin from where the heart was extracted, and the tied straps behind the head and back of the flayed skin.

In rituals performed for the regeneration of the earth, vegetation, and fertility, people were **sacrificed,** sometimes after mock gladiatorial combat, and their hearts removed and their skin peeled and donned by a priest until the day it fell off. Sometimes the old and dried skin would be thrown in a hole in the earth, or in a **cave.** The shedding of the skin would represent the sloughing off and the consumption of the skin of seeds and the sprouting of new plants.

XOCHICALCO (Shoh-chee-**kahl**-koh). This word is a place name in **Nahuatl** meaning "Place of the House of Flowers." This large and fortified site in Morelos, Mexico, reached its peak during the Late Classic and early Terminal Classic Periods (the Epiclassic in central Mexico, or ca. A.D. 800–900) when more interregional interaction, intensified **warfare,** and the downfall of many **Mesoamerican** polities was occurring. Xochicalco's monumental architecture and larger residential compounds rest on a steep hill and are encircled with multiple defensive walls. Recent mapping and excavations at the site and adjacent hilltops uncovered intriguing evidence that the construction of residential units and defensive wall systems may reflect internal lineage or ward divisions, plus segmented political structure.

Archaeological investigations have also uncovered domestic areas, craft production zones, and administrative structures. The manufacture of **obsidian** artifacts and the political importance of this center rose with the dissolution of the **Teotihuacan** state. The monumental architecture and art of this important center point to strong influence from Teotihuacan, the **Maya,** the **Zapotecs,** Veracruz, **west Mexico,** and central Mexican states. A principal pyramid at Xochicalco exhibits central Mexican talud-tablero architecture and carved feathered serpents (**Quetzalcoatl**), plus Maya-style human figures in the stone facade. The abandonment of the site may have been because of increased warfare, sociopolitical fragmentation, or economic and political competition with the rising **Toltec** state.

Y

YARUMELA. An important archaeological site in central Honduras on the eastern periphery of the **Maya** area. The architecture and material culture at Yarumela suggests that this site more than likely was not occupied by Maya speakers, but by another ethnic and linguistic group, possibly from lower Central America. Historical sources and ethnographic data hint at the presence of Lenca and Jicaque peoples in this area, and their ancestors may have been the original inhabitants at Yarumela. The people at Yarumela also had extensive contacts with peoples in Lower Central America (such as societies in Nicaragua, El Salvador, and Costa Rica) and South America. However, the site's strongest ties seem to have been with northern Honduras where other sites are found with similar architecture and **ceramic** types.

Yarumela has a major Middle to Late Formative Period component in the archaeological record, and much of the site's monumental architecture (some of the largest pre-Hispanic buildings in the area) was built at this time. The site was occupied as early as 1000 B.C., and it had a small Late Classic population as well, and few Postclassic inhabitants. The buildings in this ancient ruin are cobble-faced structures that surround a core of earth and stone fill. Elite residences, large **temple** platforms, and residential structures are found at Yarumela.

Mapping and excavations have been carried out at the site, and archaeological work continues to unravel its hidden history. Recent studies of Yarumela's paleo-botanical remains have revealed that the ancient residents procured much of their wood and plants from the surrounding uplands, and they obtained cashew wood (and probably its fruit and seeds, although none were recovered or preserved) from South America.

YAXCHILAN (Yash-chee-**lahn**). An important Late Classic **Maya** site found on the banks of the **Usumacinta River** in lowland Chiapas, Mexico. Yaxchilan (called Lorillard City in the 19th century) is a large Maya center that is made up of many monumental stone **temples** and palaces that exhibit some of the finest examples of limestone carvings in the Maya area. These ruins are found on a bend in the river, with the turbulent waters of the Usumacinta River on three sides of the site. The emblem sign for ancient Yaxchilan is the "split sky" icon.

A ridge, and possibly a surmounting wall construction (this area needs to be surveyed), to the west of the site would have completed its highly defensible location. This would have been much desired since Yaxchilan was involved in regional conflicts and **warfare** throughout much of its history, including battles with nobles from Lacanha, Lakamtun, and **Dos Pilas.** Yaxchilan rulers interacted with elites from the sites of **Bonampak, Calakmul, Piedras Negras,** and **Tikal** according to written texts, but they probably were in contact with many other cities.

Yaxchilan has a large number of impressive stone masonry buildings, many with their walls and roofs intact. An acropolis is located right on the riverbank, and a series of temples and structures are placed on a series of low hills directly above the river. Buildings are also found across the Usumacinta River and in Guatemalan territory. Structures 37 and 38 and Structures 40 and 41 have long stairways following rises in the terrain and leading up to the bases of the temples. Only a few of the monumental structures at Yaxchilan have been excavated, and only a small portion of the site has been mapped. The buildings at Yaxchilan have perhaps the largest number of carved door lintels in **Mesoamerica,** and stone **stelae** and **hieroglyphic** stairways are also present at the site.

Many breakthroughs in understanding Classic Maya hieroglyphic writing and culture have been made recently by art historians and epigraphers working with the carved monuments of Yaxchilan. Self-**sacrifice** and bloodletting, in which **women** pull cords through their tongues and men cut their penises in order to collect blood offerings, are shown on Yaxchilan lintels (such as Lintel 24). Classic Maya **dance** rituals and the holding of ceremonial objects are also seen on many carved lintels (1, 2, and 3, for example). Additionally, the **tomb** of a royal woman mentioned prominently in Yaxchilan hieroglyphic texts, "Lady Xoc," may have been discovered recently by Mexican archaeologists.

Of equal importance is the wealth of information on the Yaxchilan rulers, the dynastic sequence of the site, and the exploits and events in the lives of the ruling elite found in the written texts. With **calendar** dates and continuing decipherments of the texts, the reigns of Maya kings have been delimited and the times of their births, enthronements, conflicts, captive takings, ceremonies, and deaths are now known. From their name and title glyphs, some of the Yaxchilan kings are nicknamed "Shield **Jaguar** I," "Bird Jaguar," and "Shield Jaguar III." We also know that the Yaxchilan kings were visited by nobles from other sites during their coronation ceremonies and that they had subordinate lords with the title *sahal* ("feared one") who governed at smaller sites nearby. A carved stone panel at the nearby site of Piedras Negras also mentions that a Yaxchilan king arrived by canoe to participate in a ceremony and an evening feast with drink.

YUCATAN. The Yucatan peninsula was, and still is, inhabited by the Yucatec **Maya.** However, these people had contact with cities to the south, plus they dealt with the **Aztecs, Toltecs,** and others to the west through **trade** and alliances. Well-known archaeological sites in this region include **Balankanche, Becan, Calakmul, Chichen Itza,** Coba, Dzibilchaltun, Edzna, **Mayapan, Sayil,** and **Uxmal,** among others. Yucatan is characterized by its flat, rocky terrain, low scrub brush and tree forest mainly from its central to northern parts, plus its general lack of surface water. Water can mainly be found in **cenotes,** or sinkholes, **caves,** and **bajos,** or low swampy areas. The geography and climate of Yucatan contrasts sharply with the hills, jungles, swamps, and rivers of **Peten** in neighboring Guatemala. There are marked rainy and dry seasons in Yucatan, where farmers rely on **milpa** or slash-and-burn agriculture for their **diet. Salt** production and sea trade were also central to Yucatecan society.

Z

ZAACHILA. The name of an archaeological site near **Monte Alban** in the Valley of Oaxaca, Mexico, and a prominent noble house, or lineage, of the Postclassic **Zapotec** people. This ruin contains palace compounds and elite **tombs** that are similar to those found at Monte Alban and **Mitla.** Zaachila was one of the more powerful and influential Zapotec lineages in Oaxaca, and its members are listed in pictographic and **hieroglyphic codices** (especially the **Codex Nuttall**) from ancient Oaxaca.

Around A.D. 1280 a Zapotec prince, Lord 5 Flower, married a royal **Mixtec woman,** Lady 4 Rabbit, in a marriage alliance, and this is how the Zaachila lineage and house was formed. These nobles were buried in tombs at the site and in mummy bundles at the adjacent archaeological center of Mitla during the Postclassic Period. The historical and archaeological records indicate that the Zapotec and Mixtec dynasties interacted, intermarried, and **traded** heavily beginning in this period, and this allowed the Mixtec to establish settlements in the area.

ZAPOTEC (Zah-poh-tehk). Language and culture found in the central and southern portions of the state of Oaxaca in southeastern Mexico, which is distantly related to that of the nearby **Mixtec** people. Classic to Postclassic period ruins with ceremonial **plazas,** ornate stone buildings, **temples,** palaces, inscribed stone monuments (some with **hieroglyphic** texts), and richly stocked **tombs** are located in the Valley of Oaxaca. The Zapotec region varies in climate and geography from the high **mountain** valleys to the hot tropical coast, which has abundant natural resources and fertile land for **maize** agriculture. The lands and cities of the Zapotec people were highly sought after by later **Aztec** rulers and the Spanish **conquistadores** to increase their wealth, **tribute** payments, and labor pools.

There is disagreement as to when Zapotec culture is first witnessed in the archaeological record. Some archaeologists believe that the culture began in the Valley of Oaxaca by 1400 B.C., while others contend that it was not present until A.D. 200. Classic Zapotec civilization (ca. A.D. 200–900) was centered at the picturesque hilltop site of **Monte Alban** in the Valley of Oaxaca. Here, large stone temples containing tombs filled with fine **ceramics,** worked **jade,** precious metals, including **gold,** and painted murals were discovered. Some of these artifacts attest to interaction with **Teotihuacan,** the **Maya,** and the Mixtec. **Hieroglyphs** contain **calendar** round dates, names of historical rulers and captives, and descriptions of events. A Zapotec enclave was discovered at Teotihuacan in central Mexico.

Mitla is an important Postclassic site and is appreciated for the intricate geometric mosaic facades on its buildings. The archaeological and historical evidence suggests that Zapotec society was made up of rulers, **priests,** farmers, traders, craft specialists, and laborers, but that only small regional polities and loosely controlled local economies with some distant **trade** were present. Today, parts of highland Oaxaca and the Isthmus of Tehuantepec are where much of traditional Zapotec language and customs are still celebrated.

Appendix: Research Institutions

Researchers, staff, libraries, and collections from the following short list (there are too many institutions with qualified staff to mention here) of institutions may be of assistance on the subjects of this volume.

American Museum of Natural
  History
Central Park W. at 79th St.
New York, NY 10024

Arizona State Museum
University of Arizona
P.O. Box 210026
Tucson, AZ 85721

Art Institute of Chicago
Michigan Ave. at Adams St.
Chicago, IL 60603

Brigham Young University
Department of Anthropology
Provo, UT 84602

The British Museum
Great Russell St.
London, England
WC1 3DG

Centro de Investigaciones
  Regionales de Mesoamérica
  (CIRMA)
Antigua Guatemala, Guatemala
Centro América

El Colegio de Michoacán
Martínez de Navarrete 505
Fracc. Las Fuentes
59690 Zamora
Michoacán, México

Dumbarton Oaks
1703 32nd St. NW
Washington, DC 20007

Field Museum of Chicago
Roosevelt Rd. at Lake Shore Dr.
Chicago, IL 60605

Foundation for Advancement of
  Mesoamerican Studies
268 S. Suncoast Blvd.
Crystal River, FL 34429

Instituto de Antropología
  e Historia de Guatemala
12 Avenida, 11–65
Zona 1
Guatemala
Centro América

Instituto Nacional de Antropología
e Historia de México
Moneda 16 Centro, 06060
México, DF

Instituto Nacional de Antropología
e Historia de Honduras
Villa Roy
Bo. Buenos Aires
Tegucigalpa, Honduras

Klaus Renner
Wissenschaftliche Fachbuchhan-
lung & Antiquariat
D-8021 Hohenschaftlarn
Germany, Sonnenhang 8

Metropolitan Museum of Art
1000 Fifth Ave.
New York, NY 10028

Museo Nacional de Antropología
e Historia de México
Av. Paseo de la Reforma
Col. Chapultepec Polanca
Codigo Postal 11560
México, DF

Museo Nacional de Arqueología
y Etnología de Guatemala
Parque La Aurora
Zona 13
Guatemala
Centro América

Museo Popol Vuh
Universidad Francisco
Marroquín
Zona 10
Guatemala
Centro América

N. Fagin Books
459 N. Milwaukee Ave.
Chicago, IL 60610

National Geographic Society
1145 17th St., N.W.
Washington, DC 20036-4688

National Science Foundation
4201 Wilson Blvd.
Arlington, VA 22230

Peabody Museum
Harvard University
11 Divinity Ave.
Cambridge, MA 02138

Pennsylvania State University
Department of Anthropology
409 Carpenter Building
University Park, PA 16802

Royal Ontario Museum
100 Queen's Park
Toronto, ON
M5S 2C6, Canada

Smithsonian Institution
10th and Constitution Ave. NW
Washington, DC 20560

Southern Illinois University
Department of Anthropology
Carbondale, IL 62901

State University of New York
Department of Anthropology
The University at Albany
Albany, NY 12222

Tulane University
Department of Anthropology
New Orleans, LA 70118

Universidad de San Carlos
Ciudad Universitaria
Zona 12, 01012
Guatemala
Centro América

Universidad del Valle de
    Guatemala
18 Avenida 11–95
Zona 15, 01901
Vista Hermosa III
Apartado Postal No. 82
Guatemala
Centro América

Universidad Nacional
    Autónoma de México
Ciudad Universitaria Alvaro
Obregón, 04510
México, D.F.

University of Arizona
Department of Anthropology
P.O. Box 210030
Tucson, AZ 85721

University of Calgary
Department of Anthropology
2500 University Dr. NW
Calgary, AB
T2N 1N4 Canada

University of California
Department of Anthropology
Los Angeles, CA 90095

University of Colorado
Department of Anthropology
Campus Box 233
Boulder, CO 80309

University of Illinois
Department of Anthropology
109 Davenport Hall
607 S. Mathews
Urbana, IL 61801

University of Michigan
Department of Anthropology
1020 LSA
Ann Arbor, MI 48109

University of Pennsylvania Museum
33rd and Spruce Sts.
Philadelphia, PA 19104

University of Texas
Department of Anthropology
Austin, TX 78712

Vanderbilt University
Department of Anthropology
Box 6050 Station B
Nashville, TN 37235

Yale University
Department of Anthropology
P.O. Box 208277
New Haven, CT 06520

Bibliography

The history, archaeology, societies, and material culture of ancient Meso-america are diverse and complex subjects found in an exhaustive number of journal articles, books, and monographs. Thus, the sources provided in the bibliography do not constitute a complete and definitive list of the works and knowledge on ancient Mesoamerica, but they serve as starting references for people who want to learn more about this culture area and about the research that has been done. The sources given in this quick reference provide the reader with some classic works in the field in addition to some up-to-date information that is often used in scholarly publications and lectures. The strength of this bibliography rests in the number of books, most of which are new and can be checked for relevant articles, plus the lists of works in the sections on the Maya and ancient Mesoamerica in general are fairly extensive.

However, a very large body of useful references can also be found in the bibliographies of the works listed here, in older journals and books, and in library databases. The literature continues to accrue each year, thus the lists of journals, series, publication sources, and institutions given in this dictionary can be consulted for up-to-date information on ancient Mesoamerica. Most of the sources provided are found in the more widely distributed and known publications and presses, especially those of the United States. Another valuable source of data, excavation news, reading material, local organizations, and teaching aids on past Mesoamerican societies is available on computer in countless Internet sites and CD-ROM archives. A quick and complete search can be made through accessing the databases through "key words" such as Mesoamerica, Middle America, Mesoamerican archaeology and studies, Maya, Aztec, and so forth.

There are also many reference books, general source books, and text-books on Pre-Columbian Mesoamerica that synthesize many of the topics covered in this dictionary. Some well-illustrated works on ancient Mesoamerica that contain general information plus the results of recent investigations include *The Aztecs, Maya, and Their Predecessors* (Porter Weaver 1995), *The Art of Mesoamerica* (Miller 1986), *Diccionario de antropología mesoamericana: Volumes 1 and 2* (Macazaga Ordono 1985), *Encyclopedia of Ancient Mesoamerica* (Bunson 1996), *The Gods and Symbols of Ancient Mexico and the Maya* (Miller and Taube 1993), *Prehistoric Mesoamerica* (Adams 1991), and *Precolumbian Art* (Pasztory 1998).

Comprehensive but occasionally dated works, although additions and updates are continuing, on Mesoamerican prehistory and culture are found in the multivolume set *Handbook of Middle American Indians* (University of Texas Press). An all-encompassing opus on ancient Mesoamerica that contains short descriptive entries and figures and that will soon be available is *The Archaeology of Ancient Mexico and Central America: An Encyclopedia* (Evans, editor, New York: Garland Publishing, in press). The scholarly journals *Anales del Instituto Nacional de Antropología e Historia de México* (Mexico City), *Ancient Mesoamerica* (Cambridge University Press), and *Latin American Antiquity* (Society of American Archaeology), and the popular magazines *Archaeology* (Archaeological Institute of America) and *Arqueología Mexicana* (Mexico City) contain general information and current research regarding Mesoamerica.

Two newly revised publications that are often combined for college courses and general reference are *Mexico: From the Olmecs to the Aztecs* (Coe 1994) and *The Maya* (Coe 1999). These last two works contain many photos, line drawings, and general descriptions of ancient Mesoamerican sites and their histories. Two books that provide information on Mesoamerican archaeology in conjunction with discussions of the Spanish Colonial Period and present cultures are *The Legacy of Mesoamerica* (Carmack et al. 1996) and *Sons of Shaking Earth* (Wolf 1959). An excellent map of ancient Mesoamerican sites and peoples has been published by *National Geographic* since December 1997 (Map: Ancient Mesoamerica/The Mesoamericans). For videos on ancient Mesoamerica, refer to the *500 Nations* series (Warner Home Video; Burbank, CA, 1994–95), *Spirits of the Jaguar* series (Thirteen WNET, New York, 1997), and the continuous visual specials from *National Geographic*.

There are many excellent publications that cover the earliest civilizations in ancient Mesoamerica, particularly the Olmec civilization of the Gulf Coast area of Mexico. Some scholarly publications that contain much information, plus are well illustrated with drawings and photographs, include *The Olmecs* (Soustelle 1979), *The Olmec and Their Neighbors* (Benson and Coe, eds., 1981), *The Olmec World* (Benson, ed., 1995), and *Regional Perspectives on the Olmec* (Sharer and Grove, eds., 1989). The earliest peoples and villages of Mesoamerica, plus significant archaeological data and artifacts, are presented in *The Chantuto People* (Voorhies 1976), *Early Cultures and Human Ecology in South Coastal Guatemala* (Coe and Flannery 1967),

The Early Mesoamerican Village (Flannery, ed., 1976), *The Formation of Complex Society in Southeastern Mesoamerica* (Fowler, ed., 1991), and *Prehistory of the Tehuacan Valley* (Byers, ed., 1967).

Some useful and current synthetic works on widely researched regions and cultures of ancient Mesoamerica are available. To obtain information, illustrations, and bibliographies on the ancient Maya of Yucatan, southern Mexico, and Central America, see *The Ancient Maya* (Sharer 1994), *Ancient Maya Civilization* (Hammond 1982), *The Maya* (Coe 1999), and *The World of the Ancient Maya* (Henderson 1981). The results of recent research and concise summaries of excavation data and theories are found in *Lowland Maya Civilization in the Eighth Century A.D.* (Sabloff and Andrews 1993) and *The Blood of Kings: Ritual and Dynasty in Classic Maya Art* (Schele and Miller 1986). Many of these books provide excellent bibliographies. However, for a more complete set of publications, see the reference books *Maya Civilization* and *Maya Civilization 1990–1995* (Weeks 1993 and 1997, respectively).

Besides these complete volumes, photos and drawings of ancient Maya art can be accessed in the multiple tomes of the *Corpus of Maya Hieroglyphic Inscriptions* (Peabody Museum of Harvard University) and *The Maya Vase Book* (New York: Kerr Associates), both of which are continuing publications. Examples of descriptions of colonial era Maya society taken from early Spanish documents is available in *Landa's "Relación de las cosas de Yucatán"* (Tozzer 1941) and *The Quiche Mayas of Utatlan* (Carmack 1981). Studies of the societies found to the southeast of the Maya and who interacted with them are in *The Cultural Evolution of Ancient Nahua Civilizations* (Fowler 1989), *Interaction on the Southeast Mesoamerican Frontier* (Robinson 1987), and *The Southeast Maya Periphery* (Urban and Shortman, eds., 1986).

The predecessors of the Aztecs and early state-level societies in central Mexico are presented in well-illustrated and informative books called *Art, Ideology, and the City of Teotihuacan* (Berlo, ed., 1996), *The Mural Painting of Teotihuacan* (Miller 1973), *The Toltecs until the Fall of Tula* (Davies 1977), *Tula: The Toltec Capital of Ancient Mexico* (Diehl 1983), and *Urbanization at Teotihuacan, Mexico* (Millon, ed., 1973).

General summaries of the archaeology, society, material culture, and history of the Aztecs of central Mexico are found in *Aztecs: An Interpretation* (Clendinnen 1991) *The Aztecs of Central Mexico* (Berdan 1982), *Aztec Thought and Culture* (Leon-Portilla 1963), and *Everyday Life of the Aztecs* (Bray 1968). Some richly illustrated volumes on the Aztecs include *The Aztecs* (Townsend 1992), *Aztec Art* (Pasztory 1983), and *The Great Temple of the Aztecs* (Matos Moctezuma 1988). Discussions of Aztec society and the Spanish conquest from historical documents and eyewitness accounts are found at greater length in *Conquest* (Thomas 1993), *The Discovery and Conquest of Mexico* (Diaz del Castillo 1956), and *Florentine Codex* (Sahagun 1951–69).

The societies of ancient west Mexico, which traditionally have not been investigated to the extent of other parts of Mesoamerica, are currently drawing much attention from archaeologists and art historians. A new and excellent treatise of past cultures in West Mexico that has both valuable insights and large color photographs of ceramic figurines and artifacts is *Ancient West Mexico* (Townsend, ed., 1998). Other useful books on the archaeology of this subregion of Mesoamerica are *The Archaeology of West Mexico* (Bell, ed., 1974), *The Archaeology of West and Northwest Mesoamerica* (Foster and Weigand, eds., 1985), *Art prehispánico del Occidente de México* (Von Winning 1996), and *Evolución de una civilización prehispánica: Arqueología de Jalisco, Nayarit, y Zacatecas* (Weigand 1993). Information on the rival state of the Aztecs, the Postclassic Tarascan empire of West Mexico, and recent research in Tarascan archaeology, ethnohistory, and artifacts are *Taríacuri's Legacy: The Prehispanic Tarascan State* (Pollard 1993) and *The Tarascan Civilization* (Gorenstein and Pollard 1983).

For complete discussions, photographs, and drawings from archaeological projects and studies of art and architecture with ancient cultures from southeast Mexico there are many references. For the lowland and coastal societies refer to *Historia prehispánica de la Huaxteca* (Ochoa 1984), *Olmec to Aztec: Settlement Patterns in the Ancient Gulf Lowlands* (Stark and Arnold, eds., 1997), and *The Sculptures of El Tajin* (Kampen 1972). Recent publications on the highland peoples with many illustrations and cultural information include *The Cloud People* (Flannery and Marcus, eds., 1983), *The Mixtec Kings and Their People* (Spores 1967), *Zapotec Civilization* (Marcus and Flannery 1996), and *The Zapotecs: Princes, Priests, and Peasants* (Whitecotton 1977).

CONTENTS

SERIES AND JOURNALS

American Anthropologist. Journal of the American Anthropological Association.
American Antiquity. Journal of the Society of American Archaeology.
Anales del Instituto Nacional de Antropología e Historia de México. Mexico City.
Ancient Mesoamerica. Cambridge University Press.
Arqueología Mexicana. Mexico City.
Contributions to American Archaeology. Carnegie Institution of Washington. Washington, D.C.
Estudios de Cultura Maya. Mexico City.
Estudios de Cultura Nahuatl. Mexico City.
Foundation for Latin American Anthropological Research. Graz, Austria.
Handbook of Middle American Indians. Austin: University of Texas Press.
Journal de la Société des Americanistes. Paris, France.
Journal of Field Archaeology. Boston, Mass.
Latin American Antiquity. Journal of the Society of American Archaeology.
Memoirs of the Peabody Museum of Archaeology and Ethnology. Cambridge, Mass.: Harvard University.
Mesa Redonda de Palenque/Palenque Round Table. San Francisco: Pre-Columbian Art Research Institute.
Mesoamérica. Antigua, Guatemala.
Middle American Research Institute Publications. New Orleans: Tulane University.
Papers of the New World Archaeological Foundation. Provo, Utah: Brigham Young University.
Revista Mexicana de Estudios Antropológicos. Mexico City.
Simposios de investigaciones arqueológicas en Guatemala. Guatemala City: Ministerio de Cultura y Deportes.

Studies in Ancient Mesoamerica. Berkeley: University of California.
Studies in Precolumbian Art and Archaeology. Washington, D.C.: Dumbarton Oaks.
Supplement to the Handbook of Middle American Indians. Austin: University of Texas Press.
Vanderbilt University Publications in Anthropology. Nashville, Tenn.

GENERAL INFORMATION

Adams, Richard E. W. *Prehistoric Mesoamerica.* Norman: University of Oklahoma Press, 1991.
Anawalt, Patricia. *Indian Clothing before Cortés.* Norman: University of Oklahoma Press, 1981.
Bernal, Ignacio. *A History of Mexican Archaeology.* London: Thames and Hudson, 1980.
Boone, Elizabeth H. (editor). *Ritual Human Sacrifice in Mesoamerica.* Washington, D.C.: Dumbarton Oaks, 1984.
Bunson, Margaret. *Encyclopedia of Ancient Mesoamerica.* New York: Facts on File, 1996.
Carmack, Robert M., Janine Gasco, and Gary H. Gossen. *The Legacy of Mesoamerica: History and Culture of a Native American Civilization.* Upper Saddle River, N.J.: Prentice Hall/Simon and Schuster, 1996.
Carrasco, David. *Religions of Mesoamerica: Cosmovision and Ceremonial Centers.* Prospect Heights, Ill.: Waveland Press, 1998.
Caso, Alfonso. *Los calendarios prehispánicos.* Mexico City: Universidad Nacional Autónoma de México, 1967.
Closs, Michael P. *Native American Mathematics.* Austin: University of Texas Press, 1986.
Coe, Michael D. *Mexico: From the Olmecs to the Aztecs* (fourth edition). London: Thames and Hudson, 1994.
Coe, Sophie D. *America's First Cuisines.* Austin: University of Texas Press, 1994.
Edmonson, Monro S. *The Book of the Year: Middle American Calendrical Systems.* Salt Lake City: University of Utah Press, 1988.
Evans, Susan (editor). *The Archaeology of Ancient Mexico and Central America: An Encyclopedia.* New York: Garland Publishing, in press.
González Torres, Yólotl. *Diccionario de mitología y religión de mesoamérica.* Mexico City: Larousse, 1991.
Hristov, Romeo, and Santiago Genovés. "Mesoamerican Evidence of Pre-Columbian Transoceanic Contacts." *Ancient Mesoamerica* 10(2): 207–13, 1999.
Kirchoff, Paul. "Mesoamerica." *Acta Americana* 1: 92–107, 1943.
———. "Meso-america." *Heritage of Conquest,* edited by Sol Tax, 17–30. Glencoe, Ill.: Glencoe Press, 1952.
Kubler, George. *The Art and Architecture of Ancient America: The Mexican, Maya, and Andean Peoples.* New Haven, Conn.: Yale University Press, 1990.

Macazaga Ordono, Cesar. *Diccionario de antropología mesoamericana.* Mexico City: Editorial Innovación, 1985.

Malmstrom, Vincent H. *Cycles of the Sun, Mysteries of the Moon: The Calendar in Mesoamerican Civilization.* Austin: University of Texas Press, 1997.

Marquina, Ignacio. *Arquitectura Prehispánica.* Mexico City: Memorias del Instituto Nacional de Antropología e Historia, 1951.

Miller, Mary E. *The Art of Mesoamerica: From Olmec to Aztec.* London: Thames and Hudson, 1986.

Miller, Mary E., and Karl Taube. *The Gods and Symbols of Ancient Mexico and the Maya.* London: Thames and Hudson, 1993.

Muser, Curt. *Facts and Artifacts of Ancient Middle America: A Glossary of Terms and Words Used in the Archaeology and Art History of Pre-Columbian Mexico and Central America.* New York: Dutton, 1978.

Pang, Hildegard Delgado. *Pre-Columbian Art.* Norman: University of Oklahoma Press, 1992.

Pasztory, Esther. *Precolumbian Art.* Cambridge: Cambridge University Press, 1998.

Porter Weaver, Muriel. *The Aztecs, Maya, and Their Predecessors: Archaeology of Mesoamerica* (third edition). New York: Academic Press, 1995.

Prem, Hans J. "The 'Canek Manuscript' and Other Faked Documents." *Ancient Mesoamerica* 10(2): 297–312, 1999.

Schroeder, Susan, Stephanie Wood, and Robert Haskett (editors). *Indian Women of Early Mexico.* Norman: University of Oklahoma Press, 1999.

Seler, Eduard. *Collected Works in Mesoamerican Linguistics and Archaeology* (four volumes), edited by Frank Compato. Culver City, Calif.: Labyrinthos, 1993 [1904].

Taube, Karl. *Aztec and Maya Myths.* Austin: University of Texas Press, 1993.

Wauchope, Robert. *They Found Their Buried Cities.* Chicago: University of Chicago Press, 1965.

Webster, David L., Susan T. Evans, and William T. Sanders. *Out of the Past: An Introduction to Archaeology.* Mountain View, Calif.: Mayfield Publishing, 1993.

Willey, Gordon R. "Mesoamerica." In *Courses toward Urban Life,* edited by Robert Braidwood and Gordon R. Willey. New York: Viking Fund Publications in Anthropology, No. 32: 84–105, 1962.

Wolf, Eric R. *Sons of Shaking Earth.* Chicago: University of Chicago Press, 1959.

EARLY MESOAMERICAN PEOPLES

Aveleyra, L. "The Second Mammoth and Associated Artifacts at Santa Isabel Iztapan, Mexico." *American Antiquity* 22: 12–28, 1956.

Byers, D. S. (editor). *Prehistory of the Tehuacan Valley.* Austin: University of Texas Press, 1967.

Ceja Tenorio, Jorge Fausto. *Paso de la Amada: An Early Preclassic Site in the Soconusco, Chiapas.* Paper no. 49, New World Archaeological Foundation. Provo, Utah: Brigham Young University, 1985.

Coe, Michael D. "Archaeological Linkages with North and South America at La Victoria, Guatemala." *American Anthropologist* 62(3): 363–93, 1960.

————. *La Victoria, an Early Site on the Pacific Coast of Guatemala.* Papers of the Peabody Museum of Archaeology and Ethnology, vol. 53. Cambridge, Mass.: Harvard University, 1961.

Coe, Michael D., and Kent V. Flannery. *Early Cultures and Human Ecology in South Coastal Guatemala.* Washington, D.C.: Smithsonian Contributions to Anthropology 3, 1967.

Flannery, Kent V. (editor). *The Early Mesoamerican Village.* New York: Academic Press, 1976.

Green, D. F., and Gareth W. Lowe. *Altamira and Padre Piedra, Early Preclassic Sites in Chiapas, Mexico.* Paper no. 20, New World Archaeological Foundation. Provo, Utah: Brigham Young University, 1967.

Greengo, R. E., and C. W. Meighan. "Additional Perspectives on the Capacha Complex of Western Mexico." *Journal of New World Archaeology* 1(5): 15–23, 1976.

Leisure, Richard G. "Refining an Early Formative Ceramic Sequence from the Chiapas Coast of Mexico." *Ancient Mesoamerica* 9(1): 67–82, 1998.

MacNeish, Richard S., and Antoinette Nelken-Terner. "The Preceramic of Mesoamerica." *Journal of Field Archaeology* 10(1): 71–84, 1983.

Nicholson, Henry B. (editor). *The Origins of Religious Art and Iconography in Preclassic Mesoamerica.* Los Angeles: Latin American Center, 1976.

Niederberger, Christine. "Early Sedentary Economy in the Basin of Mexico." *Science* 203(4376): 131–41, 1979.

Piña Chan, R. *Tlatilco.* Serie Investigaciones, nos. 1, 2. Mexico City: Instituto Nacional de Antropología e Historia, 1958.

Pohl, Mary D., Kevin O. Pope, John G. Jones, John S. Jacob, Dolores R. Piperno, Susan D. deFrance, David L. Lentz, John A. Gifford, Marie E. Danforth, and J. Kathryn Josserand. "Early Agriculture in the Maya Lowlands." *Latin American Antiquity* 7(4): 355–72, 1996.

Rue, David J. "Archaic Middle American Agriculture and Settlement: Recent Pollen Data from Honduras." *Journal of Field Archaeology* 16(2): 177–84, 1989.

Voorhies, Barbara. *The Chantuto People: An Archaic Period Society of the Chiapas Littoral, Mexico.* Paper no. 41, New World Archaeological Foundation. Provo, Utah: Brigham Young University, 1976.

Whalen, Michael. "Reconstructing Early Formative Village Organization in Oaxaca, Mexico." *American Antiquity* 48: 17–43, 1983.

Wilson, Samuel M., Harry B. Iceland, and Thomas R. Hester. "Preceramic Connections between Yucatán and the Caribbean." *Latin American Antiquity* 9(4): 342–52, 1998.

OLMEC CIVILIZATION

Benson, Elizabeth P. (editor). *Dumbarton Oaks Conference on the Olmec.* Washington, D.C.: Dumbarton Oaks, 1968.

————. *The Olmec World: Ritual and Rulership*. Princeton, N.J.: Princeton University Press, 1995.

Benson, Elizabeth P., and Michael D. Coe (editors). *The Olmec and Their Neighbors*. Washington, D.C.: Dumbarton Oaks, 1981.

Bernal, Ignacio. *The Olmec World*. Translated by Doris Heyden and Fernando Horcasitas. Berkeley: University of California Press, 1969.

Bove, Frederic J. "Laguna de los Cerros: An Olmec Central Place." *Journal of New World Archaeology* 2(3): 1–43, 1978.

Clewlow, Carl William Jr. *A Stylistic and Chronological Study of Olmec Monumental Sculpture*. Contributions of the University of California Archaeological Research Facility no. 19. Berkeley: Department of Anthropology, University of California, 1974.

Coe, Michael D. "The Olmec Style and Its Distribution." In *Handbook of Middle American Indians* (vol. 3), edited by Robert Wauchope, pp. 739–75. Austin: University of Texas Press, 1965.

————. *America's First Civilization: Discovering the Olmec*. New York: American Heritage, 1968.

Coe, Michael D., and Richard A. Diehl. *In the Land of the Olmec* (two volumes). Austin: University of Texas Press, 1980.

de la Fuente, Beatriz. *Los hombres de piedra: Escultura olmeca*. Mexico City: Instituto de Investigaciones Estéticas, Universidad Nacional Autónoma de México, 1977.

————. "Order and Nature in Olmec Art." In *The Ancient Americas: Art from Sacred Landscapes,* edited by Richard Townsend, pp. 121–34. Chicago: Art Institute of Chicago, 1992.

Drucker, Philip. *La Venta, Tabasco: A Study of Olmec Ceramics and Art*. Bureau of American Ethnology, Bulletin 153. Washington, D.C.: Smithsonian Institution, 1952.

Gillespie, Susan D. "Llano de Jícaro: An Olmec Monument Workshop." *Ancient Mesoamerica* 5(2): 231–42, 1994.

González Lauck, Rebecca. "Proyecto arqueológico La Venta." *Arqueología* 4: 121–65. Instituto Nacional de Antropología e Historia, Mexico City, 1988.

Grove, David C. *Ancient Chalcatzingo*. Austin: University of Texas Press, 1987.

————. "Olmec Archaeology: A Half Century of Research and Its Accomplishments." *Journal of World Prehistory* 11 (1): 51–73, 1997.

Guillén, Ann Cyphers. "Investigaciones recientes en San Lorenzo Tenochtitlán, Veracruz: Temporada 1991." *Boletín del Consejo de Arqueología* 1991: 63–6. Mexico City: Instituto Nacional de Antropología e Historia, 1992.

Haslip-Viera, Gabriel, Bernard Ortiz, and Warren Barbour. "Robbing Native American Cultures: Van Sertima's Afrocentricity and the Olmecs." *Current Anthropology* 38(3): 419–42, 1997.

Joesink-Mandeville, L. R. V. "Olmec-Maya Relationships: A Correlation of Linguistical Evidence with Archaeological Ceramics." *Journal of New World Archaeology* 2(1): 30–9, 1977.

Joralemon, P. D. *A Study of Olmec Iconography*. Washington, D.C.: Dumbarton Oaks, 1971.

National Gallery of Art. *Olmec Art of Ancient Mexico.* Washington, D.C.: National Gallery of Art, 1996.

Piña Chan, Roman. *The Olmec: Mother Culture of Mesoamerica.* New York: Rizzoli, 1989.

Sharer, Robert J., and David C. Grove (editors). *Regional Perspectives on the Olmec.* Cambridge: Cambridge University Press, 1989.

Soustelle, Jacques. *The Olmecs: The Oldest Civilization in Mexico.* Norman: University of Oklahoma Press, 1979.

THE ANCIENT MAYA

Adams, Richard E. W. *Río Azul: An Ancient Maya City.* Norman: University of Oklahoma Press, 1999.

Adams, Richard E. W. (editor). *The Origins of Maya Civilization.* Albuquerque: University of New Mexico Press, 1977.

Ashmore, Wendy (editor). *Maya Lowland Settlement Patterns.* Albuquerque: University of New Mexico Press, 1981.

Ball, Joseph W., and Jennifer T. Taschek. "Late Classic Lowland Maya Political Organization and Central-Place Analysis," *Ancient Mesoamerica* 2(2): 149–65, 1991.

Berlin, Heinrich. "El glifo emblema en las inscripciones Mayas." *Journal de la Société des Americanistes* 47: 111–19, 1958.

Brady, James E. "Settlement Configuration and Cosmology: The Role of Caves at Dos Pilas." *American Anthropologist* 99(3): 602–18, 1997.

Carmack, Robert. *The Quiche Mayas of Utatlan.* Norman: University of Oklahoma Press, 1981.

Chase, Arlen, and Prudence Rice (editors). *The Lowland Maya Postclassic.* Austin: University of Texas Press, 1985.

Coe, Michael D. *Breaking the Maya Code.* London: Thames and Hudson, 1992.

———. *The Maya* (sixth edition). London: Thames and Hudson, 1999.

Culbert, T. Patrick (editor). *The Classic Maya Collapse.* Albuquerque: University of New Mexico Press, 1973.

———. *Classic Maya Political History: Hieroglyphic and Archaeological Evidence.* Cambridge: Cambridge University Press, 1991.

Danien, Elin C., and Robert J. Sharer (editors). *New Theories on the Ancient Maya.* University Museum Monograph 77. Philadelphia: University of Pennsylvania Museum, 1992.

Demarest, Arthur A. "War, Peace, and the Collapse of a Native American Civilization." In *A Natural History of Peace,* edited by Thomas Gregor, pp. 215–48. London: Vanderbilt University Press, 1996.

de Montmollin, Oliver. *The Archaeology of Political Structure: Settlement Analysis in a Classic Maya Polity.* Cambridge: Cambridge University Press, 1989.

Fash, William L. *Scribes, Warriors, and Kings: The City of Copan and the Ancient Maya.* London: Thames and Hudson, 1991.

Fedick, Scott L. (editor). *The Managed Mosaic: Ancient Maya Agriculture and Resource Use.* Salt Lake City: University of Utah Press, 1996.

Fox, John W., Garret W. Cook, Arlen F. Chase, and Diane Z. Chase. "Questions of Political and Economic Integration: Segmentary versus Centralized States among the Ancient Maya." *Current Anthropology* 37(5): 795–830, 1996.

Freidel, David, Linda Schele, and Joy Parker. *Maya Cosmos: Three Thousand Years on the Shaman's Path.* New York: William Morrow, 1993.

Graham, Ian. *The Corpus of Maya Hieroglyphic Inscriptions.* Cambridge, Mass.: Peabody Museum of Archaeology and Ethnology, Harvard University, (series).

Hammond, Norman. *Ancient Maya Civilization.* New Brunswick, N.J.: Rutgers University Press, 1982.

Hammond, Norman (editor). *Social Process in Maya Prehistory.* New York: Academic Press, 1977.

Hammond, Norman, and Gordon R. Willey (editors). *Maya Archaeology and Ethnohistory.* Austin: University of Texas Press, 1979.

Harris, John F., and Stephen K. Stearns. *Understanding Maya Inscriptions: A Hieroglyphic Handbook* (second edition). Philadelphia: University of Pennsylvania Museum, 1997.

Harrison, Peter D., and B. L. Turner (editors). *Prehistoric Maya Agriculture.* Albuquerque: University of New Mexico Press, 1978.

Henderson, John S. *The World of the Ancient Maya.* Ithaca, N.Y.: Cornell University Press, 1981.

Houston, Stephen D. *Maya Glyphs.* Berkeley: University of California Press, 1989.

———. *Hieroglyphs and History at Dos Pilas: Dynastic Politics of the Classic Maya.* Austin: University of Texas Press, 1993.

———. "The Shifting Now: Aspect, Deixis, and Narrative in Classic Maya Texts." *American Anthropologist* 99(2): 291–305, 1997.

Jones, Grant D. "The Canek Manuscript in Ethnohistoric Perspective." *Ancient Mesoamerica* 3(2): 243–68, 1992.

Joyce, Rosemary A. "The Construction of Gender in Classic Maya Monuments." In *Gender and Archaeology,* edited by Rita P. Wright, pp. 167–98. Philadelphia: University of Pennsylvania Press, 1996.

Kelley, David H. "A History of the Decipherment of Maya Script." *Anthropological Linguistics* 4(8): 1–48, 1962.

Kerr, Justin. *The Maya Vase Book* (vols. 1–5). New York: Kerr Associates, 1990–97 (series).

Knorozov, Yuri V. *The Writing of the Maya Indians (Russian Translation Series).* Cambridge, Mass.: Harvard University Press, 1967.

Kubler, George A. "Chichén-Itzá y Tula." *Estudios de cultura Maya* 1: 47–79. Mexico City: Universidad Nacional Autónoma de México, 1961.

Lee, Thomas. *Los códices Mayas.* Tuxtla Gutierez, Chiapas, Mexico: Universidad Autónoma de Chiapas, 1985.

Lounsbury, Floyd. "Astronomical Knowledge and Its Uses at Bonampak, Mexico." In *Archaeoastronomy in the New World,* edited by Anthony F. Aveni, pp. 143–68. Cambridge: Cambridge University Press, 1982.

Lowe, John W. G. *The Dynamics of the Apocalypse: A Systems Simulation of the Classic Maya Collapse.* Albuquerque: University of New Mexico Press, 1985.

Martin, Simon, and Nikolai Grube. "Maya Superstates." *Archaeology* 48(6): 41–6, 1995.

Matheny, Ray T. *El Mirador, Petén, Guatemala: Introduction.* Paper no. 59, New World Archaeological Foundation. Provo, Utah: Brigham Young University, 1993.

Maudslay, Alfred P. *Biologia Centrali-Americana: Archaeology.* London: E. Du Cane Godman and Osbert Salvin, 1889–1902.

McAnany, Patricia A. *Living with the Ancestors: Kinship and Kingship in Ancient Maya Society.* Austin: University of Texas Press, 1995.

Michels, Joseph W. *The Kaminaljuyu Chiefdom.* University Park: Pennsylvania State University Press, 1979.

Milbrath, Susan. *Star Gods of the Maya: Astronomy in Art, Folklore, and Calendars.* Austin: University of Texas Press, 2000.

Miller, Mary E. *The Murals of Bonampak.* Princeton, N.J.: Princeton University Press, 1986.

———. *Maya Art and Architecture.* London: Thames and Hudson, 1999.

Palka, Joel W. "Sociopolitical Implications of a New Emblem Glyph and Place Name in Classic Maya Inscriptions." *Latin American Antiquity* 7(3): 211–27, 1996.

———. "Reconstructing Classic Maya Socioeconomic Differentiation and the Collapse at Dos Pilas, Peten, Guatemala." *Ancient Mesoamerica* 8(2): 293–306, 1997.

Proskouriakoff, Tatiana. "Historical Implication of a Pattern of Dates at Piedras Negras, Guatemala," *American Antiquity,* vol. 25(4): 454–75, 1960.

———. *An Album of Maya Architecture.* Carnegie Institution of Washington, publication 558. Washington, D.C.: Carnegie Institution of Washington, 1962.

———. *Maya History.* Austin: University of Texas Press, 1993.

Reents-Budet, Dorie. *Painting the Maya Universe: Royal Ceramics of the Classic Period.* Durham, N.C.: Duke University Press, 1994.

Sabloff, Jeremy A., and E. Wyllys Andrews V (editors). *Late Lowland Maya Civilization: Classic to Postclassic.* Albuquerque: University of New Mexico Press, 1986.

Sabloff, Jeremy A., and John S. Henderson (editors). *Lowland Maya Civilization in the Eighth Century A.D.* Washington, D.C.: Dumbarton Oaks, 1993.

Schele, Linda, and David Friedel. *A Forest of Kings: The Untold Story of the Ancient Maya.* New York: William Morrow, 1990.

Schele, Linda, and Peter Mathews. *The Code of Kings: The Language of Seven Sacred Maya Temples and Tombs.* New York: Scribner, Simon and Schuster, 1998.

Schele, Linda, and Mary E. Miller. *The Blood of Kings: Ritual and Dynasty in Classic Maya Art.* New York: George Braziller, 1986.

Sharer, Robert J. *The Ancient Maya* (fifth edition). Stanford, Calif.: Stanford University Press, 1994.

Stephens, John Lloyd, and Frederick Catherwood. *Incidents of Travel in Central America, Chiapas, and Yucatan.* New York: Dover, 1962.

Stuart, David S. "The Rio Azul Cacao Pot: Epigraphic Observations on the Function of a Maya Ceramic Vessel," *Antiquity* 62: 153–57, 1988.

Taube, Karl A. *The Major Gods of Ancient Yucatan.* Washington, D.C.: Dumbarton Oaks, 1992.

Tedlock, Dennis (translation). *Popol Vuh.* New York: Simon and Schuster, 1985.

Thompson, J. Eric S. *Maya History and Religion.* Norman: University of Oklahoma Press, 1970.

————. *Maya Hieroglyphic Writing: An Introduction.* Norman: University of Oklahoma Press, 1971.

————. *A Commentary on the Dresden Codex.* American Philosophical Society Memoir 93, Philadelphia, 1972.

Tozzer, Alfred M. *Landa's "Relación de las cosas de Yucatán": A Translation.* Papers of the Peabody Museum of American Archaeology and Ethnology, vol. 18. Cambridge, Mass.: Harvard University, 1941.

Villacorta, J. A., and C. A. Villacorta. *Códices Maya.* Guatemala City: Tipografía Nacional, 1930.

Weeks, John M. *Maya Civilization.* New York: Garland Publishing, 1993.

————. *Maya Civilization 1990–1995: A Research Guide (Volume 2).* Lancaster, Calif.: Labyrinthos, 1997.

Willey, Gordon. *Prehistoric Maya Settlements in the Belize Valley.* Papers of the Peabody Museum of American Archaeology and Ethnology, vol. 54. Cambridge, Mass.: Harvard University, 1965.

ANCIENT MEXICO

Aveni, Anthony F. *Skywatchers of Ancient Mexico.* Austin: University of Texas Press, 1980.

Boone, Elizabeth H. "Pictorial Codices of Ancient Mexico." In *The Ancient Americas: Art from Sacred Landscapes,* edited by Richard Townsend, pp. 197–209. Chicago: Art Institute of Chicago, 1992.

Boone, Elizabeth H. (editor). *The Art and Iconography of Late Post-Classic Central Mexico.* Washington, D.C.: Dumbarton Oaks, 1982.

Coe, Michael D. *The Jaguar's Children: Preclassic Central Mexico.* New York: Museum of Primitive Art, 1965.

Crespo González, Norberto. "Archaeological Investigations at Xochicalco, Morelos: 1984 and 1986." *Ancient Mesoamerica* 6(2): 223–36, 1995.

Diaz del Castillo, Bernal. *The Discovery and Conquest of Mexico.* Translated and edited by Alfred P. Maudslay. New York: Farrar, Straus, and Giroux, 1956.

Garcia Cook, Angel. "The Historical Importance of Tlaxcala in the Cultural Development of the Central Mexican Highlands." In *Archaeology,* edited by Jeremy A. Sabloff, pp. 244–76. Supplement to the *Handbook of Middle American Indians,* vol. 1. Austin: University of Texas Press, 1981.

Hassig, Ross. *Trade, Tribute, and Transportation: The Sixteenth-Century Political Economy of the Valley of Mexico.* Norman: University of Oklahoma Press, 1985.

Heizer, R. F., and J. A. Bennyhoff. "Archaeological Investigation of Cuicuilco, Valley of Mexico." *Science* 127: 232–3, 1958.

Hirth, Kenneth G. "Urbanism, Militarism, and Architectural Design: An Analysis of Epiclassic Sociopolitical Structure at Xochicalco, Morelos." *Ancient Mesoamerica* 6(2): 237–50, 1995.

León-Portilla, Miguel. *Pre-Columbian Literatures of Mexico.* Norman: University of Oklahoma Press, 1969.

Lombarto de Ruíz, Sonia, Diana López de Molina, and Daniel Feal Molina. *Cacaxtla: El lugar donde muere la lluvia en la tierra.* Mexico City: Instituto Nacional de Antropología e Historia, 1986.

MacNeish, Richard S. (general editor). *The Prehistory of the Tehuacan Valley* (five volumes). Austin: University of Texas Press, 1972.

McCafferty, Geoffrey G. "Reinterpreting the Great Pyramid of Cholula, Mexico." *Ancient Mesoamerica* 7(1): 1–18, 1996.

McVicker, Don. "The 'Mayanized' Mexicans," *American Antiquity,* 50: 82–101, 1985.

Mountjoy, Joseph, and David A. Peterson. *Man and Land in Prehispanic Cholula.* Vanderbilt University Publications in Anthropology no. 4. Nashville, Tenn., 1973.

Nicholson, Henry B., and Eloise Quiñones Keber (editors). *Mixteca-Puebla: Discoveries and Research in Mesoamerican Art and Archaeology.* Lancaster, Calif.: Labyrinthos, 1994.

Plunket, Patricia, and Gabriela Uruñuela. "Preclassic Household Patterns Preserved under Volcanic Ash at Tetimpa, Puebla, Mexico." *Latin American Antiquity* 9(4): 287–309, 1998.

Robertson, Donald. "The Cacaxtla Murals." In *Fourth Palenque Round Table, 1980,* edited by Merle Greene Robertson and Elizabeth P. Benson, pp. 291–302. San Francisco: Pre-Columbian Research Institute, 1985.

Sanders, William T., Jeffrey R. Parsons, and Robert Santley. *The Basin of Mexico: Ecological Processes in the Evolution of a Civilization.* New York: Academic Press, 1979.

Seler, Eduard. *Códice Borgia,* (three volumes). Mexico City: Fondo de Cultura Economica, 1963.

Smith, Michael E., and Cynthia Heath-Smith. "Waves of Influence in Postclassic Mesoamerica? A Critique of the Mixteca-Puebla Concept." *Anthropology* 4(2): 15–50, 1980.

Smith, Virginia G. *Izapa Relief Carving: Form, Content, Rules for Design, and Role in Mesoamerican Art History and Archaeology*. Washington, D.C.: Dumbarton Oaks, 1984.

Stuart, George E. "Mural Masterpieces of Ancient Cacaxtla." *National Geographic* 182(3): 120–136, 1992.

CENTRAL AMERICA

Andrews, E. Wyllys V. *The Archaeology of Quelepa, El Salvador*. Middle American Research Institute Publication 42. New Orleans: Tulane University, 1976.

Baudez, Claude, and Pierre Becquelin. *Archéologie de los Naranjos*. Collection Etudes Mésoamericanistes, vol. 11. Mexico City: Mission Archéologique et Ethnologique Française au Mexique, 1973.

Boone, Elizabeth, and Gordon R. Willey (editors). *The Southeast Classic Maya Zone*. Washington, D.C.: Dumbarton Oaks, 1988.

Demarest, Arthur A. *The Archaeology of Santa Leticia and the Rise of Maya Civilization*. Middle American Research Institute, Publication 52. New Orleans: Tulane University, 1986.

Dixon, Boyd. "Prehistoric Political Change on the Southeast Mesoamerican Periphery." *Ancient Mesoamerica* 3(1): 11–26, 1992.

Fowler, William R. Jr. *The Cultural Evolution of Ancient Nahua Civilizations*. Norman: University of Oklahoma Press, 1989.

Fowler, William R. Jr. (editor). *The Formation of Complex Society in Southeastern Mesoamerica*. Boca Raton, Fla.: CRC Press, 1991.

Graham, John A. "Discoveries at Abaj Takalik, Guatemala." *Archaeology* 30(3): 196–7, 1977.

Healy, P. F. "The Cuyamel Caves: Preclassic Sites in Northeastern Honduras." *American Antiquity* 39: 435–47, 1974.

Joyce, Rosemary A. *Cerro Palenque: Power and Identity on the Maya Periphery*. Austin: University of Texas Press, 1991.

Kidder, A. V., J. D. Jennings, and E. M. Shook. *Excavations at Kaminaljuyu, Guatemala*. Carnegie Institution of Washington, Publication 561, Washington D.C., 1946.

Lange, Frederick W., and Doris Z. Stone (editors). *The Archaeology of Lower Central America*. Albuquerque: University of New Mexico Press, 1984.

Lee, Thomas A. Jr. *The Artifacts of Chiapa de Corzo, Chiapas, Mexico*. Paper no. 26, New World Archaeological Foundation. Provo, Utah: Brigham Young University, 1969.

Pahl, Gary (editor). *The Periphery of the Classic Maya Realm*. Berkeley: University of California Press, 1987.

Parsons, A. L. *Bilbao, Guatemala: An Archaeological Study of the Pacific Coast Cotzumalhuapa Region.* Milwaukee, Wisc.: Milwaukee Public Museum, 1969.

Robinson, Eugenia (editor). *Interaction on the Southeast Mesoamerican Frontier: Prehistoric and Historic Honduras and El Salvador.* B.A.R. International Series no. 327. Oxford: British Archaeological Reports, 1987.

Schortman, Edward M., and Patricia A. Urban. "Late Classic Society in the Rio Ulua Drainage, Honduras." *Journal of Field Archaeology* 22(4): 439–58, 1995.

Sharer, Robert. *The Prehistory of Chalcuapa, El Salvador* (three volumes). Philadelphia: University of Pennsylvania Press, 1978.

Sheets, Payson D. *The Ceren Site: A Prehistoric Village Buried by Volcanic Ash in Central America.* Fort Worth, Tex.: Harcourt Brace Jovanovich, 1992.

Sheets, Payson D. (editor). *Archaeology and Volcanism in Central America.* Austin: University of Texas Press, 1983.

Stone, Doris. *The Archaeology of Central and Southern Honduras.* Papers of the Peabody Museum of Archaeology and Ethnology, vol. 49(3). Cambridge, Mass.: Harvard University, 1957.

Thompson, J. Eric S. *An Archaeological Reconnaissance in the Cotzumalhuapa Region, Escuintla, Guatemala.* Publication 574. Washington, D.C.: Carnegie Institution of Washington, 1948.

Urban, Patricia A., and Edward M. Schortman (editors). *The Southeast Maya Periphery.* Austin: University of Texas Press, 1986.

Voorhies, Barbara (editor). *Ancient Trade and Tribute: Economies of the Soconusco Region of Mesoamerica.* Salt Lake City: University of Utah Press, 1989.

Wonderley, Anthony. "The Land of the Ulua: Postclassic Research in the Naco and Sula Valleys, Honduras." In *The Lowland Maya Postclassic,* edited by Arlen Chase and Prudence Rice, pp. 254–69. Austin: University of Texas Press, 1985.

TEOTIHUACAN

Berlo, Janet Catherine (editor). *Art, Ideology, and the City of Teotihuacan.* Washington, D.C.: Dumbarton Oaks, 1996.

Berrin, Kathleen (editor). *Feathered Serpents and Flowering Trees: Reconstructing the Murals of Teotihuacan.* Seattle: University of Washington Press, 1988.

Castro Cabrera, Ruben, George Cowgill, and Saburo Sugiyama. "El Proyecto Templo de Quetzalcoatl y la práctica a gran escala del sacrificio humana." In *La época clásica: Nuevos hallazgos, nuevas ideas,* edited by A. Cardos de Méndez, pp. 123–46. Mexico City: Instituto Nacional de Antropología e Historia, 1990.

Cowgill, George. "Rulership and the Ciudadela: Political Inferences from Teotihuacan Architecture." In *Civilization in the Ancient Americas,* edited by Richard M. Levanthal and Alan L. Kolata, pp. 313–43. Albuquerque: University of New Mexico Press, 1983.

Headrick, Annabeth. "The Street of the Dead . . . It Really Was: Mortuary Bundles at Teotihuacan." *Ancient Mesoamerica* 10(1): 69–86, 1999.

Heyden, Doris. "An Interpretation of the Cave underneath the Pyramid of the Sun in Teotihuacan, Mexico." *American Antiquity* 40: 131–47, 1975.

Kubler, George. "The Iconography of the Art of Teotihuacan." *Studies in Precolumbian Art and Archaeology,* no. 4. Washington, D.C.: Dumbarton Oaks, 1967.

Langley, James C. *Symbolic Notation of Teotihuacan.* B.A.R. International Series no. 313. Oxford: British Archaeological Reports, 1986.

López Austin, Alfredo, Leonardo López Austin, and Saburo Sugiyama. "The Temple of Quetzalcoatl at Teotihuacan: Its Possible Ideological Significance." *Ancient Mesoamerica* 2(1): 93–106, 1991.

Miller, Arthur G. *The Mural Painting of Teotihuacan.* Washington, D.C.: Dumbarton Oaks, 1973.

Millon, René. "Teotihuacan: City, State, and Civilization." In *Supplement to the Handbook of Middle American Indians,* vol. 1, edited by Victoria R. Bricker and Jeremy A. Sabloff, pp. 198–243. Austin: University of Texas Press, 1981.

Millon, René (editor). *Urbanization at Teotihuacan, Mexico.* Austin: University of Texas Press, 1973.

Pasztory, Esther. "The Natural World as Civic Metaphor at Teotihuacan." In *The Ancient Americas: Art from Sacred Landscapes,* edited by Richard Townsend, pp. 135–46. Chicago: Art Institute of Chicago, 1992.

————. *Teotihuacan: An Experiment in Living.* Norman: University of Oklahoma Press, 1998.

Sanders, William T., and Joseph W. Michels (editors). *Teotihuacan and Kaminaljuyu: A Study in Prehistoric Culture Contact.* University Park: Pennsylvania State University Press, 1977.

Santley, Robert S. "Obsidian Trade and Teotihuacan Influence in Mesoamerica." In *Highland-Lowland Interaction in Mesoamerica: Interdisciplinary Approaches,* edited by Arthur G. Miller, pp. 69–124. Washington, D.C.: Dumbarton Oaks, 1983.

Séjourné, Laurette. *Arquitectura y pintura en Teotihuacan.* Mexico City: Siglo XXI Ediciones, 1966.

Storey, Rebecca. *Life and Death in the Ancient City of Teotihuacan.* Tuscaloosa: University of Alabama Press, 1991.

Taube, Karl A. "The Teotihuacan Spider Woman," *Journal of Latin American Lore* 9(2): 107–89, 1983.

Winning, Hasso von. *La iconografía de Teotihuacan, los dioses y los signos* (two volumes). Mexico City: Universidad Nacional Autonóma de México, 1987.

ZAPOTECS, MIXTECS, AND OAXACA

Bernal, Ignacio. "Exploraciones en Coixtlahuaca, Oaxaca." *Revista Mexicana de Estudios Antropológicos* 10: 5–76, 1948–49.

Blanton, Richard E. *Monte Alban: Settlement Patterns at the Ancient Zapotec Capital.* New York: Academic Press, 1978.

Byland, Bruce, and John Pohl. *In the Realm of Eight Deer: The Archaeology of the Mixtec Codices.* Norman: University of Oklahoma Press, 1994.

Caso, Alfonso. "Zapotec Writing and Calendar." In *Handbook of Middle American Indians,* vol. 3, part 2, general editor, Gordon Willey, pp. 931–47. Austin: University of Texas Press, 1965.

————. *El Tesoro de Monte Alban.* Memorias del Instituto Nacional de Antropología e Historia no. 3, Mexico City, 1969.

Flannery, Kent V., and Joyce Marcus (editors). *The Cloud People: Divergent Evolution of the Zapotec and Mixtec Civilizations.* New York: Academic Press, 1983.

Joyce, Arthur A. "Interregional Interaction and Social Development on the Oaxaca Coast." *Ancient Mesoamerica* 4(1): 67–84, 1993.

Joyce, Arthur A., and Marcus Winter. "Ideology, Power, and Urban Society in Pre-Hispanic Oaxaca." *Current Anthropology* 37(1): 33–86, 1996.

Marcus, Joyce. "Zapotec Writing." *Scientific American* 242: 50–64, 1980.

Marcus, Joyce, and Kent V. Flannery. *Zapotec Civilization: How Urban Society Evolved in Mexico's Oaxaca Valley.* London: Thames and Hudson, 1996.

Monaghan, John. "Sacrifice, Death and the Origins of Agriculture in the Vienna Codex," *American Antiquity* 55: 559–69, 1990.

Nuttall, Zelia. *The Codex Nuttall: Facsimile of an Ancient Mexican Codex Belonging to Lord Zouche of Haryngworth.* Peabody Museum of American Archaeology and Ethnology. Cambridge, Mass.: Harvard University, 1902.

Paddock, J. *Ancient Oaxaca: Discoveries in Mexican Archaeology and History.* Stanford, Calif.: Stanford University Press, 1966.

Spencer, Charles. *The Cuicatlan Canada and Monte Alban: A Study of Primary State Formation.* New York: Academic Press, 1982.

Spores, Ronald. *The Mixtec Kings and Their People.* Norman: University of Oklahoma Press, 1967.

————. *The Mixtecs in Ancient and Colonial Times.* Norman: University of Oklahoma Press, 1984.

Troike, Nancy P. "Fundamental Changes in the Interpretations of the Mixtec Codices," *American Antiquity* 43(4): 553–68, 1978.

Urcid, Javier. "The Pacific Coast of Oaxaca and Guerrero: The Westernmost Extent of Zapotec Script." *Ancient Mesoamerica* 4(1): 141–66, 1993.

Whitecotton, Joseph W. *The Zapotecs: Princes, Priests, and Peasants.* Norman: University of Oklahoma Press, 1977.

Zeitlan, Robert N. "Pacific Coastal Laguna Zope: A Regional Center in the Terminal Formative Hinterlands of Monte Albán." *Ancient Mesoamerica* 4(1): 85–102, 1993.

THE TOLTECS

Acosta, Jorge R. "Resumen de las exploraciones arqueológicas en Tula, Hidalgo." *Anales del Instituto Nacional de Antropología e Historia* 8: 37–116, 1956.

————. "Interpretación de algunos de los datos obtenidos en Tula relativos a la época tolteca." *Revista Mexicana de Estudios Antropológicos* 14: 75–110, 1956–57.

Davies, C. Nigel. *The Toltecs until the Fall of Tula.* Norman: University of Oklahoma Press, 1977.

————. *The Toltec Heritage from the Fall of Tula to the Rise of Tenochtitlan.* Norman: University of Oklahoma Press, 1980.

Diehl, Richard A. *Studies of Ancient Tollan: A Report of the University of Missouri Monographs in Anthropology* no. 1. Columbia, Mo.: Department of Anthropology, University of Missouri, 1974.

————. *Tula: The Toltec Capital of Ancient Mexico.* London: Thames and Hudson, 1983.

Diehl, Richard A., and R. A. Benfer. "Tollan, the Toltec Capital." *Archaeology* 28, no. 2: 112–24, 1975.

Diehl, Richard A., Roger Lomas, and Jack Wynn. "Toltec Trade with Central America." *Archaeology* 27: 182–7, 1974.

Healan, Dan M. "Architectural Implications of Daily Life in Ancient Tollan." *World Archaeology* 9(2): 140–56, 1977.

Healan, Dan M. (editor). *Tula of the Toltecs.* Iowa City: University of Iowa Press, 1989.

Healan, Dan M., Janet M. Kerley, and George J. Bey III. "Excavation and Preliminary Analysis of an Obsidian Workshop in Tula, Hidalgo, Mexico." *Journal of Field Archaeology* 10(2): 127–46, 1983.

Jimenez Moreno, Wigberto. "Tula y los Toltecas segun las fuentes historicas." *Revista Mexicana de Estudios Antropologicos* 5, 79–83. Mexico City, 1941.

THE AZTEC EMPIRE

Baird, Ellen T. *The Drawings of Sahagún's Primeros Memoriales: Structure and Style.* Norman: University of Oklahoma Press, 1993.

Berdan, Frances. *The Aztecs of Central Mexico: An Imperial Society.* New York: Harcourt Brace College Publishers, 1982.

Berdan, Frances F., and Patricia Rieff Anawalt (editors). *The Codex Mendoza* (four volumes). Berkeley: University of California Press, 1992.

Boone, Elibabeth H. *The Aztec World.* Washington, D.C.: Smithsonian Institution Press, 1996.

Boone, Elizabeth H. (editor). *The Aztec Templo Mayor.* Washington, D.C.: Dumbarton Oaks, 1987.

Bray, Warwick. *Everyday Life of the Aztecs.* New York: G. P. Putnam, 1968.

Broda, Johanna, David Carrasco, and Eduardo Matos Moctezuma (editors). *The Great Temple of Tenochtitlan: Center and Periphery in the Aztec World.* Berkeley: University of California Press, 1987.

Brumfiel, Elizabeth M. "Elite and Utilitarian Crafts in the Aztec State." In *Special-*

ization, Exchange, and Complex Societies, edited by Elizabeth M. Brumfiel and Timothy Earle, pp. 102–18. Cambridge: Cambridge University Press, 1987.

———. "Figurines and the Aztec State: Testing the Effectiveness of Ideological Domination." In *Gender and Archaeology*, edited by Rita P. Wright, pp. 143–66. Philadelphia: University of Pennsylvania Press, 1996.

Brundage, B. C. *A Rain of Darts: The Mexica Aztecs*. Austin: University of Texas Press, 1972.

Carrasco, David (editor). *To Change Place: Aztec Ceremonial Landscapes*. Boulder: University of Colorado Press, 1991.

Carrasco, Pedro. *The Tenochca Empire of Ancient Mexico: The Triple Alliance of Tenochtitlan, Tetzcoco, and Tlacopan*. Norman: University of Oklahoma Press, 1999.

Caso, Alfonso. *The Aztecs, People of the Sun*. Norman: University of Oklahoma Press, 1958.

Clendinnen, Inga. *Aztecs: An Interpretation*. Cambridge: Cambridge University Press, 1991.

Davies, C. Nigel. *The Aztecs: A History*. New York: MacMillan, 1973.

Diaz del Castillo, Bernal. *The Discovery and Conquest of Mexico*. New York: Farrar, Straus, and Cudahy, 1956.

Galván Villegas, Luis Javier. *Aspectos generales de la arqueología de Malinalco, estado de México*. Instituto Nacional de Antropología e Historia, Colección Científica, no. 137, Mexico City, 1984.

Gillespie, Susan. *The Aztec Kings*. Tucson: University of Arizona Press, 1989.

Hassig, Ross. *Aztec Warfare*. Norman: University of Oklahoma Press, 1988.

Hodge, Mary G., and Michael E. Smith (editors). *Economics and Polities in the Aztec Realm*. Austin: University of Texas Press, 1994.

Kellogg, Susan. "The Woman's Room: Some Aspects of Gender Relations in Tenochtitlan in the Late Pre-Hispanic Period." *Ethnohistory* 42(4): 563–76, 1995.

Klein, Cecilia F. "The Identity of the Central Deity on the Aztec Calendar Stone." *Art Bulletin* 58: 1–12, 1976.

Leon-Portilla, Miguel. *Aztec Thought and Culture*. Norman: University of Oklahoma Press, 1963.

Matos Moctezuma, Eduardo. *The Great Temple of the Aztecs*. London: Thames and Hudson, 1988.

Pasztory, Esther. *Aztec Art*. Norman: University of Oklahoma Press, 1999.

Sahagun, Bernardino de. *Florentine Codex: General History of the Things of New Spain* (12 volumes). Sante Fe, N.M.: School of American Research, 1951–69.

Smith, Michael E. "The Aztec Marketing System and Settlement Pattern in the Valley of Mexico," *American Antiquity* 44: 110–25, 1979.

Thomas, Hugh. *Conquest: Montezuma, Cortés, and the Fall of Old Mexico*. New York: Simon and Schuster, 1993.

Townsend, Richard F. *State and Cosmos in the Art of Tenochtitlan*. Washington, D.C.: Dumbarton Oaks, 1979.

———. *The Aztecs*. London: Thames and Hudson, 1992.

Wolf, Eric R. (editor). *The Valley of Mexico*. Albuquerque: University of New Mexico Press, 1976.

NORTH AND WEST MEXICO

Aveni, Anthony F., H. Hartung, and J. C. Kelley. "Alta Vista (Chalchihuites), Astronomical Implications of a Mesoamerican Ceremonial Outpost at the Tropic of Cancer." *American Antiquity* 47: 326–35, 1982.

Bell, Betty (editor). *The Archaeology of West Mexico*. Ajijic, Mexico: Sociedad de Estudios Avanzados del Occidente de Mexico, 1974.

Boehm de Lameiras, Brigitte, and Phil C. Weigand (editors). *Origen y desarrollo en el occidente de Mexico*. Zamora, Mexico: El Colegio de Michoacán, 1992.

Cabrero G., Maria Teresa. "Cultura arqueológica de Bolanos (Zacatecas y Jalisco): Una frontera cultural." *Ancient Mesoamerica* 2(2): 193–204, 1991.

Craine, Eugene R., and Reginald C. Reindrop (editors). *The Chronicles of Michoacán*. Norman: University of Oklahoma Press, 1970.

Di Peso, Charles C. *Casas Grandes: A Fallen Trading Center for the Gran Chichimeca*. Amerind Foundation Publication 2(9). Flagstaff, Ariz.: Northland Press, 1974.

Doolittle, William E. "Settlements and the Development of 'Statelets' in Sonora, Mexico." *Journal of Field Archaeology* 11(1): 13–24, 1984.

Ericson, J. E., and T. G. Baugh (editors). *The American Southwest and Mesoamerica: Systems of Prehistoric Exchange*. New York: Plenum Press, 1993.

Folan, William (editor). *Contributions to the Archaeology and Ethnohistory of Greater Mesoamerica*. Carbondale: Southern Illinois University Press, 1985.

Foster, Michael, and Phil Weigand (editors). *The Archaeology of West and Northwest Mesoamerica*. Boulder, Colo.: Westview Press, 1985.

Furst, Peter T. "West Mexican Art: Secular or Sacred?" In *The Iconography of Middle American Sculpture*, pp. 98–133. New York: Metropolitan Museum of Art, 1973.

Gorenstein, Shirley, and Helen P. Pollard. *The Tarascan Civilization: A Late Pre-Hispanic Cultural System*. Vanderbilt University Publications in Anthropology, no. 28, Nashville, Tenn., 1983.

Hosler, Dorothy. *The Sounds and Colors of Power: The Sacred Metallurgical Technology of Ancient West Mexico*. Cambridge, Mass.: MIT Press, 1994.

Kan, Michael, Clement Meighan, and Henry B. Nicholson. *Sculpture of Ancient West Mexico*. Los Angeles: Los Angeles County Museum of Art, 1970.

Kelley, J. C. "Settlement Patterns in North-Central Mexico." In *Prehistoric Settlement Patterns in the New World*, edited by Gordon R. Willey. New York: Viking Fund Publications in Anthropology, no. 23, pp. 128–39, 1956.

Kelly, I. *Ceramic Sequence in Colima: Capacha, an Early Phase*. Anthropological Papers of the University of Arizona, no. 37. Tucson: University of Arizona Press, 1980.

Pollard, Helen Perlstein. *Tarícuri's Legacy: The Prehispanic Tarascan State.* Norman: University of Oklahoma Press, 1993.

Porter, Muriel N. "Excavations at Chupícuaro, Guanajuato, Mexico." *Transactions of the American Philosophical Society,* 46(5): 514–637. Philadelphia, 1956.

Rilley, Carroll L., and Basil C. Hedrick (editors). *Across the Chichimec Sea: Papers in Honor of J. Charles Kelley.* Carbondale: Southern Illinois University Press, 1978.

Rodríquez Betancourt, Felipe. "Desarrollo cultural en la región de Mezcala-Tetela del Río." In *Arqueología y etnohistoria del estado de Guerrero,* pp. 155–70. Mexico City: Instituto Nacional de Antropología e Historia, 1986.

Townsend, Richard (editor). *Ancient West Mexico: Art and Archaeology of the Unknown Past.* Chicago: Art Institute of Chicago, 1998.

Tudela, Jose (editor). *Relación de Michoacán (1541).* Madrid: Aguilar, 1956.

Von Winning, Hasso. *The Shaft Tomb Figures of West Mexico.* Southwest Museum Papers, no. 24. Los Angeles: Southwest Museum, 1974.

———.*Arte prehispánico del Occidente de México.* Zamora, Mexico: El Colegio de Michoacán, 1996.

Warren, Benedict J. *The Conquest of Michoacan.* Norman: University of Oklahoma Press, 1985.

Weigand, Phil C. "The Prehistory of the State of Zacatecas." In *Anuario de historia zacatecona,* edited by C. E. Sanchez, pp. 2–41. Zacatecas, Mexico: Universidad Autónoma de Zacatecas, 1977.

———.*Evolución de una civilización prehispánica: Arqueología de Jalisco, Nayarit, y Zacatecas.* Zamora, Mexico: El Colegio de Michoacán, 1993.

Williams, Eduardo. *Las piedras sagradas: Escultura prehispánica del occidente de México.* Zamora, México: El Colegio de Michoacán, 1992.

Wooseley, A. C., and J. C. Ravesloot (editors). *Culture and Contact: Charles C. DiPeso's Gran Chichimeca.* Albuquerque: University of New Mexico Press, 1993.

ANCIENT VERACRUZ AND THE GULF COAST

Arnold, Philip J. III. "An Overview of Southern Veracruz Archaeology." *Ancient Mesoamerica* 5(2): 215–22, 1994.

Arnold, Philip J. III, Christopher A. Pool, Ronald R. Kneebone, and Robert S. Santley. "Intensive Ceramic Production and Classic-Period Political Economy in the Sierra de los Tuxtlas, Veracruz, Mexico." *Ancient Mesoamerica* 4(2): 175–92, 1993.

Berlin, Heinrich. *Archaeological Reconnaissance in Tabasco.* Washington, D.C.: Carnegie Institution of Washington, 1953.

Bruggemann, Jurgen Kurt. *Zempoala: El estudio de una ciudad prehispánica.* Colección Científica no. 232. Instituto Nacional de Antropología e Historia, Mexico City, 1991.

Coe, Michael D. "Archaeological Synthesis of Southern Veracruz and Tabasco." *Handbook of Middle American Indians* (vol. 3), edited by Robert Wauchope, pp. 679–715. Austin: University of Texas Press, 1965.

Curet, Antonio. "Regional Studies and Ceramic Production Areas: An Example from La Mixtequilla, Veracruz, Mexico." *Journal of Field Archaeology* 20(4): 427–40, 1993.

Garcia Payon, J. *El Tajín: Guía Oficial.* Mexico City: Instituto Nacional de Antropología e Historia, 1957.

Goldstein, Marilyn M. *Ceremonial Sculpture of Ancient Veracruz.* Brookville, N.Y.: Hillwood Art Gallery, Long Island University, 1987.

Justeson, John S., Terrence Kaufman. "A Decipherment of Epi-Olmec Hieroglyphic Writing." *Science* 259: 1703–11, 1993.

Kampen, Michael E. *The Sculptures of El Tajin, Veracruz, Mexico.* Gainesville: University of Florida Press, 1972.

Méluzin, Sylvia. "The Tuxtla Script: Steps Toward Decipherment Based on La Mojarra Stela 1." *Latin American Antiquity* 18: 283–97, 1992.

Ochoa, Lorenzo. *Historia prehispánica de la Huaxteca.* Mexico City: Universidad Nacional Autónoma de México, 1984.

Proskouriakoff, Tatiana. "Varieties of Classic Central Veracruz Sculpture." *Contributions to American Anthropology and History* 58: 61–121. Publication no. 606. Washington, D.C.: Carnegie Institution of Washington, 1954.

Santley, Robert S., and Philip J. Arnold III. "Prehispanic Settlement Patterns in the Tuxtla Mountains, Southern Veracruz, Mexico." *Journal of Field Archaeology* 23(2): 225–50, 1996.

Santley, Robert S., Philip J. Arnold III, and Christopher A. Pool. "The Ceramic Production System at Matacapan, Veracruz, Mexico." *Journal of Field Archaeology* 16: 107–32, 1989.

Stark, Barbara L. *Settlement Archaeology of Cerro de las Mesas, Veracruz, Mexico.* Monograph no. 34. Los Angeles: Institute of Archaeology, University of California, 1991.

Stark, Barbara L., and Philip J. Arnold III (editors). *Olmec to Aztec: Settlement Patterns in the Ancient Gulf Lowlands.* Tucson: University of Arizona Press, 1997.

Wilkerson, S. Jeffrey K. "Man's Eighty Centuries in Veracruz," *National Geographic* 158(2): 203–31, 1980.

———. *El Tajin: A Guide for Visitors.* Xalapa, Veracruz, Mexico, 1987.

Winfield Capitaine, Fernando. *La Estela 1 de La Mojarra, Veracruz, México.* Washington, D.C.: Center for Maya Research, 1988.

COMPARATIVE AND THEORETICAL WORKS

Benson, Elizabeth P. (editor). *Death and the Afterlife in Pre-Columbian America.* Washington, D.C.: Dumbarton Oaks, 1975.

———. *Mesoamerican Sites and World Views.* Washington, D.C.: Dumbarton Oaks, 1981.

Berlo, Janet C. (editor). *Text and Image in Precolumbian Art.* B.A.R. International Series no. 180. Oxford: British Archaeological Reports, 1983.

Berlo, Janet C., and Richard A. Diehl (editors). *Mesoamerica after the Decline of Teotihuacan*. Washington, D.C.: Dumbarton Oaks, 1989.

Blanton, Richard E., and Gary Feinman. "The Mesoamerican World System." *American Anthropologist* 86: 673–82, 1984.

Blanton, Richard E., Gary M. Feinman, Stephen P. Kowalewski, and Peter N. Peregrine. "A Dual-Processual Theory for the Evolution of Mesoamerican Civilization." *Current Anthropology* 37(1): 1–14, 1996.

Blanton, Richard E., Stephen A. Kowalewski, Gary Feinman, and Jill Appel. *Ancient Mesoamerica: A Comparison of Change in Three Regions*. Cambridge: Cambridge University Press, 1987.

Carrasco, David. *Religions of Mesoamerica: Cosmovision and Ceremonial Centers*. New York: Harper and Row, 1990.

Chase Diane Z., and Arlen F. Chase (editors). *Mesoamerican Elites: An Archaeological Assessment*. Norman: University of Oklahoma Press, 1992.

Claassen, Cheryl, and Rosemary A. Joyce (editors). *Women in Prehistory: North America and Mesoamerica*. Philadelphia: University of Pennsylvania Press, 1997.

Conrad, Geoffrey W., and Arthur A. Demarest. *Religion and Empire: The Dynamics of Aztec and Inca Expansionism*. Cambridge: Cambridge University Press, 1984.

Dahlgren, Barbro (editor). *Historia de la religión en Mesoamérica y áreas afines*. Mexico City: Universidad Nacional Autónoma de México, 1987.

Demarest, Arthur A., and Geoffrey W. Conrad (editors). *Ideology and Pre-Columbian Civilizations*. Santa Fe, N.M.: School of American Research Press, 1992.

Galinat, W. C. "The Evolutionary Emergence of Maize." *Bulletin of the Torrey Botanical Club* 102(6): 313–24, 1975.

Gasco, Janine, Greg C. Smith, and Patricia Fournier-García. *Approaches to the Historical Archaeology of Mexico, Central and South America*. Monograph 38. Los Angeles: The Institute of Archaeology, University of California, 1997.

Hammond, Norman (editor). *Mesoamerican Archaeology: New Approaches*. Austin: University of Texas Press, 1974.

Hassig, Ross. *War and Society in Ancient Mesoamerica*. Berkeley: University of California Press, 1992.

Heizer, R., and John Graham (editors). *Observations on the Emergence of Civilization in Mesoamerica*. Monograph no. 11. Berkeley: Contributions of the University of California Archaeological Research Facility, 1971.

Hellmuth, Nicholas M. *Pre-Columbian Ball Game: Archaeology and Architecture*. Providence, R.I.: Foundation for Latin American Anthropological Research, 1975.

Hirth, Kenneth G. (editor). *Trade and Exchange in Early Mesoamerica*. Albuquerque: University of New Mexico Press, 1984.

Kowalski, Jeff K. (editor). *Mesoamerican Architecture as a Cultural Symbol*. Oxford: Oxford University Press, 1996.

Mangelsdorf, Paul C. *Corn: Its Origin, Evolution and Improvement.* Cambridge, Mass.: Harvard University Press, 1974.

Manzanilla, Linda (editor). *Unidades habitacionales mesoamericanas y sus áreas de actividad.* Serie Antropológica 76. Mexico City: Universidad Nacional Autónoma de México, 1986.

Marcus, Joyce. "The Origins of Mesoamerican Writing." *Annual Review of Anthropology* 5: 35–67, 1976.

————. "On the Nature of the Mesoamerican City." In *Prehistoric Settlement Patterns,* edited by Evon Vogt and Richard M. Leventhal. Albuquerque: University of New Mexico Press, 1983.

————. *Mesoamerican Writing Systems: Propaganda, Myth, and History in Four Ancient Civilizations.* Princeton, N.J.: Princeton University Press, 1992.

Messenger, Lewis C. Jr. "Ancient Winds of Change: Climatic Settings and Prehistoric Social Complexity in Mesoamerica," *Ancient Mesoamerica* 1(1): 21–40, 1990.

Miller, Virginia E. (editor). *The Role of Gender in Precolumbian Art and Architecture.* Lanham, Md.: University Press of America, 1988.

Mock Boteler, Shirley (editor). *The Sowing and the Dawning: Termination, Dedication, and Transformation in the Archaeological and Ethnographic Record of Mesoamerica.* Albuquerque: University of New Mexico Press, 1998.

Ringle, William M., Tomás G. Negrón, and George J. Bey III. "The Return of Quetzalcoatl: Evidence for the Spread of a World Religion during the Epiclassic Period." *Ancient Mesoamerica* 9(2): 183–232, 1998.

Sanders, William T., and Barbara J. Price. *Mesoamerica: The Evolution of a Civilization.* New York: Random House, 1968.

Sanders, William T., and David Webster. "The Mesoamerican Urban Tradition," *American Anthropologist* 90: 521–46, 1988.

Santley, Robert S., and Kenneth G. Hirth (editors). *Household, Compound, and Residence: Studies of Prehispanic Domestic Units in Western Mesoamerica.* Boca Raton, Fla.: CRC Press, 1993.

Scarborough, Vernon L., and David R. Wilcox (editors). *The Mesoamerican Ballgame.* Tucson: University of Arizona Press, 1991.

Wilk, Richard R., and Wendy Ashmore (editors). *Household and Community in the Mesoamerican Past.* Albuquerque: University of New Mexico Press, 1988.

Willey, Gordon R., and Jeremy A. Sabloff. *A History of American Archaeology.* San Francisco: W. H. Freeman, 1980.

About the Author

Joel W. Palka (B.A., Northern Illinois University, 1987; Ph.D., Vanderbilt University, 1995) is assistant professor of anthropology and Latin American studies at the University of Illinois–Chicago, where he has taught since 1996. He was a visiting assistant professor at Vanderbilt University from 1995–96, where he taught courses in Mesoamerican art and archaeology. He is also adjunct curator in anthropology at The Field Museum in Chicago, where he studies collections of material culture from Mesoamerica. His research specialties and interests include cultural evolution, social organization, social inequality, settlement patterns, Mesoamerican ethnohistory, Maya history and archaeology, and Maya hieroglyphic writing. He is also a member of the Society of American Archaeology, the American Anthropological Association, and the Chicago Maya Society.

Dr. Palka has undertaken archaeological investigations in Classic Maya ruins in Honduras and Guatemala and has lived and traveled extensively throughout Mexico and Central America. He has directed excavations in the northern rainforests of Guatemala as a Fulbright Scholar and Vanderbilt University Mellon Grant recipient, and he currently is the director of a historical and archaeological project sponsored by the University of Illinois–Chicago, Foundation for the Advancement of Mesoamerican Studies, Sigma Xi: The Scientific Research Society, National Endowment for the Humanities, and the National Geographic Society that examines indigenous culture change of the 19th-century Lacandon Maya of lowland Chiapas and Guatemala. Dr. Palka has written numerous articles in English and Spanish regarding his work on Classic Maya civilization and the 19th-century Lacandon. His dissertation *Classic Maya Social Inequality and the Collapse at Dos Pilas, Peten, Guatemala* is being prepared for publication by Vanderbilt University Press. He has also reviewed books and articles for *Latin American Antiquity, Visual Anthropology, Ancient Mesoamerica,* and *Ethnohistory.*